ACC. No. BK3
CLAS. 7S1...
...COLLEGE
ORDER No. 03901

KT-545-494

This book is due for return on or before the last date shown below.

3 1 MAY 2002

-1 NOV 2002

-5 DEC 2003

3 0 NOV 2004

1 5 DEC 2011

-5 OCT 2012

1 6 APR 2013

1 0 JAN 2014

3 0 JAN 2014

The Later Morandi
Still Lifes 1950–1964

Guggenheim Collection
ril–13 September 1998

Don Gresswell Ltd., London, N21   Cat. No. 1207   DG 02242/71

BK35040

Peggy Guggenheim Collection

Deputy Director: Philip Rylands

Curator: Fred Licht

Administrator: Renata Rossani

Conservator: Paul Schwartzbaum

Officer for Membership and Special Events: Claudia Rech

Accountant: Laura Micolucci

Accounting Assistant: Gabriella Andreatta

Deputy Director's Assistant: Chiara Barbieri

Assistant for Development and Public Affairs: Beate Barner

Assistant for Information Technology: Fabio Lanza

Retail Operations Manager: Roberta Chiarotto

Inventory Manager: Fabio Bobatz

Shop Assistant: Elena Reggiani

Maintenance: Siro de Boni

Security: Alessandro Claut, Franco Pugnalin, Daniele Regolini, Oliviero Scaramuzza

 This exhibition has been organized together with the **Galleria dello Scudo, Verona**

Exhibition project and organization: Massimo Di Carlo, Laura Mattioli Rossi, Massimo Simonetti

Historical-critical co-ordination, selection of works: Laura Mattioli Rossi with the contribution of Massimo Di Carlo, Flavio Fergonzi, Maria Mimita Lamberti, Franz Armin Morat, Giuseppe Panza di Biumo, Marilena Pasquali

Catalog edited by: Massimo Di Carlo, Laura Mattioli Rossi, Marilena Pasquali

Essay and contributions by: Maria Mimita Lamberti, Laura Mattioli Rossi, Franz Armin Morat, Giuseppe Panza di Biumo, Marilena Pasquali, Fausto Petrella, Joseph J. Rishel, Angela Vettese

Catalog of works: Flavio Fergonzi

Technical entries: Laura Lorenzoni

Biography: Lorenza Selleri

Image research: Laura Lorenzoni, Francesco Sandroni, Lorenza Selleri

Conservation of works: Gianni Rossi, Milano

Transport: Sattis Trasporti Internazionali srl, Venezia

Insurance cover by

 Assicurazioni Generali S.p.A.

The operations and programs of the Peggy Guggenheim Collection are supported by:

INTRAPRESÆ COLLEZIONE GUGGENHEIM

Aermec	**Gruppo Imation Italia**
Arclinea	**Istituto Poligrafico**
Automotive Products	**e Zecca dello Stato**
Italia	**Leo Burnett**
Banca Antoniana	**Luciano Marcato**
Popolare Veneta	**Rex Built-In**
Barbero 1891	**Sàfilo Group**
Bisazza	**Swatch**
DLW AG	**Wella**
Gruppo 3M Italia	**Zucchi - Bassetti Group**

Management by Michela Bondardo Comunicazione

Official carrier: Alitalia

The Trustees of the Solomon R. Guggenheim Foundation gratefully acknowledge the **Regione Veneto** for the annual subsidy that assures the effective operation of the Peggy Guggenheim Collection

The Later MORANDI

Still Lifes
1950–1964

edited by Laura Mattioli Rossi

Mazzotta

For the fundamental contribution they made to this initiative, we are grateful to:
Maria Teresa Fiorio, Director of the Civiche Raccolte d'Arte, Milan; Mina Gregori,
President of the Fondazione di Studi di Storia dell'Arte Roberto Longhi, Florence;
Franz Armin Morat, President of the Morat-Institut für Kunst und Kunstwissenschaft, Freiburg.
Special thanks go to Marilena Pasquali, Director of the Museo Morandi, Bologna, for the vital
contribution she made. We are grateful to Paola Marini, Director of the Civici Musei, Verona,
and to Lorenzo Sassoli de Bianchi, President of the Istituzione Galleria d'Arte Moderna,
Bologna, for their precious and unstinting collaboration.

Our deepest gratitude to Antonio and Domenico Catanese, Alessandro d'Urso, Marta and
Paola Giovanardi, Laura Mattioli and Gianni Rossi, Daniele Pescali, and all the private
collectors who generously permitted us to include works they own in this show.
Claudia Gian Ferrari, Paola and Tiziano Forni, Luisa Laureati, and Giulio Tega also made
fundamental loans possible.

We also thank: Rosalba Amerio Tardito, Art Historical Supervisor of the Ministry of Cultural
Assets; Filippa Aliberti Gaudioso, Superintendent of the Department of Artistic and
Historical Assets of the Veneto Region; Cristina Acidini, Superintendent Vicar of the
Department of Artistic and Historical Assets of the Provinces of Florence, Pistoia and Prato;
Giorgio Bonsanti, Superintendent of the Opificio delle Pietre Dure e Laboratori di Restauro,
Florence; Andrea Emiliani, Superintendent of the Department of Artistic and Historical
Assets of Bologna, Ferrara, Forlì and Ravenna; Luisa Arrigoni, Art Historical Director of the
Superintendency of Artistic and Historical Assets, Milan; Fabrizio Pietropoli, Art Historical
Supervisor of the Superintendency of Artistic and Historical Assets of the Veneto Region.

Graziano Ghiringhelli provided us with a great deal of information that helped to make this
show a reality, and additional research was carried out at: the Ente Esposizione Nazionale
Quadriennale d'Arte archive, Rome; the Fondazione di Studi di Storia dell'Arte Roberto
Longhi archive, Florence; the Galleria Il Milione archive, Milan; the Giovanardi archive,
Milan; the Giuseppe Marchiori archive, Lendinara; the Mattioli archive, Milan;
the Morat-Institut für Kunst und Kunstwissenschaft archive, Freiburg; the Museo Morandi
archive, Bologna; Archivio del '900 (Maurizio Fagiolo dell'Arco), Rome; Archivio Storico
delle Arti Contemporanee della Biennale (ASAC), Venice; Archivio Storico del Cinema / AFE,
Rome; the Vitali archive, Milan; the Biblioteca dell'Accademia di Brera, Milan; the Biblioteca
d'Arte del Castello Sforzesco, Milan; the Biblioteca d'Arte dei Musei Civici - Galleria Civica
d'Arte Moderna e Contemporanea, Turin; the Biblioteca d'Arte del Museo di Castelvecchio,
Verona; the Biblioteca Civica, Verona; the Biblioteca Comunale, Milan; the Biblioteca
Nazionale Braidense, Milan; Documenta Archiv, Kassel; the Frick Art Reference Library,
New York; the Schweizerische Landesbibliothek, Bern; the New York Public Library, New York.

We are grateful for the advice we received from: Giacomo Agosti, Giuseppina Baffi,
Pierluigi Bagatin, Emanuela Barilla, Gabriella Belli, Maria Benedetti, Renata Bollea,
Mariarosa Bricchi, Anna Cappanera Pescali, Paolo Cardazzo, Doriana Comerlati, Michele
Cordaro, Floriano De Santi, Silvia Evangelisti, Maurizio Fagiolo dell'Arco, Luigi Ficacci,
Cecilia Filippini, Gisella Floersheim, Giorgio Galli, Ginevra Grigolo, Sergio Grossetti,
Werner Haftmann, Linda Kovarich, Leo Lionni, Omero Locatelli, Giorgio Marini, Patrizia
Minghetti, Massimo Minini, Vittoria Pallucchini Pelzel, Silvana Pasquin, Domenico and Laura
Pertocoli, Enrica Petrarulo, Elio Pinottini, Mario Ravagnan, Federico Rollino, Maria Livia
Rossi, Ennio Sandal, Erich Steingräber, Michael Strauss, Nico Stringa, Bruno Trombetti,
Marisa Vescovo, Enrico and Franca Vitali, Sara Vitali, Leslie Waddington, Maria Silva Zanini,
Carlo Zucchini.

The Peggy Guggenheim Collection grasped the opportunity to present this exhibition for several reasons. Firstly it is a model of how exhibitions of this kind should be curated, with its close attention to quality, numbers, and art-critical cohesiveness. Secondly, the exhibition helps us to understand with unprecedented and admiring clarity Giorgio Morandi's art in a period, his last, which is sometimes dismissed as too prolific, even facile. Thirdly, the long-term loan to the Peggy Guggenheim Collection of paintings from the Gianni Mattioli Collection includes six rare and beautiful early works by Morandi. One of these, a still life with two bottles and a fruit bowl of 1916, is often admired as Morandi's first masterpiece. This refers in part to its intrinsic quality, but surely also alludes to the fact that it is the premonition, the prototype of Morandi's mature compositional format and preferred subject matter, the table-top still life—precisely in fact those paintings so rigorously selected, scrutinized and sorted in this jewel of an exhibition. But the main reason of course is that it reveals to us what we all know, but will feel more strongly after seeing this exhibition: that Morandi is a great twentieth-century master to whom the epithet "genius" can safely be applied.

I would like therefore to extend my congratulations to the curator of the exhibition, Laura Mattioli Rossi, to her colleague Flavio Fergonzi, who contributed his scholarship and connoisseurship to the catalog, and to Massimo Di Carlo, who organized the exhibition in its first venue at the Galleria dello Scudo, Verona. I am grateful to both Laura Mattioli Rossi and Massimo Di Carlo for sharing my enthusiasm and for going to considerable trouble, together with Laura Lorenzoni of the Galleria dello Scudo, to enable the installation of the exhibition in Venice. It has been a pleasure to work with Gabriele and Bianca Mazzotta on the Venice edition of the catalog. The owners of the paintings in the show—the lenders—have been deprived of the pleasure of having Morandi's masterpieces near them for longer than they at first anticipated. Thank you, most warmly, to all of them.

Finally I would like to acknowledge all those who make possible the exhibitions at the Peggy Guggenheim Collection, and this one in particular. The Regione Veneto has loyally and consistently subsidized the programs of the Collection since 1981. The individual members of the Peggy Guggenheim Collection Advisory Board contribute annually to museum operations, thus fueling and encouraging what I trust is perceived as a vital and energetic organization. Assicurazioni Generali, so proudly identifiable with the emblem of the Lion of St Mark, has generously insured Morandi's paintings for their Venetian sojourn. Intrapresæ Collezione Guggenheim, the association of Italian companies that support the Peggy Guggenheim Collection on an annual basis, and whose names, like those of the Advisory Board, are published in this catalog, make possible the planning of our exhibitions with the happy confidence that the funding is in place.

Thomas Krens
Director
Solomon R. Guggenheim Foundation

This volume is the English language edition of the catalog published for the exhibition *Morandi ultimo. Nature morte 1950–1964* held in the Galleria dello Scudo, Verona, from 14 December 1997 to 28 February 1998

Note to the Reader
Each time an oil painting, watercolor, drawing or etching by Giorgio Morandi is mentioned or reproduced in this volume, the catalogues raisonnés and respective publication numbers are given, abbreviated as follows:

Pasquali no.	Pasquali M., *Morandi. Acquerelli. Catalogo generale*, Electa, Milan, 1991
Pasquali-Tavoni no.	Pasquali M., Tavoni E., *Morandi. Disegni. Catalogo generale*, systematic cataloging, dating and iconographic comparisons by M. Pasquali in collaboration with L. Selleri, Electa, Milan, 1994
Vitali no.	Vitali L., *Morandi. Catalogo generale*, Electa, Milan, 1977, 2 vols. (2nd ed. expanded, 1983)
Vitali etchings no.	Vitali L., *Giorgio Morandi. Opera grafica*, Einaudi, Turin, 1957, with 113 plate illustrations (2nd ed. expanded and corrected, 1964; 3rd ed. expanded and corrected, 1978; 4th ed. expanded, 1989)

Layout: Bruno Trombetti
Cover: Fulvio Ariani

© 1998 Giorgio Morandi - by SIAE

© 1998 Edizioni Gabriele Mazzotta
Foro Buonaparte 52 - 20121 Milano

© 1998 Galleria dello Scudo
Via Scudo di Francia 2, 37121 Verona

ISBN 88-202-1279-X

Contents

Giorgio Morandi in a photograph by Mario De Biasi, 1959.

Giorgio Morandi: Questions of Method

Laura Mattioli Rossi

In 1963, just a few months before Giorgio Morandi's death, Lamberto Vitali was writing his introduction to the monograph published by Edizioni del Milione. His opening words read: "The writer of this note would be happy if . . . it could be useful for some future biographer of Morandi (but perhaps the book on Morandi will come about only in fifty years time, when views will be more settled and many facts, the reason and importance of which those of us who have witnessed them are uncertain about, will become clear)."[1] Thirty-five years after these words were written, this exhibition now suggests a new interpretation of Morandi's work, focused on the last phase of his career, from the post-war period up to his death. Attention will be given to the still lifes with objects—considered the central theme of the artist's investigations, leaving aside the flowers and landscapes—painted from 1950 (the year in which, in the heat of post-war reconstruction, Morandi's new stylistic path seems to be defined) until 1964, when his last period was ended, characterized by an increasingly diaphanous use of paint.[2]

To write "the book on Morandi," as Vitali called it, is not the aim of this show, even as far as the Bolognese artist's late work is concerned. What it does intend to do is to make the most of the historical distance that time has placed between us and the works, in two ways: to test and deepen our understanding of the still lifes of the fifties and sixties by following strictly an art historic approach, and to ask certain basic questions about the meaning and value of these paintings, questions that inevitably involve the very concept of history as applied to artistic output, as well as the methods of art criticism.

While 1964, the year of Morandi's death, saw the publication of two seminal texts, the monographs by Lamberto Vitali and by Francesco Arcangeli (besides those of Marco Valsecchi and Alberto Martini),[3] in the following years exhibitions were held all over the world in rapid succession, beginning with the retrospective in Bologna in 1966 and continuing through to the centennial show in 1990 and the shows organized in Milan and in Japan[4] between 1989 and 1990. In the past two years alone there have been four monographic exhibitions dedicated to the artist.[5] Thus, it might almost seem difficult to say or suggest something new about Giorgio Morandi.

A look at the rich array of literature on Morandi shows how the fame of this great master of Italian art—which began to grow up around him already in the second half of the thirties and was consolidated in the fifties thanks to the post-war writings of Francesco Arcangeli, Cesare Gnudi, Roberto Longhi, and Giuseppe

Raimondi,[6] as well to his success with collectors—has so greatly influenced later criticism that it is almost always anthological in scope and celebratory in tone. Apart from certain recent thematic shows,[7] interest has always been in Morandi's career as it unfolded, stressing certain of the earliest paintings influenced by Cézanne, the Metaphysical and "Valori Plastici" periods, and works of the twenties and thirties. Despite a general appreciation of the later works, in particular the landscapes, and a recognition of Morandi's rigorous experimentation, a characteristic of his work up to the time of his death, resulting in a continual renewal of his expressive means,[8] critics have tended not to investigate his activity from the fifties onwards (perhaps unconsciously put off by the number of works),[9] considering it simply an unbroken continuation of his previous investigations.

According to this view, after his brilliant debut in the second decade of the century, seen in a few surviving canvases, Morandi reached his full maturity in the twenties and thirties, producing etchings as well as oil paintings. He continued this artistic course after the Second World War in a way that was completely coherent with the poetics he had already amply set out. Emblematic of this critical view is the fact that, in the historical panorama of Italian art of this century shown at the CIMAC in Milan, Morandi was, with a monographic room, presented together with Arturo Martini, Mario Sironi, and Filippo de Pisis as documentation of the period of the Fascist dictatorship. The only painting later than 1950 belonging to the Milan civic collection, the splendid *Still Life* with a yellow drape of 1952 (Vitali no. 831), present in this show, is exhibited together with the rest of the Vismara collection, of which it is a part, in Via Palestro.

However, the later work of the Bolognese master shows some striking innovations, ideas that were to bear fruit in time. The sheer number of works is enough to create a sense of embarrassment—as I have already hinted—among critics used to concentrating their attention on a few emblematic paintings of his earlier output. In fact, the catalogue raisonné of the oil paintings curated by Vitali shows that Morandi painted 603 works between 1910 and 1947 and some 772 from 1948 until his death.[10] Thus more than half of Morandi's production comes from

Three still lifes of 1914–15 (from left, Vitali nos. 13, 18, 23), belonging respectively to the Giovanardi collection, the Musée National d'Art Moderne in Paris, and the Mattioli collection. They are the earliest example in absolute of a composition in which Morandi painted the same objects—a rectangular box, a pitcher, a bottle and/or a clock case—from various viewpoints.

this period; therefore, after having ascertained their quality (which, anyhow, has never been questioned by the critics and of which the painter himself was the greatest censor) it might reasonably be held that this is the period of greatest creative richness in the painter's life.

By now Morandi enjoyed the esteem of critics and collectors in an Italy characterized by full economic growth and the desire to forget the drama of the war and the years under Fascism. In such a climate, the artist seems to have found a greater confidence in himself and a new serenity which translated into a chromatically clear and luminous color range and a fertile creative impulse. The large number of paintings he produced in these years may further be explained by his working methods and the very meaning of the works: this is strictly linked to the undertaking of *series*, that is, numerous pictures of similar subjects differentiated by variations of different kinds. In this show six out of a total of ten of the 1952 "yellow drape" series illustrate this new way of working.

The first two very similar, specular still lifes date from 1923 (Vitali nos. 79 and 80), though upon close inspection, the still lifes of 1914–15 in the Giovanardi collection in the Musée National d'Art Moderne in Paris and in the Mattioli collection (respectively cataloged by Vitali as nos. 13, 18, and 23) prove to depict the same objects—a rectangular box, a jug, a bottle and/or clock-case—from different viewpoints, from the front and from the side, above and below, near and far. More than one version of the same model appears in 1927–29.[11] From 1939–40 he begun to take up with greater frequency the repetition of the same composition, changing the position of one or other object and the distance from it. In these last years the variations are also related to the format (as in *Still Life* Vitali no. 260, which is the oval version of the *Still Life* Vitali no. 259) or the subject plane (in the *Still Life* Vitali no. 265 part of the canvas is taken up by the table whose presence is only hinted at in *Still Life* Vitali no. 263) and they were also extended from the still life to the landscape, as in the two views of Bologna under the snow (Vitali nos. 283, 284); later on this procedure would be applied to flower paintings as, for example, may be seen in certain pictures of 1950 (Vitali nos. 728, 730).

After 1940 the repetition of the same subject became more frequent. In certain paintings part of the composition, for instance the right half, remains unchanged while the left half and the distance change (as in the still lifes, Vitali nos. 291, 293–296). In others (as in the still lifes, Vitali nos. 314–318 and 320) the grouping of the objects changes while the viewpoint moves across from the center to one side. From this point onwards the painter seems to want to try systematically the various possibilities latent in the model, multiplying the number of paintings inspired by the same theme, for example in the still lifes of shells from 1943 (Vitali nos. 433–435 and 439–443). The succession of canvases, then, documents the long sequences of transformations of the same composition in progress, as occurs in the still lifes Vitali nos. 488–493 of 1945,

In the years 1939–40, Morandi took up the repetition of similar compositions, changing the format, framing or the subject plane.
In the *Still Life* of 1940 (Vitali no. 265) at the Nationalgalerie of Berlin, part of the canvas is taken up by the table, the presence of which is only hinted at in the *Still Life* of the same year (Vitali no. 263, right), in a private collection.

and nos. 514–523 of 1946 which narrate various moments of a single history. From 1948 the problem of variations on a single theme develops enormously and imposes itself as a *modus operandi*, so much so that, from this date on, we must consider as exceptions those works which cannot be related to some series. Changes in tonality then came to be added to those of format, composition, distance, as well as horizon line and the subject plane. It almost seems as though the wish to try out the various possible variations on the same subject became a new element in the still life genre, the pictorial equivalent of the musical variations on a theme whose great master was Johann Sebastian Bach. Although this almost obsessive way of working on a single model, characteristic of Morandi's activity after the Second World War, has so far roused no particular interest among critics, as if it were the monotonous repetition of themes already elaborated previously, this does not mean that it is not rich with philosophical meaning inherent to the artistic act.

In three still lifes of 1941, in private collections (from top, Vitali nos. 314, 315, 316), the grouping of the objects varies, while the viewpoint shifts from the center to one side, using an approach that foreshadows the *series*.

For many centuries, starting with the early Renaissance, western culture has conceived the work of art as a meaningful moment in a historical process determined by progress;[12] Vasari himself in his *Lives* codified this process into its first, second, and third phases, corresponding to the rebirth, development, and perfection of art. The individual work of art occupies a precise moment in history. The more it incorporates preceding elements, resolves them in a new way, and opens up paths for the future, the greater its artistic value. It is, therefore, considered one of the links of a chain—that of art history—and its value is defined by the epithet "masterpiece," alluding not just to the aesthetic content but also to an ability to be a central element in the development of artistic progress.

Even the historical avant-gardes maintain this concept of the masterpiece, and this is fundamental both for the individual efforts of the artists and for the group. For the whole of the first half of this century, the focus has been on summing up reality whether by proposing a new world to replace seemingly meaningless forms (as in the case of the "Futurist reconstruction of the universe") or by destroying a reality that offers no other possibilities for meaning apart from the absurd (as in the case of Dada). Furthermore, this logic has since the end of the eighteenth century permeated museums and private collections formed around series of works considered *exemplary*. Morandi himself seems to have shared in it for most of his activity, particularly during his Metaphysical period when he produced few but carefully considered works. But from the early fifties, starting with the idea of the series, he abandoned the idea of creating masterpieces. Walter Benjamin had theorized the death of the aura, something belonging to the unique and historically determined artistic object, as a result of the advent of photography and, above all, of cinema, which were reproducible and aimed at the masses.[13] Morandi instead pursued in practice, within painting itself and within a historical genre such as the still life, the death of the aura, because he no longer believed that reality—multiple, discontinuous, and subject to the relative position of the observer and the arbitrary choices of the painter—could still be represented by an emblematic and unitary act.

Some conclusions can be drawn from these considerations. First of all, by abandoning the concept of the masterpiece, Morandi took his distance from the idea of progress that permeates not only classical art but even the historical avant-gardes and most of the production of this century, at the same time placing himself automatically outside "art history" as traditionally understood (this argument will be further developed below). In the second place, the undifferentiated repetition of the same title—*Still Life*—for all the compositions matches all the coeval or later works designated as *Untitled*, in other words the greater part of contemporary artistic production. In the third place, his interest in watercolors, a characteristic of his last years, is also explained by abandoning, along with the

Still Life, 1916 (Vitali no. 27).
New York, The Museum of Modern Art.

concept of the masterpiece, every distinction between materials, the artist is able to confer on these tiny works on paper the same importance as his oil paintings and to create a completely autonomous genre even when he repeats the same subjects.

It does not seem legitimate to interpret the series as a search for perfection through an increasing scale of values, even if it is natural that in Morandi's output some works are more successful than others. Working on his series Morandi varies the composition of the objects, the proportions of the canvas, the spectator's viewpoint, the framing of the visual field, the study of the relationship between the model, the formats, and the views. The chromatic quality of the whole and of the individual details also creates a system of variables. And with this system of variables and all the possibilities and contradictions that it contains, Morandi considers himself capable of expressing his obsessive search for absolute beauty. Multiplicity, the fleeting relativity of the phenomenal world in which each object is contingent (in itself, in relation to every other object, to time, to light, to the spectator. . .), never collapses into confused chaos, the parent of anxiety, but conveys meaning because it encloses in itself an absolute value to which it also alludes.

This is why Morandi never took that apparently small step to abstraction: on the contrary he stated in an interview of 1957 that "nothing is more abstract. . . than reality."[14] Instead he faced courageously the problem of a world experienced by contemporary culture in an intrinsically discontinuous and fragmentary way, giving up a conception of the work of art as an emblematic and representative act in a global sense; he wanted to maintain in painting the contradiction between representation of real objects and abstract forms, between colors referring to the natural world and purely painterly tonal values because the mind of man, the eye and hand of the painter are the only possible meeting point between passing and phenomenal reality and the absolute.[15] Morandi achieves this result through a second highly innovative element present in the paintings of his last years: a new construction of space and the elements it contains.

Just as the series are part of the development of an idea already latent in the Cubist-influenced works of 1914–15 and which occasionally resurfaces during the twenties and thirties and became fully established after the Second World War, so Morandi's new handling of space in the fifties and sixties has its roots in the canvases of the second decade of the century. Morandi seems to have returned to meditate on the paintings of 1916, in particular on the still lifes Vitali nos. 27, 28, and 29[16] in which the subject plane and the horizon line are only

In the fifties, Morandi seems to have returned to meditate on the paintings of 1916, especially the three still lifes now in the Museum of Modern Art (above), the Mattioli collection and a private collection (from left, Vitali nos. 28 and 29), where the subject plane and the horizon line are only indicated by horizontal lines, and there are no oblique depth lines. The only diagonals are constituted by the shadows and the table supports in the New York painting, and have a compositional rather than three-dimensional value, well-suited to the stylized shapes of the objects.

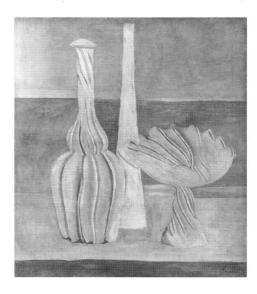

indicated by horizontal lines, and completely lack the oblique lines of depth (the only diagonals constituted by shadows and by the table supports in the New York painting have a compositional and not three-dimensional value). Moreover, the objects, depicted with a thin and transparent material conjuring up thoughts of frescos, become stylized forms related to the canvas's two-dimensions.

The long interim between the spatial problems suggested by these works and the artist's return to them in the canvases of the last period began with the Metaphysical paintings of 1918, such as the still lifes in the St. Petersburg Hermitage (Vitali no. 37) and formerly in the Jucker collection (nos. 38 and 39), of which the "spatial container" is an explicit component. We are dealing with a "spatial container" purposely ambiguous and incongruous—in accordance with Metaphysical poetics—which is always upheld by a Cartesian concept of infinite space.[17] Three-dimensionality negates the canvas surface and turns it into a "transparent glass" beyond which there opens a painterly reality different to that found in nature.

From this time on the importance of the table on which the objects are placed grows. In *Still Life*, 1918, formerly in the Jucker collection (Vitali no. 40), the round table top suspended in emptiness detaches itself from the walls of the room indicated with lines that are perpendicular rather than oblique; it also functions as a "perspectival fig-leaf," according to Panofsky's definition, because it hides the point at which the lines meet, which otherwise would appear incongruous. With the close of the Metaphysical period, the perspectival view of the base underlines more than ever the concrete presence of the object and stands out as a fundamental element of the composition, as in *Still Life*, 1920 (Vitali no. 51), in which the central leg of the table is clearly indicated, while it is overlooked, instead, in the 1918 Metaphysical painting (Vitali no. 40). In two works dating from 1919 (Vitali nos. 47 and 48) the subject plane consists of an ottoman firmly drawn along the lines of the sepulchre in Piero della Francesca's *Resurrection of Christ* in Borgo San Sepolcro. The presence of a table on which the objects are placed is a constant of all the output to follow, whether it is emphasized, as in the two still lifes with glass and knife of 1920 (Vitali nos. 54 and 55), in the still life of 1926 which belonged to the Alberto Della Ragione collection (Vitali no. 114), in the compositions with a basket of 1927 (Vitali nos. 115 and 116) and in that with a jug of 1940 (Vitali no. 265)—to give just a few examples— or whether it is just hinted at, as in the still life with jug and oil lamp of 1923 (Vitali no. 79), or in one even richer in objects of 1927 (Vitali no. 117), where the front edge coincides with the front plane of the image, or in the two paintings

The long interim between the two-dimensionality declared in the paintings of 1916 and the artist's return to it in the canvases of the last period began with the Metaphysical paintings of 1918, such as the *Still Life* formerly in the Jucker collection (Vitali no. 38), of which the "spatial container" is an explicit component.

In the *Still Life* of 1919 on deposit at the Museo Morandi (Vitali no. 47) the subject plane consists of an ottoman, the intensely sculptural quality of which is a clear reference to the sepulchre in Piero della Francesca's *Resurrection of Christ* in Borgo San Sepolcro.

In the *Still Life* of 1918, formerly in the Jucker collection (Vitali no. 40), the round table top stands out against the wall of the room indicated by lines that are perpendicular rather than oblique; it also functions as a "perspectival fig-leaf," as it hides the point at which the lines meet, which otherwise would appear incongruous.

With the close of the Metaphysical period, the perspectival view of the base stands out as a fundamental element of the composition. In this *Still Life* of 1920 (Vitali no. 51), private collection, the central leg of the table is clearly indicated, while it is overlooked in the painting of 1918 (Vitali no. 40).

with white bottles of 1940 (Vitali nos. 256 and 257). In all these cases the subject plane gives an important indication of the whole composition and marks out the depth.

In the paintings done between 1930 and 1936, characterized by thick layers of paint, all the elements, including the base plane, are reduced to the common denominator of the paint, as seen, for example, in *Still Life* of 1936 (Vitali no. 208).

From 1941 the presence of the table is more allusive than concrete (as in the still lifes Vitali nos. 294, 295, and 296, which not by chance constitute one of the first series), and Morandi begins to replace traditional three-dimensional space with a space that is mental and psychological rather than physical. The position of the horizon line is now determined above all by its relationship with the two-dimensional aspects of the composition, as in the series of 1941 (Vitali nos. 314–318 and 320), where it underlines and ideally continues the curved line marked by the neck of the bottle. The compositional valence of the oblique line of depth is accentuated in the still lifes of 1948 (Vitali nos. 621–626) as is the double and ambiguous definition of the subject plane and of the limit of the composition, while in the tight grouping of objects in the still lifes of 1949 (Vitali nos. 682–699), the same procedure has evolved to the point of transforming itself into a precise vertical line.

At the beginning of the fifties, a slow but inexorable process of abstraction finally culminates in the disappearance of the "spatial container," and the recovery of the two-dimensionality of the canvas, along with the importance of the paint itself, which tends to a lighter chromatic range, dominated by grays and a bright and diffused light.

The objects are no longer placed on a table in a three-dimensionality accentuated by contrasts between shade and light; the edges of the surface are left undefined and the diagonals of depth are not indicated. The background wall, too, is painted as a flat surface without any perspectival implications. In the foreground there often appears the thickness of the base which, however, is far higher than it should be in relation to the visible portion of the horizontal surface. Thus, an incongruity of viewpoints is created between the various parts of the painting; some things are shown frontally (the thickness of the base, the objects, the lower wall) and others are more or less seen from above (the subject plane, some of the objects). All this gives the image a strong sense of ambiguity—generally seen as the legacy of his Metaphysical period—which is resolved thanks to the two-dimensional compositive relationship.

The thickness of the table, on which the objects rest, and the background are seen as three chromatic bands which increase in height as their tonality diminishes from darkness to light; the viewer's eye reads them as the coordinates of the setting in which the objects are placed, but the purely pictorial nature of the visual simulation is so evident as to make us aware of this interpretative act.

The thickness of the base, accentuated far beyond reality, takes on the function of a parapet dividing the physical space in which the viewer stands from the pictorial space present in the picture; this qualifies as a mental space both because it has been invented by the painter according to the work's internal logic, and because it is interpreted and constructed by the eye and the mind of the observer. The immediate reference is to the stone parapet present in many of the paintings created in northern Italy at the end of the fifteenth century—portraits or representations of the Madonna and Child—in which this element has the analogous role of a threshold between the physical and natural space of the viewer and the space of the "artificial perspective" invented by the painter, alluding to the paradisiac world.

The horizon line too is an element related to the composition of the forms more than to a demarcation of the plane defining the depth. It divides the painting into two mutually proportional parts which are also related to the dimensions of the canvas: at times it is placed about halfway down the canvas, as in *Still Life* of 1953–54 (Vitali no. 895) which is almost square, or it may be three quarters of the way above the base, as in a work of the same period (Vitali no. 896), characterized by an extremely elongated format. Its continuous and contiguous relationship with the horizontal lines seen in the composition's objects further underlines its double role and two-dimensional valence. (Both works mentioned are on show at this exhibition.)

In this new pictorial context Morandi systematically confronts the problem of how objects are arranged in depth: they seem to superimpose or "slide" themselves vertically over each other and take on a spatial value above all with regards to color, dark for the forms lying further back and lighter for those towards the front (as in *Still Life*, 1953, Vitali no. 848 to be seen in the show), keeping indefinite and therefore highly ambiguous the view of the upper objects. Already for some time, right angles had been banished from Morandi's paintings; even his rectangular cans have wavy outlines which make it difficult to define precisely their position and orientation. Not by chance Morandi's favorite theme is that of bottles, so much so that he was nicknamed the "bottle painter;" and in fact

In the tight grouping of objects in these still lifes of 1949, private collection (from left, Vitali nos. 684, 686), the line that defines the edge of the table also takes on the function of the edge of the composition, becoming a precise vertical line.

In the fifties, Morandi accentuates the thickness of the table on which the objects rest far beyond reality; it is seen as a flat band of color, as in the *Still Life* of 1957 (Vitali no. 1044, private collection), and it takes on a function analogous to that of the parapet in the *Madonna and Child* by Giovanni Bellini in the Accademia Carrara at Bergamo; the parapet divides the physical space in which the viewer stands from the pictorial space of the picture.

bottles, vases, and cylindrical cans are curved elements that can be shown perspectively with a certain margin of ambiguity, eliminating the diagonals of depth on which are based the checkerboard-like grid so dear to the painters of the early Renaissance, a device that allowed them to reproduce the distance between things and the viewer into a metric-proportional system.

The compositions painted by Morandi in these years appear as sets of objects which are individually characterized, identified by paint applied in flat expanses and modelled by easily recognizable brushstrokes. The result is that they are isolated from each other and surrounded by emptiness indicated by dark and shapeless areas between them. In this way the painter seems to wish to make a point of denying "the space that exists before bodies," theorized by Descartes but understood a long time before him through Renaissance perspective;[18] between bodies and space there exist substantial antinomies corresponding to that between being and non-being and for this reason the paint and two-dimensionality of the work turn out to be the only elements that allow the objects to be integrated with space.

In the fifties Morandi used oil paint in a way that was completely new with respect to the preceding periods, above all with regard to the layers of material that, towards the middle of the thirties, destroyed the form of the objects with heavy brushstrokes. A single tonality passes from the objects to the background and only a different *ductus* creates distinctions, rich with shimmering effects of light.

In the sixties the paint became ever thinner and more rarefied, almost as though it wished to abandon the physical to become immaterial thought, while the brush-mark became ever more uncertain in describing the form of things. Often there remain on the canvas small unpainted spaces, as though no sooner had the image been suggested than it no longer needed to be completely described and could left in an unfinished state, due to an extreme expressive sobriety. By exalting the physical aspects of "making art" and the conventions that painting must use in order to express itself, Morandi unequivocally detaches the still life genre—which for him was the artistic act *par excellence*—from the reign of *mimesis* and leads it to that of *poiesis*, that is, from the imitation of the real world to the creation of a poetical world which draws sustenance from the former through the mind and the hand of man.

A clear and diffused light that Morandi obtains and controls by means of a complicated system of white curtains made for this purpose removes from his still lifes the idea of a temporally-defined situation (for example, an artificial nocturnal light rather than natural daylight), and places them once again in a rarefied mental space. Shadows, when they occur, do not follow physical laws but take on a weight similar to that of the objects, and they too present themselves as marks of color on the surface.

The absence of perpendiculars of depth removes any reference points for visual orientation and for understanding the dimensions of the objects, which can only be imagined, thus conferring on the still life, taken from the real world but alienated with respect to it, an *absolute* value (in the etymological sense) of time and space. In fact there remain undefined the relations between the inclinations of the planes, which we know from experience to be ninety degrees, but which the painting shows in an incongruous way; likewise, the dimensions of the table or its distance from the wall are unknown. The picture seems to propose distances tending to infinity, but infinity does not enter into the experience of our senses and contrasts with the reduced model used by Morandi, which in some way we imagine. In this way a different dimension, both infinite and absolute, mysteriously emerges from the work and transforms the simplicity and the poverty of the subjects, whose "fragmentary" character is underlined by the use of series.

Leaving to Maria Mimita Lamberti and Flavio Fergonzi the task of investigating in their essays in this catalog the newest aspects of Morandi's post-1950 activity from a formal point of view and tracing their internal development, I would like to return to the question that gave rise to the idea of this show, that is, how the last paintings of Morandi should be considered within twentieth-century art.

Giorgio Morandi died in June 1964, when Robert Rauschenberg won first prize at the Venice Biennial and when Pop Art was officially consecrated. This meaningful coincidence was at once appreciated by Roberto Longhi who made a note of it in his *Exit Morandi*, stating, among other things, that "the stature of Morandi can and must grow further after these last fifty years have been accordingly redimensioned."[19] Even if Longhi's appreciation of Morandi, particularly with reference to his final production, was offset by a negative evaluation of American art, the two sides in question are extremely clear—the latest production of Morandi and, on the other hand, the avant-garde—even though today the art historian's judgment might well seem reversed.

The artistic production of this century in fact is increasingly judged in relation to art history's developments, according to an idea of "progress" that pushes artists toward unrelenting evolution. This is a problem that has marked and troubled critics since the beginnings of the modern movement. As Ernst Gombrich pointed out, already in 1925 Hans Tietze had written, "The individual phenomenon had its validity, not so much in its intrinsic value, as in its place in an evolutionary chain; each thing seemed fluid and relative, resulting from the preceding phases and preparing for the later ones, not an organic whole but, rather, a document of stylistic evolution. Each artistic event was dissolved in a succession of styles and 'currents' which followed one after another with the inevitability of natural laws, the position of the work of art within a stylistic current assumed a decisive importance, and its value or lack of value seemed determined by exterior characteristics."[20] The twentieth century is thus interpreted by art history as a succession of great avant-garde movements that transform and continually push ahead the very concept of art, and in which works are important in relation to the innovative aspects they introduce into artistic practice rather than for their aesthetic value in the broadest sense. "Fine arts" have given way to "new art."

It is obvious that, if we judge from this point of view, Roberto Longhi's scale of values is overturned, with Pop Art left in charge of the field and the Bolognese painter relegated to the background. And it made no difference when Arcangeli began a courageous examination in his 1964 monograph in order to contextualize Morandi's culture and painting.[21] In fact, to counter the myth of the monk-like hermit that had grown up around the artist, which the Bolognese critic considered limiting, he made a sweeping analysis of the whole of Morandi's career in order to link it to the historical avant-garde and then to contemporary research. This interpretation, which remains the best of its kind, has led to various attempts at linking Morandi to other contemporary artists, above all Italians, but it has not gained currency in international circles. For art history, as codified in text books, and galleries and museums, Morandi has remained an outsider, alienated from the great movements that created modern art. However, inexplicably, the popularity of Morandi has not diminished either with the public or with critics, as can be seen from the uninterrupted sequence of monographic shows since 1964 until today, or with collectors.[22] Perhaps, at this point in the century, both the problem of the meaning of Morandi's painting and the value of the avant-garde movements ought to be revised in the light of a redefinition of "art history."

Already in 1983 Hans Belting put forward this methodological problem in his fundamental essay *Das Ende der Kunstgeschichte?* (1983), in which he deplored how the usual approaches are unable to offer an exhaustive answer to artistic production.[23] Riegl's *Kunstwollen*, Panofsky's iconology or Longhi's hermeneutics, no less than Gombrich's psychology of stylistic change and Hausser's sociology of art are unable to give a definitive reading of the work in itself and only create abstract schemes in which the artists themselves feel prisoners. With regard to this Belting quotes the performance of Hervé Fischer in the Centre Pompidou's Petite Salle in Paris on 15 February 1979, in which the painter symbolically cut a white cord suspended at eye height and solemnly declared that "the history of art is finished" and "innovation has already died in advance. It falls within the myth of the future."[24] In order to escape from this proclaimed crisis of the discipline, which disarms both the critic and the public in front of what seems more than ever the enigma of art, it is not enough to abandon stylistic-historical schemes that by now seem to be empty containers, unable to contain the complexity of the object.

In this context Belting himself has suggested some highly interesting solutions. First of all he underlines that "all those art historians who have formed the discipline have basically held themselves aloof from modern art. Those, instead, who have faced up to modernity avoid developing general interpretative models . . . as a consequence there is an analogous break in the artistic field and in the art historical discipline."[25] After a well-stated analysis of the complex relationship between ancient, modern, and contemporary art he hopes for a new synoptic vision of inherent problems,[26] strengthened by a greater awareness of the fact that we all look at the art of the past through the eyes (I would say the telescope) of contemporary culture. "The history of style can no longer be simply substituted by social history," he states, precisely because each "approach that overlooks the form of the work of art, or that does not make it the main object of analysis is, to say the least, uncertain."[27] After this strong plea to reconsider, even by way of an interdisciplinary point of view, the work in itself, at the end of his study Belting appears to be substantially doubtful about the future of contemporary art.[28]

His perplexities seem to be echoed by a sense of bewilderment that pervades the majority of the public, even a cultured public, in the face of the most recent art, besides a state of general confusion as far as critical evaluation is concerned: the eclectic mix of opinions is worrying. Apart from the objective difficulties in following the evolution of contemporary art—difficulties as much due to lack of information as to the comprehension of an "innovation" frenetically undergoing further changes—there are three elements that seem to me decisive in creating this uncertain situation. The first, one that derives from the historical type of criterion that evolved in the nineteenth century and to which the words of Hans Tietze referred, consists in dealing with works of art according to a classifying criterion while overlooking their intrinsic value and meaning. The second interprets them as historical documents, endowed with anthropological clues to the political, economic, and social situation but substantially extraneous to any kind of aesthetic evaluation. The third, which derives from the first two, refers to the loss of meaning of aesthetic values in contemporary criticism. The category of beauty has been overcome by relativity, by the idea that "beauty is in the eye of

These three still lifes of 1963 (from left, Vitali nos. 1298, 1299, 1300, private collection) show how with the procedure of the *series* Morandi's painting stands outside of the traditional concept of "art history" as a continual evolutionary process sustained by the idea of progress to turn into an exquisitely linguistic exploration of its media and meanings.

Morandi with Roberto Longhi in a photograph of the early sixties (courtesy Museo Morandi archive, Bologna).

the beholder." In this variable situation, where by now there is no kind of fixed point on which to build an aesthetic, the historical approach seems the only basis on which to erect the discipline of criticism.

The present crisis in painting in the real sense of the term has contributed decisively to the uncertainty of the situation, which seems to promise, more than "the death of art history," the "death of art." Here too Belting's hypotheses are of great interest.[29] He considers easel painting a genre which came to maturity in the historical situation of the thirteenth century and which was destined to die after having exhausted its real function, as happened with Greek tragedy, with the epic, and with opera.

It is in this context of widespread concern over the disappearance of painting, which is seen as "the death of art," and the disappearance of the concept of beauty itself that we should place consideration of Morandi as the last-ditch defender of the glorious Italian painting tradition and the upholder of eternal values dear to all the leading art historians, beginning with Roberto Longhi and Lamberto Vitali. Longhi's authority strongly conditioned Italian criticism until halfway through the sixties. And just as he envisaged the genius of Masaccio "emerging fully armed and defined from the painting's brain"[30] like Minerva from Jove's forehead, so Vitali interpreted Morandi as an isolated painter without teachers or fellow travelers, writing in 1961: "Morandi is not a contemporary painter," in fact, "he has never been a contemporary painter."[31] Vitali thus qualified Morandi as a character quite outside history in general and the history of art in particular. But such a definition as a painter outside time—even his own time—is unacceptable for today's critics, deeply aware as they are that each work is historically determined.[32] However, it is necessary to underline that Morandi never contradicted these words as, on the other hand, he had contradicted Arcangeli's attempt to contextualize his activity, especially that of the last period, nor did he close himself up in an obstinate and dark silence, as he had done when he wanted to disassociate himself from the dispute between supporters of realistic, politically involved painting and those of "pure art," accepting the freedom to turn to abstraction as an autonomous choice, a quarrel that had affected him first hand just after the war.[33] While not wishing to attribute to Morandi phrases he would never have said, we can still reasonably suppose that he felt himself above the problems discussed by the critics of his time, above all in Italy. As I

Morandi in his Bologna studio with Lamberto
Vitali in a photograph by Leo Lionni, 1955
(courtesy Enrico Vitali).

have tried to explain when discussing the series, he had radically moved away
from the current concept of art history. Through books and his own small
collection of antique art he looked at the masterpieces of the past in a "dia-
chronic" way, linked to a search not for eternal and aesthetic "beauty," but for a
language able to give sense and meaning to painterly form. For this reason he was
quite free to turn to Giotto, Masaccio, Chardin, Seurat, or Cézanne without
feeling they were unrelated to the problems he was dealing with; in fact he
considered them all fellow workers in his linguistic exploration of significant
form.

We must now look at how Morandi's work can be placed in the field of
contemporary research and which methodological links with other painters can
help us today to understand better the hidden but substantial innovations of his
still lifes. A more profound reply to this will be given in the essays in this catalog
by Giuseppe Panza di Biumo, Joseph J. Rishel, and Angela Vettese. For the
moment I will limit myself to giving a few indications of a general character.

As Belting has written, artists rather than critics determine the development of
artistic practice and, therefore, of art history.[34] In looking at the art of the past we
ask questions that derive from our present experiences and we see what the
artists of our own times point out to us. So, in looking at contemporary interests,
it is often possible to see clearly what the decisive elements are. Contrary to what
we usually think, Morandi is fairly well-known abroad thanks to his later work,
which was immediately sought after for private and public collections. For the
most part, the rare Metaphysical works and the paintings from the Fascist period
remained in Italy and, being less accessible, have had less effect. The fact that
numerous contemporary American artists have looked on the later Morandi as a
master—just as the Cubists looked on Cézanne—ought to provide us with food
for thought.

The original choice of the still life as the principle, even sole subject of his
painting places Morandi in direct relation to the idea that art can develop from
art itself. This idea, which gave rise to the epithet "modern," began with the

break that occurred in the last decades of the nineteenth century when the work of art tended to drop its traditional expressive or representative meanings in order to take on increasingly the conventional value of linguistic research, according to what Filiberto Menna has called "the analytic path of modern art."[35] For centuries considered a minor subject with respect to "history painting," as well as to portraiture and to religious themes, and relegated to the sphere of imitation from life, of illusionist technical virtuosity, of compositional ability, the still life seemed destined to speak above all the symbolic language of *vanitas* if not the simpler one of decoration. With the arrival of modern art the problems of color, composition, and the appearance of what is painted become fundamental and constitute the problem of being and of appearing as well as the linguistic problem and painting and of art in general. In fact during the nineteenth century art lost its main traditional functions, that is, the devotional function in an increasingly secular context, the celebratory function, which shifted from the portrait to photography and the mass media, the didactic function, which was taken up by the communications media, and the decorative one which was absorbed by industry and architecture. The function of philosophical meditation on itself, on man, and on the world seems to have become the only alternative left to art that can give it sense and guarantee its survival. And so, from having been a minor genre, the still life became the favoured theme for the meditation of art on itself, on its expressive means, and on its meanings. It is in this genre that the relationship with painters of the past and with art history was concretely verified; on the other hand it is here that the most clamorous innovations also regarding the use of materials occurred. The whole history of modern art passes through the still life—from Cézanne to Picasso, from Cubism to Dadaism, from Metaphysics to Surrealism and Pop Art. To have painted in this genre right from the beginning and to have explored it with unswerving dedication certainly meant for Morandi never abandoning an investigation that placed him at the heart of the problems of modern and contemporary art.

The theme of the object is the essential element within the still life genre. The famous bottles, boxes, coffee pots and all the rest that we see today in the Museo Morandi in Bologna are not humble and unassuming things that were once a part of a daily life lived without emphasis or noise and which might be defined as objects of "affection:" they are the objects of painting. Chosen for their form and color, covered in a thick layer of dust that eliminates the memory of their function in order to replace it with sheerly tonal values, these objects are often found to have been painted, in their turn, inside, outside, and along their edges, like the big white Mantuan oil-bottle that is seen time and again in Morandi's canvases and which he had painted with a dark line around its base. So they are objects for painting, symbols of life offered to our thoughts, related through their concreteness and poetry to other artists who have abandoned two-dimensionality of the canvas in order to cross the threshold of sculpture without depriving themselves of color, such as Robert Rauschenberg, Jasper Johns, Stuart Arends, or Lawrence Carroll.

The fact that he never abandoned traditional technical means—canvas, brushes, and paint—suggests that Morandi wanted to verify and analyze them through a pre-existing ancient tradition and to compare himself with both contemporary artists and with the artists of the past. So a discussion of materials is of particular importance. He always gave a great deal of attention to the technical aspects of his work. His mastery of etching is known to all. No less important is the skill with which he himself stretched his canvases and ground colors for his paint. He considered these to be highly important aspects and never wanted to delegate them to industry and buy ready-made products.

As I have said, in his last years his paint became thinner and inconsistent, as did the preparation of the canvas which became so thin as to allow light to filter

A photograph by Leo Lionni from the early sixties, taken in Morandi's studio; the objects painted by the artist make up a composition for a still life.

through it. Certainly nothing could be more different from the thick paint layers of the Art Informel group to whom Morandi had so violently objected to being compared by Arcangeli. This new way of applying paint evidences the *ductus* of the brushstrokes—in other words a further technical aspect of picture making—and, more generally, the two-dimensionality of the support, giving importance to all the materials making up the painting. So at all levels painting is proposed as a special place for philosophically meditating on man and on the world, thoughts that cannot be translated into words—with which Morandi, anyway, was notoriously avid. His argument is not made *with* materials in some kind of incarnation of Neo-Platonic ideas, but *from* the materials which make up its intrinsic substance. This attention to the technical side of things which Morandi constantly cultivated, especially in his last period, is in harmony with both the latest tendencies of art criticism, which is now beginning to use for its own purposes the outcome of scientific analyses in the field of restoration,[36] and a large part of contemporary artistic investigation, which, in contrast to the flood of mass and multimedia information, further underlines the importance of technical and handicraft techniques.

This linguistic kind of meditation accompanies the creative process of the *series*, the theoretical implications of which I have amply spoken. I must stress that both approaches place Morandi at the center of the most innovative artistic debates of the fifties and sixties. The following examples illustrate my point. The *series* can easily be related to Warhol's *Flowers*, in which not only the same subject but the identical image are repeated in different variations of color, or to Josef Albers' *Homages* which propose ad infinitum the same image in various chromatic versions explained by long notes on the back of the canvas. Even though apparently quite different, Morandi's painting is close to that of Agnes Martin in its self-referential aspects, in its use of materials and in the methodical investigation of variants in a rigorously codified sign system.

These thoughts on this exhibition, as already occurred with *Boccioni 1912 Materia*,[37] had their roots not in any academic training, but in my long cohabitation with Morandi's paintings. In fact, apart from brief periods, I have always had paintings by him in my home, above all those from the second decade of this century and from his last period. Forced to stay in bed for some months, I had in front of me the *Still Life* with bottles and fruit of 1916, now exhibited in the

The paintings by Morandi in the Gianni Mattioli collection in the apartment in Via Senato 36, Milan, in a fifties photograph (courtesy Mattioli archive, Milan).

Peggy Guggenheim collection in Venice. Looking at that painting for such a long time made me aware of what enormous complexity was hidden behind such apparent simplicity.

Other Metaphysical paintings, those by Carrà for instance, reveal their message after a short period of time, almost as though it were a literary message. Morandi's painting, instead, is a visual argument that is explicated at various levels and that passes from the world of the senses to that of philosophy. Such reflections have become further complicated by questions arising from my period of teaching art criticism at the Carrara academy in Bergamo: what art history can be written today and what is the position of certain artists such as Morandi? The experience of contemporary art, above all American, has had a great clarifying effect. From a direct comparison I became aware that late-period Morandi, more than any other modern Italian artist, can live happily alongside the other recent works that, in my home, have taken the place of the Futurists that belonged to my father. So I would invite the visitor to linger over the still lifes exhibited in this show, to observe them at length, because this is the only way that one can *experience* Morandi's poetics.

[1] L. Vitali, *Giorgio Morandi pittore*, Edizioni del Milione, Milan, 1964, p. 5. Printing was finished on 25 January 1964.

[2] In considering the master's later period his extremely dramatic last three oil paintings have been ignored because they were tragically left unfinished at the time of his death (still lifes, Vitali nos. 1341–1343). Morandi himself spoke of their "new ideas." Of these "new ideas" and of his dismay at the fact that they were destined to remain forever unfinished, Roberto Longhi spoke in his necrology "Exit Morandi," *Paragone*, Florence, no. 175, July 1964.

[3] Vitali, *Giorgio Morandi pittore*; F. Arcangeli, *Giorgio Morandi*, Edizioni del Milione, Milan, 1964; M. Valsecchi, *Morandi*, Garzanti, Milan, 1964; A. Martini, *Giorgio Morandi*, series *I maestri del colore*, Fabbri, Milan, 1964.

[4] *L'opera di Giorgio Morandi*, ed. by G.A. Dell'Acqua, R. Longhi and L. Vitali, exh. cat., Palazzo dell'Archiginnasio, Bologna, 30 October–15 December 1966; *Giorgio Morandi 1890–1990. Mostra del centenario*, ed. by M. Pasquali, exh. cat., Galleria Comunale d'Arte Moderna, Bologna, 12 May–2 September 1990; *Morandi e Milano*, ed. by various authors, exh. cat., Palazzo Reale, Milan, 22 November 1990–6 January 1991; *Giorgio Morandi*, ed. by M. Garberi, exh. cat., The Museum of Modern Art, Kamakura, 18 November–24 December 1989, then traveled to Okada, Fukuyama, Tokyo and Kyoto in 1990.

[5] I would point out, among the most recent, those held respectively at Palazzo Martinengo, Brescia, from December 1996 to February 1997, curated by Marilena Pasquali; at the Musée Maillol, Paris, in the same period; at the Museu de Arte of São Paulo from February to March 1997; and at the Art Gallery of New South Wales, Sydney, in May 1997.

[6] F. Arcangeli, *12 opere di Giorgio Morandi*, Edizioni del Milione, Milan, 1950; C. Gnudi, *Morandi*, Edizioni U, Florence, 1946; R. Longhi, Presentation of the solo show at the Galleria Il Fiore in Florence, spring 1945; Raimondi often wrote about Morandi from 1947 to 1951, amongst others the articles "Le cose dell'uomo nell'opera di Morandi," *La Fiera Letteraria*, Rome, 27 November 1949, and "La congiuntura metafisica Morandi-Carrà," *Paragone*, Florence, no. 19, July 1951.

[7] *Morandi: i fiori*, curated by M. Pasquali and V. Rubiu, exh. cat., Palazzo Pubblico, Magazzini del Sale, Siena, 1st November 1990–6 January 1991; *Giorgio Morandi. L'immagine dell'assenza*, curated by M. Pasquali, Grizzana Morandi, 22 July–2 October 1994, dedicated to the landscapes of the war years 1940–44.

[8] F. Gualdoni, "L'ultimo Morandi," M. Semff, "Gli ultimi paesaggi di Morandi," in *Giorgio Morandi 1890–1990. Mostra del centenario*, pp. 45–50 and 51–56.

[9] Arcangeli, on page 312 of his monograph of 1964 (see note 4), speaks of about 175 photographs spread on the floor in front of him and which strike him for the "amazing insistence on the themes."

[10] L. Vitali, *Morandi. Catalogo generale*, Electa, Milan, 1977, 2 vols.; 2nd expanded ed., 1983.

[11] Still lifes, Vitali nos. 115 and 116 of 1927; Vitali no. 117 of 1927, no. 128 of 1928, no. 138 of 1929; Vitali nos. 145 and 146 of 1929.

[12] Regarding this see E.H. Gombrich, *Arte e progresso. Storia e influenza di un'idea*, Laterza, Rome-Bari, 1985 (Eng. ed. *Ideas of Progress and Their Impact on Art*, Mary Duke Biddle Foundation, New York, 1971); H. Belting, *La fine della storia dell'arte o la libertà dell'arte*, Einaudi, Turin, 1990, with bibliography (German ed. *Das Ende der Kunstgeschichte?* Deutscher Kunstverlag, Munich 1983).

[13] W. Benjamin, *L'opera d'arte nell'epoca della sua riproducibilità tecnica*, Einaudi, Turin, 1966 (German ed. *Das Kunstwerk im Zeitalter seiner technischen Reproduizierbarkeit*, Suhrkamp Verlag, Frankfort, 1955).

[14] The interview with Morandi was recorded on 25 April 1957 for "The Voice of America" (Presto Recording Corporation Paramus, New Jersey).

[15] In the 1957 interview Morandi said: "What we see is, I believe, creation, the artist's intervention, whenever he is able to eliminate those diaphragms or conventional images that are interposed between him and things."

[16] In this evolution of space the flower paintings represent a chapter apart, even though an important one. An infinite and abstract space already characterizes *Flowers* of 1916 formerly in the Jesi collection (Vitali no. 26) and the 1917 canvas from the Mattioli collection (Vitali no. 31); it is still to be found in the Metaphysical period *Flowers* of 1920 (Vitali no. 56) where the modeling of the subject is fully confirmed. In the twenties, for example in *Flowers* of 1924 (Vitali no. 87), the space surrounding the vase is only defined by the light which creates a kind of niche analogous to the spatial dimension of the canopy of a gothic statue.

[17] For the concept of "infinite space" as the basis of Renaissance perspective and, more generally, on perspective as a stylistic period the fundamental text remains that of E. Panofsky, *La prospettiva come "forma simbolica" e altri scritti*, Feltrinelli, Milan, 1966 (German ed. *Die Perspektive als "Symbolische Form,"* B.G. Teubner, Leipzig-Berlin, 1927).

[18] Ibid., p. 30 ff.

[19] Longhi, *Exit Morandi*.

[20] Gombrich, pp. 80–81.

[21] Morandi's violent reaction to Arcangeli's text, which could only be published after the artist's death, is documented in the letters published by P. Mandelli as part of "Storia di una monografia," *Accademia Clementina. Atti e Memorie*, Bologna, no. 35–36, 1995–96.

[22] As I write, the José Luis and Beatriz Plaza collection is up for sale by auction at Sotheby's, London (8–9 December 1997), but the sales so far registered—such as those of the Morat-Institut collection at Sotheby's, London, on 28 November and 1st December 1995, and the etchings from the Plaza collection at the same auction house in New York on 16 May 1997—have seen decidedly high prices.

[23] Belting, pp. 14–21.

[24] Ibid., pp. 3–4.

[25] Ibid., pp. 31–32.

[26] Ibid., p. 41.

[27] Ibid., p. 27.

[28] Ibid., pp. 48–56. Belting seems perplexed above all by Post-modernism and by an art "condemned to carry out the postulates of an already over-possessive criticism" (p. 55).

[29] Ibid., p. 40.

[30] R. Longhi, "Fatti di Masolino e di Masaccio," *Critica d'Arte*, Florence, no. XXV–XXVI, July-December 1940.

[31] L. Vitali, *Giorgio Morandi*, Olivetti, Ivrea, 1961.

[32] Today every work seems more "historically determined," not just because of such elements as culture, taste, and tradition, but also thanks to the choice and use of materials to which art historians dedicate increasing attention.

[33] See A. Trombadori, "Serietà e limiti di Morandi," *Rinascita*, Rome, May-June 1945, pp. 156 ff.

[34] Belting, p. 11.

[35] See F. Menna, *La linea analitica dell'arte moderna. Le figure e le icone*, Einaudi, Turin, 1975.

[36] The flood in Florence in 1966, with the consequent damage to the artistic heritage of the city, was a landmark in the history of restoration. Since then there has been a systematic increase in chemical, physical, stratigraphic analyses etc. on works as part of their conservation. From the seventies onward the results of these analyses have excited even more interest on the part of art historians who have begun to ask themselves new questions about materials and ways of making works. At the moment critics seem to be interested in aspects ranging from purely stylistic ones to the complexity of the work as artefact. A particularly significant example of this evolution is seen in the readings of Piero della Francesca's *Pala di Brera*, beginning with the writings of Roberto Longhi and arriving at *La Pala di San Bernardino di Piero della Francesca. Nuovi studi oltre il restauro*, ed. by F. Trevisani and E. Daffra, Centro Di, Florence, 1997.

[37] The exhibition, curated by me, was held at the Galleria dello Scudo, Verona, from 8 December 1991 to 16 February 1992; it was then shown at the Fondazione Antonio Mazzotta, Milan, in the spring of 1995. The catalog contained contributions by Marisa Dalai Emiliani, Antonello Negri, Fausto Petrella, Marco Rosci, Aurora Scotti; the technical entries of the works exhibited were by Leonardo Capano and Sergio Marinelli.

The Conventions and Convictions of a Painting Genre

Maria Mimita Lamberti

Books and Paintings in Via Fondazza

Georges Braque, *Violon, verre et couteau*, 1910. Prague, Národni Galeri. Reproduced with the title *Still Life* in *La Voce*, December 1911.

"Still life is our dictionary, and also our Treatise on harmony and our book of grammar. . ."
(Henri des Prureaux, "Della natura morta," *La Voce*, Florence, 22 June 1911)

Henri des Prureaux's definition of still life was undoubtedly a revelation for the young Morandi, as well as a stimulus to make that "most humble and aristocratic genre his own. Following the example of Chardin and Cézanne, the still life surely provided his painterly intelligence with a field free of ambiguity about content. The modern still life, "daughter of the spirit of analysis and of individualism" was indicated as the matrix for "abstract, almost occult painting, something that should never leave the studio."[1]

In December of that same year, and again in *La Voce*, des Prureaux developed this theme, publishing the first photos of Cubist paintings. Among these was Braque's oval still life, now in Prague, which in its play of mirror reflections is similar to an experiment by Morandi of 1912 (Vitali no. 4).

In obedience to the purity recommended in the magazine Morandi was always to call his works by the anodyne title of "still life." He insisted on this neutral and already academic label even when his dialectic series of individual paintings and his elusive depiction of objective data might have suggested a term such as "composition," which is so widely used among abstractionists.

If in some cases critics have grouped certain paintings by referring to a shared detail (for example in the still lifes featuring a drape), this is only a kind of studio usage which the artist himself never publicly confirmed. *Still Life* and nothing more; what counted was the picture, the painting (or rather, the work process): this was what Morandi repeated in interviews. His acceptance of such a neutral and traditionally academic term seemed to protect rather than disturb him, like the old fashioned and unchanging formulas of courtesy which he used in his letters. Morandi, afraid of giving offence, once said to Francesco Paolo Ingrao after years of friendship, "You must excuse me if I use the formal *Lei* instead of *tu*, but I also use *Lei* with Lamberto Vitali."[2] A formal education, or form as education, might be the correctly ambiguous formulas of these defenses, both as a man and as an artist.

Like the secret space of the studio, the still life genre, in its apparent monotony and above all in the importance it placed on the identity and recognizability of the obsolete objects chosen by Morandi, risked becoming a kind of cage, a scheme for judging the content first and only later its stylistic qualities. This was apparent in the scorching letter that Licini wrote to Marchiori after visiting the Rome Quadrennial in 1939: the artist's identification with his objects was mistaken for nostalgia for humble kitsch *à la* Gozzani.[3] To paraphrase a beautiful phrase Cesare Garboli wrote about Penna's poetry, we might answer that, "as the dazzling and splendid history of an obsessive neurosis" Morandi's painting "has nibbled at all the walls of his prison."[4]

Paul Cézanne, *Pichet et fruits*, 1900–1906. Winterthur, Sammlung Oskar Reinhart.

Even if, instead of applying the traditional label of "still lifes," or "silent lifes" as Isabella Far de Chirico preferred, we were to refer to Morandi's paintings by the evocative titles of recent exhibitions based on this theme—from *Der stille Dialog* (1978) to the *Objects of Desire* (1997)—little would be gained in terms of understanding Morandi's repertoire. A paradoxical attempt to describe bottles, worn cups, and chipped vases as *Gemälte Schätze* (painted treasures) would perhaps serve, in its jarring dissonance, to underline how ironic such a choice would be. Just think of the difficulty in recognizing such an elusive object as the clock-case that appears in some still lifes of 1914 and which so firmly negates a content-orientated reading of painting.

The elementary analysis of the still lifes of Le Douanier Rousseau is the second pole of this deliberately low-key choice of humble nineteenth-century objects, like an ironic junk-dealer's stock-taking list not so different from the Florentine roast-chestnut sellers' signs which elicited the same amazement for the naïf in Soffici as Le Douanier's paintings. From the beginning Morandi's objects are *trouvés*, marginal, provocative choices that, cannot be rendered explicable by forced references to the standard decadent poets. Baudelaire, a poet much loved by turn of century artists, dedicated a whole poem to a perfume flask,[5] including these two fascinating lines, "Je suis un vieux boudoir plein de roses fanées, / Où gît tout un fouillis de modes surannées."[6] Among other things this parallel, which has a funerary aura, with its wardrobes and drawing-rooms hiding mementos and old-fashioned objects, a tomb and a common grave, and the weight of the artist's memories and thoughts, is already to be found in the ideas evoked by the title itself, *Spleen*: boredom, detachment, a sense of the emptiness and uselessness of everyday life which a reading of Baudelaire may have focused in Morandi's mind, at least in his youth, when he was trapped by family obligations and frustrated by his wretched job as a drawing teacher in an elementary school (Morandi always rejected with disdain the obsequious epithet of "maestro" as a result of these years).[7]

The still life by Le Douanier Rousseau of 1910, formerly in the collection of Ardengo Soffici. Private collection.

Luigi Magnani used to tell a story confirming that the poverty of Morandi's objects was deliberate: when, at Magnani's insistence, Morandi agreed to paint a still life with musical instruments (Vitali no. 313), he substituted the precious instruments that had been lent to him with a little guitar and a trumpet, toys he had bought at a fair (both today conserved in the Morandi museum, Bologna). This unusual still life at first subverted Magnani's intentions, but then went beyond them by making an open reference to such a great precedent as Chardin's *Les attributs de la musique*, now in the Louvre. In fact it is only in this case (one of particular difficulty for Morandi, struggling with a theme imposed on him from the outside) that the reference to Chardin can be precisely identified: not only in the horizontal guitar, frontally placed towards the viewer, but in the wind instrument placed diagonally above it, as well as the raised surface on which the whole rests and the descending belt. These recur both in Chardin's decoration (originally a panel placed above a door) and in the elongated form of Magnani's picture.

Even if overturned, not only by referring to the non-cultural language of children's toys but in the details (the guitar is rotated from right to left, the belt can be seen behind the supporting plane. . .) these quotations from Chardin are, what is more, the only ones that can be easily recognized in Morandi's output.

Because he was a painter who reacted so acutely to visual experience that he practically nullified his own language (he confessed that he could not paint for some days after visits to shows), Morandi transformed all input after a long process of meditation: any study of works undeniably influenced by Chardin ends by leaving a wide margin of autonomy with the barest of contacts (certain volumetric relationships, the double axis of identical objects in a rhythmic whole, the planar layout, the tonal researches into white, the light and play of shadows. . .).[8] Morandi had been well aware of Chardin's role as inventor of the modern self-referential still life and forerunner of Cézanne's revolution ever since he had read the letters by des Prureaux and Soffici in *La Voce*.[9] The artist himself wrote in a letter to Bartolini: "I would be only too happy to achieve a tenth of what Chardin created."[10] In the heat of the controversy over the Quadrennial, Bartolini, poisonously pointed out Chardin's precedents, to then hurl the unfair accusation of plagiarism: "And I repeat that sometimes Morandi lifted the subject of a painting by Chardin in its entirety: as he also did when he etched the beautiful print of the pears, apples and muscat grapes, one of those that I praised . . . but praised when I did not yet know that the etching was derived from the painting *Fruit* in the Reinhart collection at Winterthur. Morandi, among other things, has never been to France, but he saw Chardin from photos of paintings by Chardin that he kept pinned up on the walls of his studio in 1932."[11] While the direct comparison of the Chardin with Morandi's etching demonstrates the complete lack of foundation of this insinuation, in any case it is interesting to hear of the reproductions of Chardin's works pinned to the walls of Morandi's studio; in fact, Bartolini had already mentioned this detail elsewhere, but here he gives a precise date, 1932.[12]

In 1932 Valori Plastici published in Paris, in French, a monograph on Chardin edited by André de Ridder and illustrated with ninety-six black and white reproductions,[13] including all his major paintings in the Louvre as well as, under the title *Fruits*, the Winterthur still life (pl. LXXVII).[13] The book was printed in November 1931 in Spoleto in a limited edition. Morandi's copy, however, is not only intact—and therefore the plates cannot have been cut out of it—but a letter found inside it proves that it was not sent from Florence to the painter until 1939.[14] Of course this is not sufficient to rule out the de Ridder edition as a possible source for the Chardin iconography known by Morandi in the early thirties: given the close relationships between the two documented by the Bro-

Jean-Baptiste-Siméon Chardin, *Les attributs de la musique*, 1765. Paris, Musée du Louvre.

Still Life, 1941 (Vitali no. 313). Mamiano di Parma, Fondazione Magnani Rocca.

glio archive from 1932, the publisher, whom the artist had already asked for a photograph of Cézanne's *La maison du pendu*, might well have supplied him with some of the volume's clichés while the book was being printed in Spoleto.[15] Even though de Ridder's text is full of biographical observations on Chardin that could be applied as they stand to Morandi's habits and quirks, it should be noted that in the copy found today in the Morandi museum in Bologna the only marks in the margins dating from after the Second World War (and there is no reason to doubt that they are by Morandi) highlight techniques for preparing canvases and for laying down color.[16]

Obviously, the artist's approach to the illustrations was different: he never made direct quotations but limited himself to a lengthy study of the compositional schemes. This was Morandi's longstanding habit, and it had always permitted him to draw the greatest advantage from black and white photographs of inaccessible works. The 1932 book (chronologically the first of the four texts kept in the library)[17] confirms, among the most obvious references, *La tabagie*, a still life that for its play of sharp volumes and the presence of the large jug seems to interact with various of the painter's works of the twenties.[18]

Jeune homme construisant un château de cartes is well documented in de Ridder's reproductions: in 1956 when Morandi went to Winterthur he studied the picture at length and observed the detail of the cards on the table, probably verifying a construction that had already caught his attention in photographs.[19] And, although the 1932 book documented the Hermitage variant of *Jeune homme jouant avec des cartes*, it is, for the moment, mere speculation that Morandi knew of the replica of this painting that arrived in the Uffizi in 1951.

The detail of the house of cards (in a horizontal parallelepipid form in the Reinhart version, like a stage wing in that of the Uffizi) can be related to various of Morandi's still life schemes (such as the extreme foreground of the two still lifes of 1953, Vitali nos. 891 and 892), but so can his habit of hand-constructing cardboard boxes, now conserved in the Morandi museum, to be used in his still lifes together with milk containers and bottles, repainted or zoned with paint.

The artist's work on his chosen objects is analogous to hand-building things, a way to alter real data in view of his plans for a painting. It is not different from Morandi's dust, about which so many fascinating words have been spent (dust as the basis of tonal play, as the sign of time passing, like the sand through an hourglass, or, instead, the suspension of events; again, as the extreme *vanitas*

Jean-Baptiste-Siméon Chardin, *La tabagie*, ca. 1737. Paris, Musée du Louvre.

Jean-Baptiste-Siméon Chardin, *Fruits*, 1758. Winterthur, Sammlung Oskar Reinhart.

Still Life with pears and grapes of 1927 (Vitali etchings no. 36).

From Morandi's library: the monograph on Chardin by André de Ridder published in Paris in 1932 with the reproduction of *Jeune homme construisant un château de cartes* of ca. 1735. Winterthur, Sammlung Oskar Reinhart.

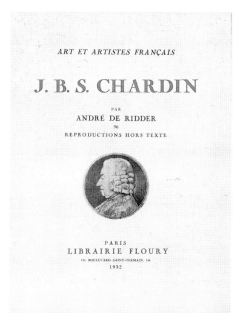

vanitatum or even the equivalent of snow softening the features of a landscape). Further evidence of Morandi's relationship with the still lifes set up on the three surfaces in front of the two easels in his studio, is the change in relative size between the real objects and the painted ones (a notable scale reduction which, in his last years, led to an unusually reduced format even with respect to easel painting). It is as though the painter observed "so-called nature" by reversing the binoculars already used at Grizzana in order to distance the landscape subjects; an alienation perhaps suggested by a note by Pascoli to his *Fanciullino* ("Little Boy"), a poem that Morandi's sisters, who were school teachers, must have known by heart. The passage did not escape Pasolini in his graduate thesis, even though he did not see its connection with Morandi's method, known to only a few: "Do you have some binoculars? Point them on the countryside, on a house, a town. Look through the right end: that is prose. Look through the other end: that is poetry. The first has more details and is more distinct. The second more vision, and more . . . poetry."[20]

Bartolini, in his usual derisive tones, referred to Morandi as a fake, Pascoli-like "little boy," and perhaps this was meant to refer not only to the image spread by the critics but also to specific knowledge of reading or conversations that took place in Via Fondazza when they were still friends.[21]

Just as Pascoli the critic offers clues to the reasons behind Morandi's technique so, with an apparent paradox, a literary interpretation of Morandi's choice of objects might come from Cézanne's well-known words about the physiognomy of a sugar bowl, which transforms the still life into a portrait and the compositional relationships into an intimate dialogue between things.[22]

The existential unease underlying what seems so cosy and homelike has its most moving comment in a private confession of Matisse: the choice of objects the painter depicts while experiencing them is not a neutral act but the projection into the things of a feeling (and a need) for tenderness "without the risk of suffering from them, as happens in life."[23]

Still Life, 1935 (Vitali no. 892). Whereabouts unknown.

> Marcello – Say, I see you have a magnificent Morandi.
> Steiner – Ah yes: he's the painter I love most. The objects are immersed in a dream-like light, eh? And yet they are painted with detachment, precision, and a rigor that makes them almost tangible. You can say it's an art in which nothing happens by chance.
> (Federico Fellini, *La dolce vita*, 1960)

Scene photograph of Fellini's film *La dolce vita*, 1960: Mastroianni standing before the enlarged reproduction of the 1941 *Still Life* formerly in the Jucker collection (Vitali no. 305). (Courtesy Archivio Storico del Cinema / AFE, Rome, and Ugo Brusaporco.)

In all the anecdotes about Morandi I have never heard a reference to his going to see the movies. So I think we can exclude that the then seventy-year-old painter ever saw *La dolce vita*, despite the scandal and fame that accompanied its release; but perhaps a friend mentioned to him how, in the fictitious and emblematic collection of the intellectual Steiner, a recognizable Morandi still life was the object preferred for aesthetic comment over the copies of Rouault, Casorati, and Ferrazzi hung on the set.

It is not hard to imagine the restrained reaction of the moody artist at such a reference ("enormous" was his comment about contemporary excesses). Furthermore, had he actually seen the film we can imagine his grin, not just at the innocent banality of the dialog between Steiner and Marcello, but for the incorrect reproduction of the picture, disrespectful, at the very least, of an art "in which nothing happens by chance." In fact, in order to make the copy visible the scene designer had altered its proportions, not just enlarging it but changing its format from horizontal to vertical. Despite these variations we can easily recognize the "magnificent Morandi" in Steiner's Roman home as the *Still Life* painted in 1941 (Vitali no. 305) in the Jucker collection in Milan. It is only from the photographs of the set that we can recognize another Morandi, hung in the library under *The Two Sisters* by Casorati: the *Still Life* of 1929, formerly in a collection in Jesi and later moved to Brera (Vitali no. 143).

In another emblematic film of 1960, *La notte* by Michelangelo Antonioni, once again with Marcello Mastroianni as the lead actor, another still life by Morandi (lent by Galleria il Milione) appears in its original state on the walls of Pontano's studio.[24]

In the interior decoration of Italian movies Morandi's bottles are an easily recognizable sign: for Antonioni they indicate a modern and economically stable Milanese context (in the same scene the other recognizable works are a Campigli, a large Sironi, and some sculptures by Somaini); for Fellini, and for his co-writers Tullio Pinelli and Ennio Flaiano, the (copied) picture served to suggest the owner's position in an intellectual circle whose values were about to be wiped out by a corrupt society (in fact, the existential breakdown of Steiner, the owner of the Morandi and the refined player of Bach, explodes in the sudden and dramatic decision to kill himself and his two children).

The stereotype seen in both films proposes two real and actual facts in Morandi's career: on the one hand, the monopoly of the Milanese market, as a result of a purposely rationed supply of works, and the consequent selective policy of prices and buyers in answer to a greater demand than the supply. On the other hand, the position manned by intellectuals in defense of Morandi presented him as a difficult, élite painter, a rare and precious craftsman whose sophisticated language could only be deciphered and understood by very few. In the simplification of both films the presence of a painting by Morandi concentrated within the limits of an object the figure of a painter preferred by an élite, in terms both of money and of quality.

Perhaps more interesting than Antonioni's truth is Fellini's fiction, a fiction,

Alain Cuny (above) and Leonida Répaci (right) in another scene photograph of Fellini's film *La dolce vita*. On the right two works can be made out: a still life of 1929 (Vitali no. 143) and the painting by Felice Casorati *The Two Sisters* of 1921. (Courtesy Archivio Storico del Cinema / AFE, Rome, and Ugo Brusaporco.)

what is more, that Fellini went searching for with method and conviction, reconstructing, as is well-known, entire exteriors in Cinecittà in Rome. Even if there was no lack of Morandis in Roman collections (some of them actually in the movie world, such as those of De Sica and Zurlini), certain questions arise about the enlargement of the Jucker still life with respect to the Jesi one: it was then a painting nineteen years old but one of the few, in the fifties, that could easily be reproduced by means of a photographic plate then in circulation.[25]

Perhaps chosen for its clear and legible arrangement of vertical elements (the bottle, the vinegar bottle, the gas lamp), the still life corresponds to a notion that linked the artist to his objects, a widespread view of Morandi summed up somewhat too succinctly in a popular handbook after the war: "MORANDI GIORGIO. . . . He paints almost exclusively still lifes (especially bottles and the like), landscapes, some self-portraits and no figures."[26] This still refers to the ancient battle over genres, but above all it schematizes Morandi's career as one locked into a timeless dimension by its scarce or nonexistent renewal of subjects, an idea repeated in other parts of the text (published in 1949), and underlined above all by the choice of images: just one work of 1946 and all of three from 1919–20, even though not just of bottles.[27]

The choice of the still life with bottles, dated yet still meant to set the tone for Steiner's house, may not therefore be blamed on a tired prop manager's carelessness, but instead reflects the lack of visibility (and awareness) of the new postwar Morandi, a situation that extended even to the art world.

It might be said that in Italy the cultural bet on Morandi had been closed with the successes and the polemics that grew out of the 1939 Quadrennial in Rome, about which both detractors and admirers had then fixed their parameters of judgment (even the excited political climate after the Second World War had, with regard to Morandi, been anticipated in 1939 by the young artists of the "Corrente"). This judgmental immovability was accompanied by the objective difficulty of seeing, either directly or in reproduction, Morandi's new works, which might have changed the critical view of the painter as by now belonging to the past. This view was common to the opposing factions even though it oscillated between a pauperist or crepuscular reading of the content (defended either in a quietly lyrical manner or opposed because of its poverty of meaning) and the ivory tower of the sublime model of art for art's sake (once discussed in post-Fascist political circles as Crocian alterity, but now accused of being bourgeois lack of commitment). The urgent needs of artists and critics, when measured against these stereotypes, pushed in other directions: political debate, the tensions between abstraction and figuration, discussions about realism, technical and expressive renewal, and all of this seemed to happen in the absence of Morandi, too often accused of being out of date by now, or even completely silenced.

In 1963, a year before his death but at a moment when his production had arrived at an extraordinary linguistic freedom, it was possible to read a public distancing from "post-Morandi naturalism" in a kind of posthumous judgment from a revolutionary court of current affairs: ". . . we are no longer in the age of the Macchiaioli nor of dissoluteness nor even of Brücke-like or Blaue Reiter-like expressionism or of post-Morandi naturalism. This is a far more serious time where painting has other tasks than being anecdotal, illustrative, romantically sentimental, atmospherically intimate, or objectively photographic."[28] Not very generous definitions, but above all not correct when measured against the paintings, better known today than to the critics and the public of the time.

Nicolas de Staël, *Nature morte au fond bleu*, 1955. Antibes, Musée Picasso, gift of Françoise de Staël.

Even Carlo Ludovico Ragghianti, friend and companion during the war years in Bologna, found he had to complain of the lack of visibility of the new, post-war work of Morandi. He wrote that he did not know the works very well, much less the sequences of series that were making them far more significant. As a demonstration of the oligopolis which he would later openly denounce,[29] Ragghianti plublished new works by Morandi in only two issues of the art magazine *Sele Arte* which he directed: in 1957 a montage places three works from the twenties together with the 1957 *Still Life* (Vitali no. 1033) from the New York show and the one—rather striking with its two lone objects, a two-colored box and a Persian bottle, placed way up in the foreground, and its unusually long format of 41.5 × 22 cm—from the same year (Vitali no. 1062). Three years later, in the fall of 1960 there was a color plate showing a watercolor of Grizzana from 1959, while on a black and white page two small still lifes also dating from 1959 (Vitali nos. 1159 and 1163) were placed together.[30]

The two contrasting monographs, the authorized one by Lamberto Vitali and the other, unauthorized one by Arcangeli represent a case apart, as far as knowledge of Morandi's work is concerned.[31] It is impossible to compare the two here, but it is sufficient to remember how in Arcangeli's book, completed in 1961 and printed three years later, the most recent work reproduced was the 1959 *Still Life* (Vitali no. 1152), while the text arrived as far as two landscapes "from this late fall:" probably the 1961 *Landscape* (Vitali no. 1251) and, the very "strong, almost bad-mannered, painted straight off almost like a Munch," 1961 *Landscape* (Vitali no. 1252).

The 1960 *Still Life* (Vitali no. 1202) loaned by Galleria Il Milione for Antonioni's film *La notte*.

While the general outline of the plates and the critical-biographical notes remained unchanged, between the book planned by Arcangeli for Il Milione and the one signed by Vitali in 1964, the lack of plates of these two landscapes in the Morandi-approved edition seems a further and intentional taking of distance from Arcangeli's hyper-contemporary reading. A more detailed examination could of course show that other plates expunged are from among the works best loved by Arcangeli and underlined by his comments. They are genuine deletions from Vitali's orthodox repertory, ratified by the painter at the moment when he intended to give his blessing to the public image of his artistic career through the new monograph.[32]

An evaluation of the real consistency, more modest in Italy than abroad, of Morandi's effective participation in exhibitions, not of a retrospective kind, but

Still Life, 1955 (Vitali no. 943), the only work by Morandi selected for the 1964 Venice Biennial.

Landscape, 1961 (Vitali no. 1252).
Private collection.

as an active painter at the height of his maturity, might hold surprises, yet objectively speaking, it would net affect his aura of extraordinariness and complexity. And this in the context not of a drop in the painter's productivity (on the contrary, in his last years of life it is the sheer number of works that impresses), but on the monopoly on the Italian market, restricted to a precise waiting list of collectors and closed off to foreign outlets (Ghiringhelli certainly did not need to exhibit the latest Morandis in order to sell them).

This reserve was further accentuated by the painter's aversion to public events, as well as his persistent bad habit of declaring he painted very little ("seven or eight pictures a year" was a recurring phrase throughout his life, but it is not born out by the catalogue raisonné). However, mention of the extremely limited production of works, as legendary as the artist's misanthropy, is to be found in all interviews with the elderly painter, far more than one might expect from these circumstances, even though by and large they were interviews conceded, with polite openness, to non-Italian scholars and journalists.

A reconstruction of the activity and of the construction of the image of Morandi in the last two decades of his life puts in doubt not only the provincial vision of a painter enclosed in his beloved yet hated Bologna, but also the old and persistent image, along the lines of that of Soffici, of a local painter, first of all, and then only afterward an Italian one: instead he seems clearly international in terms of his decisions regarding exhibitions and the press during the fifties and sixties.[33]

If anything, the paradox of the later Morandi was in being less noted and acknowledged in Italy than abroad: the example of a contemporary who was extremely interested in Morandi was, not by chance, Nicolas de Staël, whom Arcangeli considered a kindred soul of Morandi and who was exhibited in the same refined American circles.[34] If this is valid as a small proof, in the 31st Venice Biennial in 1964, which opened on June 20 (two days after Morandi's death), the only painting by him in the international section *Arte d'oggi nei musei*, was a still life of 1955 lent by the Museu de Arte Moderna in Rio de Janeiro (Vitali no. 943).[35] In the retrospective at the 1966 Biennial, where post-war Morandis made up over a quarter of the oils shown in the eight rooms, this percentage (25 out of a total of 83) changed dramatically in the catalog: out of eight plates the only post-war painting reproduced was once again the *Still Life* of 1957 (Vitali no. 1062). Notable for embarrassment disguised as emotion was Roberto Longhi's choice to publish in the catalog the text he had written to present the solo show by Morandi at the Galleria Il Fiore in Florence in April 1945.

The distancing is, however, quite explicit in the brief introduction where Longhi isolated the artist's output from the context of current art—present in the Biennial—thus highlighting a kind of primacy of the works produced from 1919 until the breaching of the Gothic Line in 1943 with respect to the "additions of the last twenty years." There was an historical perspective, then, but a highly polemical one with a strong misoneistic streak. At the end of this introduction, where without a doubt one of the targets is Arcangeli's visceral contemporaneity, Longhi anyhow finds himself in a retrograde position even with respect to Morandi's final production: "In re-reading this brief essay, and noting that the Florentine show covered a period, from 1919 until 1943, similar to the one that predominates in the Venice selection, apart from the additions from the past twenty years, I hope that this might still serve as an introduction to today's public, also in order to remove Morandi from a context in which he found himself involved by force of circumstances and about which, unfortunately, it is no longer possible to have an answer from him, apart from the one implicit in his work."[36]

Already in his letter of 1962 to Arcangeli, which was to end bitterly the question

From *Sele Arte*, no. 33, November-December 1957: two still lifes of 1957 (from top, Vitali nos. 1033 and 1062), in a sampling of works by Morandi.

of the Morandi monograph, Longhi had admitted that his dissent was based on opposing value judgment about modern movements: positive on the part of the forty-seven year old critic, "basically skeptical and negative" on that of the seventy-two year old master.[37] In this sense Morandi was proposed as an antidote and admonishment to "all those deviations of an abstractionist tendency," while, with the exception of the Cubists, Klee, and Soutine, any other possible comparison or reference to other names in contemporary art "near or at a tangent to Morandi was rejected."

If, in the context of Morandi's production, we compare the selection of his works in the Longhi collection with, for example, the works belonging to Venturi, the former shows a clear preference for an assertive and non-problematic Morandi: it is a classic defensive proviso slashing the knot linking tradition (above all of life and habit) to the refined modernity of the results, leaving aside the artist's own poetics, which are what really make this painter unique in our time.[38]

[1] For Henri des Prureaux, a French painter with a villa at Montughi, friend of Soffici and of Papini, the owner of two important pictures by Gauguin, see J.F. Rodriguez, *La réception de l'Impressionnisme à Florence en 1910*, Istituto Veneto di Scienze, Lettere ed Arti, Venice, 1994, pp. 143–151.

[2] F.P. Ingrao, "Ricordo di Giorgio Morandi," in *Quaderni morandiani n. 1: Morandi e il suo tempo*, by various authors, Mazzotta, Milan, 1985, p. 47.

[3] This well-known letter marks the distance between the author and his old friend, "sent to sleep by the opium of Soffici, Oppo and company," but without doubting his talent. Instead, Licini says that he suffers for "this backward path, from Cézanne to Chardin and beyond," in the name of their intense friendship during their early years in Bologna (see the letter to Marchiori of 3 March 1939 in O. Licini, *Errante, erotico, eretico. Gli scritti letterari e tutte le lettere*, ed. by G. Baratta, F. Bartoli, Z. Birolli, Feltrinelli, Milan, 1974, pp. 142–143).

[4] C. Garboli, *Penna Papers*, Garzanti, Milan, 1984, p. 38.

[5] The "maudit" aspect of the Bolognese "boys"—Licini, Morandi, and Vespignani—is shown by a contemporary photograph, while Licini wrote to Morandi himself in 1927: "Do you remember our gang and the nights we lived through?" (Licini, pl. 8 and p. 104). The poetic preferences of Licini, from Leopardi to Baudelaire, studied by Gino Baratta (ibid., pp. 33–41) seem to have been shared by Morandi.
For the poem quoted, see C. Baudelaire, *Les fleurs du mal. Spleen et idéal, XLVIII: Le Flacon*: "En ouvrant // . . . // dans une maison déserte quelque armoire / Pleine de l'âcre odeur des temps, poudreuse et noire, / Parfois on trouve un vieux flacon qui se souvient / D'où jaillit toute vive une âme qui revient. // Mille pensers dormaient, chrysalides funèbres, / Frémissant doucement dans les lourdes ténèbres, / Qui dégagent leur aile et prennent leur essor, / Teintés d'azur, glacés de rose, lamés d'or. // . . . // Ainsi, quand je serai perdu dans la mémoire / Des hommes, dans le coin d'une sinistre armoire / Quand on m'aura jeté, vieux flacon désolé, / Décrépit, poudreux, sale, abject, visqueux, fêlé, // Je serai ton cercueil, aimable pestilence!"

[6] Baudelaire, LXXVI: *Spleen*: "J'ai plus de souvenirs que si j'avais mille ans. // Un gros meuble à tiroirs encombré de bilans, / De vers, de billets doux, de procès, de romances, / Avec de lourds cheveux roulés dans des quittances, / Cache moins de secrets que mon triste cerveau, / Qui contient plus de morts que la fosse commune. / . . . / Je suis un vieux boudoir plein de roses fanées, / Où gît tout un fouillis de modes surannées, / Où les pastels plaintifs et les pâles Boucher, / Seuls, respirent l'odeur d'un flacon débouché."

[7] Emilio Cecchi described the emotional state of Morandi in 1918, "after six months of acute cerebral anaemia," in his *Taccuini* (Mondadori, Milan, 1976, p. 294) and, above all, in a letter to his wife of 6 June 1918. His words suggest an unusual interpretation of the artist's existential malaise (as well as of works that were later lost) in that year: "I visited Bacchelli for some time and went with him to see the painter Morandi whose snow-covered, 'Secessionist' landscape you will remember seeing in the Pizzirani room. He is an ailing, weary, worn-out kind of man who lives in a run-down house with the smell of inherited misfortunes and illnesses, in a moldy room that is his studio, bedroom, everything. He has some strange drawings: still lifes of flowers painted in tempera with the chalky, washed-out colors of stencils, silky-grays, pink, olive green etc., things which are fairly finished. He is more lyrical in some landscapes and portraits, but also more bent to borrowing things from El Greco and Derain. Altogether, there is a lot of morbidity, as well as a touch of freshness and classicism, in those still lifes which I told you about" (E. Cecchi, *Lettere da un matrimonio*, ed. by M. Ghilardi, Sansoni, Florence, 1990, p. 28).

[8] In 1958 Morandi said of Chardin that in his opinion he was the greatest of all still life painters. He added that Chardin never relied on trompe-l'œil effects; on the contrary, with his pigments, his forms, his sense of space and his "matière," he was able to suggest a world that involved him personally (E. Roditi, *Dialogues on Art*, Secker & Warburg, London, 1960, p. 56).

[9] The article by des Prureaux appeared in June 1911 while a year later it was Soffici who took an interest in Chardin: see A. Soffici, "Commentario del Louvre. Giornata seconda (Chardin)," *La Voce*, Florence, 11 July 1912.
For Chardin's reputation see E. Riccomini, "Morandi e i suoi 'congegneri,'" in *Quaderni morandiani n. 1*, pp. 13–18.

[10] Quoted by M. Pasquali in "Morandi e il dibattito artistico degli anni Trenta," in *Quaderni morandiani n. 1*, p. 117.

[11] L. Bartolini, "Diario romano. Dedicato alla critica ermetica," *Quadrivio*, no. 21, Rome, 19 March 1939. The etching by Morandi mentioned here is *Still Life with Pears and Grapes*, 1927 (Vitali etchings no. 36).
This article, the second of four published by Bartolini (and not three as might appear from the notes to "Carteggio Brandi-Morandi 1938–1963," ed. by M. Pasquali, in C. Brandi, *Morandi*, introduction by V. Rubiu, Editori Riuniti, Rome, 1990), was drawn to my attention by Paolo Rusconi, who wrote an essay on it to be published shortly in *Acme* with the title "Cronaca del caso Bartolini-Morandi alla Quadriennale del 1939."

[12] L. Bartolini, "Un pittore tra i pittori della Quadriennale," *Quadrivio*, no. 16, Rome, 12 February 1939 (now to be consulted in Brandi, pp. 157–158): "And sometimes Morandi even etched well: as when he etched the muscatel grapes and the ripe pears (so-called winter pears, with a rough skin). However, even this derives from Chardin . . . . And so Morandi

himself, and quite rightly, never hid his admiration for Chardin. I even remember that he had pinned up in his studio photos of pictures of still lifes by Chardin (little boxes, vases, bottles; or else sweet muscat grapes, winter pears, and strawberries)."

[13] The volume (A. de Ridder, *J.B.S. Chardin*, Librairie Floury, Paris, 1932) is part of the series "Art et artistes français," but the copyright belongs to the publishing house Valori Plastici, Rome.

[14] Tucked inside the book belonging to Morandi (it is copy no. 1508) was found a letter from the Beltrami bookshop, Florence, dated 15 March 1939. In answer to an inquiry from the painter of the 14th of the month, it states, "The monograph on Chardin was sent to you on the request of Messrs Valli = Via Lamarmora 19 = Florence." As it is impossible to cross-check (Morandi's letters are still being cataloged), we can imagine that this expensive book was a gift to Morandi on the part of someone who had seen his studio and knew his preferences.

[15] See E. Coen, "Morandi tra Soffici e Broglio," in *Quaderni morandiani n. 1*, p. 107: "The correspondence between Broglio and Morandi was to continue until 1932, the date of the last letter from Morandi kept in the Broglio archives. Morandi made a strange request to Broglio on the eve of a journey to Paris (letter dated 9 January 1930): 'I would like to ask a favor of you. For some time I have wanted a photo of a painting by Cézanne in the Louvre. It is *La maison du pendu . . .*'"

[16] In de Ridder's copy conserved in the Morandi library there appear, marked in ballpoint pen (and therefore after the Second World War), the following comments on the technique: "In Chardin the canvas is usually 'medium-grained and given a heavy coating which helps the fixing of the impasto characteristic of his way of working.' First of all it was treated with glue, and then covered with a thin coat of oil paint which was almost always a mixture of lead white and brownish red, and which was given to the artist in this state so he could start work at once. It was a ready-prepared surface, dark and solid. First of all Chardin laid down the darker parts and then applied the half tones, threw down here and there a lighter tone, and then, finally, returned to the more lively parts and to the shadows in order to create (the result of patient work) those harmonies that only he was capable of producing." Further: "The great secret of Chardin is to be found in a homogeneous range of colors. Seemingly monotonous, it reveals itself to be quite complex when you seize its subtleties. They are many and yet are absorbed into an overall harmony. The painter obtains such a unison thanks to his knowledge of reflections, since every color in some way acts as a mirror for another, and all are reflected in soft gradations, and strong contrasts are avoided or at once softened" (de Ridder, p. 59).

[17] The other texts belonging to Morandi are: B. Denvir, *Chardin*, Flammarion, Paris, 1950; *Hommage à Chardin*, exh. cat., Galerie Heim, Paris, June-July 1959; P. Rosenberg, *Chardin*, Skira, Geneva, 1963.

[18] The most interesting comparison with *La tabagie* is the etching *Large Still Life with a Lamp on the Right* (Vitali etchings no. 46) and it was suggested as an example in *Morandi e Milano*, exh. cat., ed. by various authors, Palazzo Reale, Milan, 22 November 1990–6 January 1991, p. 49. Visually the heart of the comparison is the jug with the handle turned to the right: the etching, though, reproduces in reverse earlier works by Morandi, such as the still lifes dated by Vitali between 1927 and 1929 (Vitali nos. 117, 128, 138). So there is a tangle of questions to unravel about: the order of the dates suggested by Vitali, the three paintings and the etching, the Chardin-like theme and its development.

[19] In de Ridder there are present, under various titles, four paintings by Chardin inspired by this subject: the one in the Louvre, once belonging to Lacaze (pl. VII), two examples from London (pls. LX and LXI) with a horizontal format analogous to the example in the Reinhart collection in Winterthur (pl. LXXVIII) and the one in the Hermitage (pl. LXXVI).
The complicated question of the many paintings by Chardin with this title is investigated in *Chardin*, exh. cat., ed. by P. Rosenberg, Grand Palais, Paris, 29 January–30 April 1979, entries nos. 65 and 73.

[20] The thesis on Pascoli, which took the place of the one on art history put together with Longhi and was lost from sight in 1943, has recently been published (in P.P. Pasolini, *Antologia della critica pascoliana. Introduzione e commenti*, ed. by M.A. Bazzocchi, Einaudi, Turin, 1993). The note with the quotation from Pascoli (ibid., p. 77) reappears as "the technique of the reversed binoculars," a "Montale-like image ante litteram" with reference to the relationship between Pascoli and Montale in an essay by Pasolini in *Officina* of 1955 (ibid., p. 233): despite the relationships and assonances with the Bologna debate, I do not think this has ever been related to Morandi.

[21] In another of the articles in *Quadrivio* in 1939 Bartolini writes that he doubts that there "exists the little boy Morandi," while he is certain that "there exists instead the cautious, hidden, modest proud taciturn Morandi who knows all the Parisian fashions and who, I repeat, what with one thing and another uses some of them to satisfy that love of things foreign that nowadays, with the re-emergence of Italian art, has fallen on hard times" (Brandi, p. 158).

[22] Part of a conversation with Gasquet: "We were talking about portraits. It is thought that a sugar bowl is without a physiognomy, a soul. But it too changes every day. It is necessary to know how to accept and flatter these ladies. . . These glasses, these plates speak among themselves. Never ending chats. . ." (J. Gasquet, *Cézanne*, Bernheim-Jeune, Paris, 1926, p. 202).

Regarding the presence of the book in Morandi's library, once again it was a gift and arrived only later in the painter's library: "One of the books he liked most was the one with conversations between Cézanne and Gasquet" (Ingrao, p. 49).

[23] ". . . in the harmony I create between the objects that I keep around me, that I live among and in which I manage to repose my tenderest feelings without suffering from them, as in life" (from a letter from Matisse to Rouveyre, 6 October 1941, in H. Matisse, *Ecrits et propos sur l'art*, ed. by D. Fourcade, Hermann, Paris, 1972).

[24] The work by Morandi is the *Still Life* of 1960 (Vitali no. 1202): the small format of the picture, 20 × 30 cm, is made more imposing by a large passe-partout, typical of the taste of the times.

My thanks to Flavio Fergonzi for having given me the information about the work and for having then identified the paintings in the movie.

[25] The 1941 painting was perhaps chosen from the color plates of the recent book published by Il Milione and edited in 1957 by P.M. Bardi.

[26] R. Salvini, *Guida all'arte moderna*, "L'Arco" series, Vallecchi, Florence, 1949, p. 275.

[27] In Salvini's text the illustrations of Morandi pictures (all still lifes) are: *Still Life*, 1919 (Vitali no. 47), already reproduced in 1921 in *Valori Plastici* and in 1922 in the catalog of the Florence Primaverile, placed after a Cézanne dresser and before a similar subject by Matisse (the comparison suffers from a cropping of the format into a square and a consequent enlargement and fuzziness of the image); the Metaphysical *Still Life*, 1919 (Vitali no. 44) placed next to de Chirico for the Metaphysical period; *Flowers*, 1920 (Vitali no. 56) contrasted with a van Gogh, even though in the comment Morandi's thick rose buds are confused with "tulips," a mistake probably due to a superficial knowledge of the painting (or of botany?).

The reproductions chosen by Salvini give preference to works from the "Valori Plastici" period, but all are reproduced anyway in the plates of Cesare Brandi's monograph of 1942. The only post-war work, compared to a *Demolition* by Mario Mafai (not a comparison of content and one that is more acute than the previous ones), was the *Still Life*, 1946 (Vitali no. 538) belonging to Raimondi. This too had already appeared in a plate in the monogaph on Morandi published by Edizioni "U," Florence, 1946, with a text by Gnudi from which Salvini extracts the comment: "Morandi's is a long pose: the image slowly rises to be focussed by the interior lens;" he then remarks on "The representation of the superior and longer lasting harmony of nature and of things, felt in their silent immobility within the ample and slow rhythm of the infinite life of light" (Gnudi), and the Dantesque "sentimental atmosphere without the tint of time." Even though we ought to note that "the aura without the tint of time" (*Inferno*, Canto III, 29) refers to an infernal storm that was anything but ataraxic, so the quotation has value as an example of the literary allusions gratuitously affixed to Morandi, while (and this is more interesting) the limited choice of works reproduced, often at second hand, helps to establish an old fashioned image of his painting, even when praising it.

[28] G. Dorfles, "I pericoli di una situazione," in *Il Verri*, no. 12, Milan, December 1963, p. 4.

[29] "During his life Morandi had, as is well known, a very few established clients for whom he reserved the greater part of his output: these clients, who were more or less hoarders, distributed the work, above all after his fame on the eve of his death. Certain gifts, and some concessions after the intervention of friends, did not change this kind of monopoly which allowed him to avoid a practical involvement he did not enjoy . . ." (C.L. Ragghianti, *Bologna cruciale 1914 e saggi su Morandi, Gorni, Saetti*, Calderini, Bologna, 1982, p. 256, in which the critic republishes his essay "Morandi in listino" which had appeared in *Critica d'Arte* in 1977).

[30] Respectively in *Sele Arte*, no. 33, Florence, November-December 1957, p. 59, and no. 48, October-December 1960, p. 7 and pl. 1. These dates do not appear in the bibliography of the descriptions in Morandi's catalogue raisonné.

[31] The reasons for the dissent between Morandi and Arcangeli, which broke dramatically the Oedipus relationship between painter and critic, have been explained by the publication of their correspondence (in P. Mandelli, "Storia di una monografia," in *Accademia Clementina. Atti e Memorie*, no. 35–36, Bologna, 1995–96, pp. 315–335).

[32] In Arcangeli's text, signed by hand July 1960–December 1961, the post-war period is dealt with in less than thirty pages mostly occupied in refuting both the hypothesis of Morandi being out of date, and the parallel with Mondrian suggested by Pallucchini. Of the flood of 175 photographs of recent works placed on the floor that Arcangeli cites as a cardinal moment in his career, the Einaudi book, which ends with a work from 1959, publishes 11, a fifth of the total works reproduced. His esteem for Morandi's later period, then, is confirmed more by the choice of photographic documentation than by the critical analysis.

[33] In the 1958 interview with Roditi, checked before publication in English by Morandi himself who made various cuts (reintegrated in the French version in 1987), this aspect of success is underlined by the artist: "My only hope is to be able to enjoy the peace and quiet I need for working. But I have been robbed of this mental peace since the time, a couple of years ago, I won the prize at the São Paulo Biennial in Brazil. Now I receive more visitors from abroad in one month than I saw in the previous ten years. Besides, now I find that it is more difficult to paint, and all my visitors and the letters I must answer, keep me extremely busy. I suddenly seem to have lots of new friends and to know more people than

I've ever known before" (in Roditi, p. 58).

[34] For Arcangeli and the affinities between Morandi and de Staël see A. Emiliani, "Un'impossibile felicità," in *Nicolas de Staël*, exh. cat., ed. by D.A. Lévy, S. Studer, and S. Tosini Pizzetti, Fondazione Magnani Rocca, Mamiano di Parma, 10 April–17 July 1994, pp. 28–33.

[35] The selection of Italian painters presented by our museums places together, respectively, Cassinari, Guttuso, Licini, Spazzapan, introduced by Vittorio Viale for the Galleria Civica d'Arte Moderna in Turin; for the Galleria Nazionale d'Arte Moderna in Rome, curated by Palma Bucarelli, Burri, Capogrossi, Fontana, Prampolini, Soldati, Vedova; for Ca' Pesaro in Venice, Perocco exhibited Birolli, Morlotti, Musič, Saetti.

[36] The foreword, dated June 1966, was reprinted in R. Longhi, *Scritti sull'Otto e Novecento 1925–1966*, Sansoni, Florence, 1984, pp. 93–94; out of the nine reproductions of oil paintings there are two post-war works not seen in the Venice show: *Flowers*, 1950 (Vitali no. 719) and *Still Life*, 1954 (Vitali no. 906), this last, unfortunately, altered at the top by a graphic artist who has cropped the image in order to help his layout.

[37] The letter is published in Mandelli, pp. 333–334.

[38] In his 1957 presentation of the solo show at the World House Galleries, Lionello Venturi finds illuminating words, perhaps as a result of his own critical career, for Morandi's antinomy: "Abstract art always implies a break with tradition, and Morandi is a traditional man . . . . To discover the most refined subtleties of modern art rooted in the most humble and traditional way of feeling: this is the secret of Morandi's art, its fascination, its uniqueness, its greatness" (from *Giorgio Morandi. Retrospective. Paintings, Drawings, Etchings 1912–1957*, exh. cat., World House Galleries, New York, 5 November–7 December 1957).

Perception and Allusion in Giorgio Morandi's Mature Art

Marilena Pasquali

"A white bottle is all that remains."
Giorgio Morandi, 1962[1]

From *Style*, no. 4, 1961: one of the two work tables in the Grizzana studio. Note how in his arrangement of the model for a new composition, Morandi takes account not only of a just-finished work, hung behind the objects (Vitali no. 1232, of 1961, now at the Winterthur Kunstmuseum), but also of a previous work with a similar layout: on the lower surface is a reproduction of a *Still Life* of 1942 (Vitali no. 376). The photograph, representative of the artist's working method in his maturity, captures both the phase of perceptual *selection* of the visible—the choice and arrangement of the objects—and its *rendering* in the work of art.

For some time now critics have placed a particular value on Giorgio Morandi's works of the fifties and sixties. By then, the sixty-year-old artist had digested the lessons of the masters, re-elaborated the stimuli of the avant-garde and overcome all his existential and expressive insecurities. While abroad there is a unanimous chorus of recognition that this is the highest point of the whole of Morandi's output ("a well-drawn trajectory" Robert Longhi has said with great intuition),[2] perhaps only in Italy, and out of an old habit that we are not inclined to discuss, there are still those who consider Morandi one of the part players in the Metaphysical movement or one of the masters of the Novecento group. They do not recognize his unique role as one of the protagonists of this century's art of which he expresses the intense interior dissatisfaction as well as the aspiration (fought against, denied, betrayed and yet impossible to renounce) to beauty and harmony.

Morandi is a difficult and secret artist of "understated luminosity,"[3] and it is not possible to explain his poetry, reduce its musical flow to concepts and words, isolate its vital impulse and emotional impact. Each work of his must be seen, felt, accepted or refused at a deeply personal level. Words, even when poetry in themselves, must remain mute before these images so rich in sensations, so full of meaning, so immediate and complete in their capacity for expressive synthesis. In order to approach the world of the artist and try to understand his linguistic characteristics we can try to analyze the constructive mechanisms of the image, what Gombrich has called the representative scheme.[4]

The Method

There are three basic phases in Morandi's creative process. First of all there is prefiguration, that is the assiduous and constant conceptual activity that identifies and puts the images into focus in the *mind*. Morandi does not start from reality but arrives at it and confronts himself with it, moving from what he has within him (was it not perhaps David Hume who said that "beauty in the eye of the beholder?").

In the second place he constantly seeks contact with the visible—one of the artist's preferred words in which he reveals his complete oneness with the culture of his times—and he looks for it through perception, that is by awareness of the sensory experience, a difficult but sure bridge built between man and reality in

As was to occur in the works of Morandi's late maturity, in this nearly monochrome *Still Life* catalogued by Vitali as no. 151 and dated by him ca. 1929, but probably from a few years later, the light-color passes seamlessly from the background surface to inside the objects—open, dynamic forms captured during a continuous process of transformation.

order for man to recognize and inhabit it. For the artist this is a matter of a gestalt kind of approach, i.e. of form and the relationships between forms, of analogies and associations, of organization and spatial orientation.

And then, having renewed the pact of faith with what is visible, after having once again made use of that handle on reality that he cannot and will not leave hold of, Morandi arrives at his rendering of what he has thought of and seen, through the artistic image; this is a kind of cognitive and highly subjective reconstruction of all the data in his possession, whether conceptual, sensory, or perceptive.

There are, then, three phases in Morandi's art, each complementary to the others: prefiguration, perception, and rendering. But there is also something more, a certain something too deep to be wholly comprehended and yet too important to be overlooked even though words are quite insufficient to describe it: from the mind's intuition and through the illusion of the senses—organized in language and interpreted according to a precise method of representation—the artist arrives at evocation and vision, the first a real *call* from within, the second speculative contemplation, in gestalt terms "active exploration"[5] and, according to the theories of phenomenology, "the revelation of essence."

Yes, because Morandi, so apparently withdrawn and distant from the static of the world is, instead, far more aware of what the world thinks and says is important. If between the two world wars his aesthetic reference point was Hermeticism, in the years of his full maturity he seemed to open out his horizons even further, developing his previous intuitions in order to share, with his usual caution in making judgments, in the new cultural climate created by the affirmation of phenomenology and existentialism.[6] What he calls the "visible" is the phenomenon, the manifestation of reality, its optical, sensory appearance. But if this is the given, if this is what we can immediately grasp, then the problem is to reconstruct the real forms of which these appearances are the reflection, and identify and implement their code in order to generate a new, unprejudiced, even unhoped-for reality.

Basing himself on certain pet concepts and the force of visual impact, Morandi selects a part of the visible to represent the whole, according to a synedochic process. Then he deepens his observation until he knows the part inside and out; from here, he tries to extrapolate its form, paring it down to mathematical elements in which the phenomenon seems to shed its empirical elements in order to carry out what Husserl defines as the "eidetic reduction" to its essence. Finally he recomposes reality into a new, completely autonomous image with respect to the data he began with. He transforms its conceptualization and observation into a single aesthetic gesture into which the artist has put all of himself, complete with sensory perceptions, thinking, and imagination, that is, the capacity for inventing complex representations different from objective reality.

Once again it is Roberto Longhi who supplies a key to understanding Morandi's poetics when he reflects on the "reduction of the subject to understatement changes; the abolition in every case of the invasive subject that devours both the work and the observer. Useless objects, unfriendly landscapes, flowers in season are all sufficient pretexts for expressing himself 'in good form' and he only expresses feeling, as we well know."[7] This was written in 1945 and, obviously, cannot take into account the later works or the extraordinary interior changes that Morandi was to bring to his images in the fifties and sixties. However, it does foresee them thanks to that quantum of prophetic authority that Longhi could claim by virtue of his long friendship with the artist and his own acute critical sensibility. There seem to be two basic concepts for appreciating Morandi: the "reduction of the subject to understatement changes" and a fearless approach to the terms of form and feeling by recognizing their oneness.

The artist works *at the roots* of the image, stripping it of every embellishment and closing his mind and eyes to the lures of decoration in order to hear only the hidden heart of reality, that life-beat conserved in its every part and which he knows how to translate into form, understood not as the exterior aspect of things but the intrinsic quality of the *feeling* of the things themselves. It seems hard to use certain terms that today retain only their most banal meanings: sentiment is not sentimentality nor is it weakness in the face of the force of reason. Instead it is the ability to feel what is around one and to transform sensory data into emotions, enriching reason with imagination and adding a pinch of pathos, perhaps of light, to the grayness of everyday life.

The Artist's Gaze and the Object

The main instrument used by Morandi for achieving what can be defined a precise geometry of the soul—rigor and poetry fused in the artist's intensity of a deep feeling for reality—is the artist's gaze, the knowledge of how to look and use the eye as the main means for piercing through appearance and arriving at essence. His is a sharp eye, highly experienced and not easily fooled, but always ready, without prejudices and completely fresh in front of the same, unchanging model, as though every time were the first time.

There is a phrase by Cesare Pavese in *Dialoghi con Leucò* which expresses this process of unveiling while digging deep: "We know that the surest—and quickest—way to amaze ourselves is to stare fixedly at a given object. At one point, it will seem to us—miraculously—that we are seeing it for the first time."[8]

Flowers, 1962 (Vitali no. 1259), formerly in the José Luis and Beatriz Plaza collection, Caracas. (Courtesy Sotheby's, London.)
The small painting, dominated by shades of gray shot through with silver dust, is one of the most touching examples of the "reduction of the subject to understatement," as Roberto Longhi noted about Morandi's work. Another example of this method of working *at the roots* of the image is the *Still Life* of 1959 (Vitali no. 1158, private collection).

The lessons that Morandi was able to draw from his knowing and differentiated repetitions are as many as the works themselves. It is, for example, sufficient to consider the completely different transformations of the artist's favorite twisted white bottle, a Houdini-like character, that appears in the still lifes of 1916 and is then used again and again until it becomes the leading actor on the stage of Morandi's composition.[9] An example of this is the intense *Still Life* of 1955, present in this show, where the bottle reigns in all its splendor of pure light made yet more blinding by the density of the shadow of a dark bottle, like an altar-boy before the altar or a knight kneeling before his lord.[10]

It is well-known that every artist "sees" better or more than an ordinary observer because of his constant attention, the exercise and perfection of his eye-instrument. And Morandi's eye was certainly perfected through practice and experience. But capacity for visual understanding, his eye's natural sharpness for forms and color suggest something more. This was later refined in his visual researches into objects and landscape views, always the same ones, a kind of extra studio made of air and light and delimited only by the Apennine crests though disciplined by rules like those that reigned inside the studio in Via Fondazza and in the white room of the final period at Grizzana.

Like the *Case della Sete*, carved out against the mountain slopes, or the *Casa del Campiaro*, reduced to the simplest marks accessible to only a few, his studio objects are choosen and regrouped each time according to a specific logic within each single composition. They appear identified by an equally specific point of view: at times proudly frontal and without the shadows that might mitigate the saturated density of the image, at other times seen from above, almost giving the sensation of a sudden: plunging drop, making everything seem smaller; at yet other times it is pushed forward toward the observer, following a principle of inverted perspective distantly derived from Byzantine art. It may be amplified and seen from the bottom upward as though to make the whole bloom and every component expand; or again, it may be diagonal, dominated by a vanishing point that measures the objects rhythmically and reduces their physical aspect, often transforming them into ghosts, the shadows of an ungraspable reality.

Still Life, 1957 (Vitali no. 1026).
Private collection.
In the fully frontal composition, the image is saturated and compact, forming a nearly perfect rectangle.

Still Life, 1957 (Vitali no. 1048).
Private collection.
The "bird's eye" point of view seems purposely to compress the group of objects, perhaps with the aim of making them look smaller.

Still Life, 1955 (Vitali no. 1056), usually dated 1957.
Bologna, Museo Morandi, formerly in the Francesco Paolo Ingrao collection, Rome. The diagonal composition—which here is enhanced by a nearly circular rhythm—rarefies the physical nature of the objects, "carving out" some of them against the dark hues of those behind them and transforming them into ghostly apparitions.

Still Life, 1957 (Vitali no. 1054), formerly in the José Luis and Beatriz Plaza collection, Caracas. (Courtesy Sotheby's, London.) The forms find room in the grouping of the figure, built within a veritable spatial cage.

Perspective: Conventions and Transgressions

Morandi knows linear perspective perfectly, but he does not always use it, purposely giving life to images that contradict its rules or, rather, are separate from them. By grouping the composition in a closed space, he need not respect painterly ways of indicating the relative size of the objects—closer things are larger and distant things smaller—nor the device of apparently converging parallel lines: his painted forms *stand* in space and find their only reference in each other and in maintaining the proportions and the relationships of size of the original models, even when all of them together are subjected to an enlarging or a diminishing process. To the convergence of straight lines he prefers a parallelism of diagonals or the perpendicular crossing of Cartesian coordinates so as to construct a spatial cage in which each form finds its place in the overall scheme. The objects placed along the diagonal are as large as those in the foreground, as are those, wholly mental ones, placed on the horizon line that, rather than retreat into the background, seem to press against the foreground and become larger the higher up they are in the painting. It is worth stressing the importance of this second line—the horizon of the composition—which defines the table top and creates a layered spatial area against which the shapes of the objects stand out. Sometimes, almost as if to force the flat space into a third dimension, Morandi draws a curved horizon like that of the outlines of the mountains surrounding the Apennine houses and, in this way, envelops the forms and pushes them forward, almost making them bow down before the viewer.

By not recognizing aerial perspective as an absolute value—for which the sharper and more concentrated the light the closer the objects seem, and the more diffused it is the more they seem indistinct and far off—he shows the *Case della Sete*, which in reality are far-off in the mountains barely visible to the naked eye as two lighter marks on the thick vegetation, like two squares devoid of material,

Still Life, 1949 (Vitali no. 677).
Private collection.
Like the one of 1962 to the right (Vitali no. 1285, Siegen, Städtische Galerie), this painting testifies to Morandi's frequent violation of linear perspective: even the objects placed in diminishing order along the diagonal are as large as those in the foreground and actually seem to grow in size the higher up they are painted.

even though of great clarity of form and light. He cuts them out of their context and enlarges the mental image without natural references using the device of observing and isolating them through the lenses of a telescope or, more simply, through a round or square hole cut in a piece of white paper, used like a photographer's lens or a film director's movie camera. All of this underlines the certainty that Morandi's painting has nothing naturalistic, mimetic or referential, and that he investigates—through perspectival transgression, too, and the removal of the same, unchanging object from its context—new horizons for thought, the ever new discovery of reality's dynamic forces, recognized in the continual metamorphoses of the visible.[11]

On the other hand, he respects, even prefers, the rule of transparency—according to which whatever lets show through is in front of what shows through—and this he does in the prismatic glass objects of his earliest years just as he did in the most magical and illusory watercolors of the sixties. The principle of superimposing (and the forms hide behind each other almost to the point of melting into unexpected figures of utterly new plane geometries) and the play of light and shade give weight and depth wherever it does not contribute to the decomposition of planes and dimensions.

Still Life, 1962 (Vitali no. 1273).
Edinburgh, Scottish National Gallery of Modern Art.
Here the artist applied the perspective principle of superimposition, so that the forms hide behind one another to the point of merging into unexpected geometric figures.

Color

If it is true that, according to Gombrich, color is a quality of our sensation, then Morandi used this quality with consummate skill, whether by innate gift or learned with experience. It was Aldous Huxley who observed that "the capacity for remembering is the basis of perception," distancing himself from gestalt theories as well as from the traditional physiological and neurological approaches to the act of seeing;[12] Morandi followed the same path, memorizing colors and selecting them within his mind as active sensations, using them as perceptive clues of the first order. The colors have three characteristics: luminosity, tonality, and purity and they are all perfectly calibrated in Morandi's painting. Here everything is light, the brushstrokes and the paint itself feed on light, space breathes light, the forms absorb light, even the chromatic edges defining the objects live through varying light intensity, while the chiaroscuro reinforces the volumes of the objects and underlines their detachment from the background.

Morandi only uses harmonic and complementary colors and prefers cool hues: greens (how many are the shades of Morandian green? Would it be possible to give them all a name?), shades of gray and beige (but here there is a last spark of warmth), lilac, and violet, colors which in the last period shade into a sad black even while remaining saturated with color. At times, however, the subdued

The color-light typical of the artist is particularly manifest in his watercolors. In these two still lifes of 1959 (from left, Pasquali no. 1959/28, Bologna, Museo Morandi, and no. 1959/30, private collection) the chromatic borders delimiting the forms radiate constant luminous vibrations.

murmur of grays, whites, and ivories is shaken by the brightness of a salmon-pink can, by the advancing of the sky blue in the painted backgrounds of his still lifes, and the intrusion of straw-yellow Persian bottles. Here Morandi works by "quality contrasts," highlighting within an apparently uniform color zone a patch of strident color. His tones are never saturated but are intermediate and neutral, clean but not pure because they always contain in themselves many other, different, color possibilities, *possibilities* that perhaps the artist will not develop but that remain *within* the individual tones as enrichment and vibration. He arrives at the maximum refinement in his watercolor paintings where a veil of color is enough to suggest the form and transform the light.

Morandi also uses color to underline the depth of the things in space and to render the appearance of reality, preferring to the artificial laws of perspective the wholly sensory and fantastic fascination of color. Reinterpreting Cézanne, he fuses formal qualities and chromatic qualities in "colored volumes" (and Cesare Brandi has based his aesthetic of "positional color" on this), also transforming shadow into volume, into a new figure in space.[13] He places patches of warmer or denser color against a neutral or cool background to create detachment, diversity. Or, contrarily, he uses similar tones with slight variations of luminosity in order to plant his forms into the background or to allow them to emerge ever so slightly, as though they were being born at this moment in a metamorphic process leading from indistinctness to the greatest clarity.

Figures and Perceptive Principles

In front of such subtle yet engrossing works of art as Morandi's, we feel two contrary temptations. On the one hand there is the tendency to think of them as does Ruggero Pierantoni when he comments, "perhaps, even though it is tempting, it is unreasonable to seek a grammatical structure in the images."[14] On the other hand, however, there is a strong wish to understand something more of its structure and mechanisms, also because it is well-known that optical illusion—

Still Life of Vases on a Table, etching, 1931 (Vitali etchings no. 84).
In this etching, one may notice Morandi's early and personal application of the Kanizsa figure, or phenomenon of the "almost perceptive margins."

"perceptive error," and the imaginary projection of a complex and deceptive reality—may be seen, as it was by Richard Gregory, as a fascinating phenomenon of our experience, one that effectively serves as a bridge between art and science.[15] Without overstating the significance it could be interesting to consider what figures and principles of the psychology of perception Morandi adopted as elements inherent to his work, those dynamic factors that contribute to the growth of his visual magic. And, above all, it should be noted that such perceptive devices, although sporadically present in earlier works, increase and are refined in the paintings of his later period when the relationship with the visible becomes gradually more complex and tends towards the complete stripping away of objective data in favor of perceptive suggestions, allusions, echos.

Among the artist's favorite gestalt figures are certainly those of Rubin[16] and Kanizsa.[17] The former, which is very well-known, shows black and white figures in profile with a dual perceptive possibility: a vase or two faces placed eye to eye. Morandi plays on such ambiguities, almost as though to demonstrate the fragility of another observation of the psychology of vision according to which space between figures has no form,[18] and this he does by advancing that portion of the background enclosed between the profiles of the objects until they delineate a new and unforeseen reality. Kanizsa's figure, or the phenomenon of the *almost* perceptive margins," highlights a not-drawn white space while defining what surrounds it so that, in the positive-negative relationship, what is not there actually acquires the value of form. Morandi could not help but be fascinated by the possibilities of going beyond appearance in order to allow what was left unsaid, unseen to emerge. He often uses such figures, beginning with the well-known etching of 1931 with undrawn objects against a dark and strongly marked background and arriving at the still lifes of the fifties where a genuine dark curtain embraces the pale forms in the foreground, allowing them to surface like luminous ghosts.[19] And then, tiny refined jewels, there appear the watercolors with the Levico landscapes of 1957, where the looming shape of the chimney—which is not underlined in any other way—is carved out against the pale blue sky and the liquid green of the surrounding vegetation. In both cases the main problem is that of the relationship between the figure and the background, the keynote of Morandi's painting, as it seeks to put into focus one

Still Life, 1961 (Vitali no. 1232). Winterthur, Kunstmuseum.
Using a process similar to that of Rubin's gestalt figure, Morandi highlights a patch of the background to the point that he delineates it as a new, unexpected form (it is the area of the "inverted teardrop" created between the full shapes of the two caraffes and the handle of the one on the left).

Still Life, 1963 (Vitali no. 1322), formerly in the José Luis and Beatriz Plaza collection, Caracas. (Courtesy Sotheby's, London.)
The forms here, crowded one up against the other, are an example of the perceptive phenomenon that Kanizsa defined "amodal completion:" one figure is partially covered by another, but is perceived as a finished form, since the perceptive force tends to complete the image.

form among others while still obsessively aware of the relationships, of the analogies, the total sum of the fragment of vision that is placed before the artist's inquisitive gaze.

Once again Gaetano Kanizsa gives us a particular and interesting example of perceptive phenomena, the so-called "amodal completion" which occurs when a figure is partly covered by another and, therefore, not wholly delineated, but all the same it is seen by the viewer as a complete form.[20] Morandi is the master of allusion and of what is there but not seen, so he certainly could not overlook such an intriguing phenomenon and use in his compositions of objects, as well as in his landscapes, all the perceptive force that develops in such situations and that tends to complete the image. His forms, in fact, are conceptually and emotionally open and leave a fairly wide margin for interpretation, so it is the viewer who has to complete them on the basis of his perceptive, imaginative, and sentimental (again, in the sense of rich in emotion and psychically involved) conjectures.

And Morandi does not stop here because he also suggests the reversal of the image by constructing a system for transition between one or more figures locked into each other like the reversed facets of a single form. Once again it is the color that determines the positive and the negative, the figure and the background but, at a formal and poetic level, the figures are equivalent and complete one another.[21]

Finally, it is possible to recognize how at the base of all his works lie two perceptive principles of primary importance: those of symmetry and closure. The first tells us that a form that is symmetrical with respect to the Cartesian axes of the perceptive field is more easily understood. The second refers to the phenomenon for which, at a gestalt level, a closed form is easier to perceive than any other. Morandi lives for symmetry and order, and he offends against them only when he wants to enhance his image. And often he further strengthens the Cartesian layout of the surface by creating a further axis horizontal to the table-horizon line in order to delimit a precise chromatic and spatial area—a figure which, in turn, is in space—within the overall perceptive field.

Equally, or even more so, the artist prefers a closed form of composition, almost always contained in a simple geometric figure, while he leaves open the forms of the single objects that seem almost to migrate one into the other until they fuse into unexpected new things. But the whole is closed and compact, with just the occasional hint of imbalance seen in an object placed near the edge, or in a shadow that modifies the plane geometry in order to suggest other dimensions.

The visual impact remains sharp, apparently simple, and reduced to essentials even when in the final works the objects organized into the image open out to the background surface in order to permit the influx of the air and light which

Landscape (Levico), watercolor, 1957 (Pasquali no. 1957/15). Bologna, Museo Morandi, gift of Maria Teresa Morandi.
Adopting and developing one of Cézanne's insights (proof is offered by the watercolor shown here, *Le four à plâtre*, of 1890–94, Louvre), by isolating the vertical form of the smokestack, making it stand out against the green of the trees and the transparent blue of the sky, Morandi underlines its emptiness and what is left unsaid.

By Francesco Arcangeli

Morandi on Guido Reni of Bologna

The seventeenth-century Baroque master's retrospective exhibition is discussed with Italy's leading modern painter

Ominous shadows and bold, almost Impressionist gleams of light characterize the plague-ridden city of Bologna in a detail from Guido Reni's *Madonna of the Rosary*, ca. 1631-32.

Pinacoteca, Bologna

Only the diaphanous, sunlit upper section of Reni's *The Giving of the Keys*, 1618-20, pleased Morandi, who rejected the rest of the composition.

Morandi considers the composition of Reni's *Circumcision*, 1639—its austere postures, architecture and light-borne *putti*—as "nearly all beautiful."

It is not easy to interview Giorgio Morandi, in fact it is not easy to engage him in conversation. The block of his instinctive reticence becomes even more insurmountable when he realizes that his opinions are not intended for the closely restricted circle of his friends, but for publication. In Italy we have long since come to understand that Morandi concentrates exclusively on his still-lifes, landscapes and etchings—he makes no public pronouncements. Carrà and Soffici may air their views in print, but not Morandi. He avoids all arguments, written and verbal, he relies in absolute silence upon the message of his painting. His restraint and the conclusive quality of his achievement have earned him, in his country, the particular respect that is reserved for those who work without talking and who work well.

Actually, an artist like Guido Reni is immensely removed from Morandi's most natural interest and preference: he epitomizes the seventeenth century, not a favorite period when Morandi was young, around 1910. Giotto, Masaccio, Piero della Francesca then stood for the great Italian tradition and it is their triumphs that Morandi strove to integrate into modern forms of expression. In the early twentieth century the Baroque seemed excessively literary, its magniloquence, its slapdash descriptiveness, its impetuous theatricality were considered, in those days, obtrusive and repugnant. Too stagey for an intimist,

too oratorical for a man so laconic, the dashing brush work and spotting of the *seicento* were uncontrollably offensive to this master of color so discreet, so subdued that its richness could only be measured by its resonance within us. Even Caravaggio, whom Morandi appreciates, could not equal within his century the sobriety of Velásquez, Rembrandt and Vermeer; and—as for the seventeenth-century Bolognese—their work, in the early nineteen-hundreds, was dismissed as "literature."

Despite these prejudices of his youth, Morandi nowadays can yet discover certain formal beauties, certain inconspicuous yet exquisite passages in Reni's work.

For instance in the background of the huge, dark *Crucifixion* of the Bologna museum he singles out the small background section with distant horsemen. "If only Reni had lived in a better period"—he deplores—"he might have had a chance to reveal his true stature!" In the *Madonna of the Rosary* from the same museum he cherishes the detail of the city of Bologna desolated by the plague, all in greys and silvers, muted in tone, boldly handled.

The Guido Reni exhibition of seventy canvases and thirty drawings was installed in the handsome halls of the Archiginnasio in Bologna. I went through the show several times with Morandi who, at times, found it hard to suppress his impatience

and exasperation. For our last appointment I happened to be a few minutes late and, not seeing him at the entrance, I rushed to the last galleries where I knew I would find him among his favorites, the late "unfinished" canvases. But we shall return to this; first we must run through the paintings which, by their size and number, made Reni famous in his time.

The *Assumption of the Virgin* from S. Ambrogio, Genoa, he considers just a "machine" of little interest; the *Moses with the Tables of the Law* partially recommends itself by the dashing sketch of the small worshipers of the Golden Calf against the somber background of the mountain. "But just look at the mantle of Moses," Morandi expostulates; "it is nothing but dead paper wrapped around the figure. What's the point?" The point, of course, is that this drapery is inherent to the picture's rhetoric. But, like Matisse and Braque, Morandi has no mercy for rhetoric; he brushes aside in Reni all that is comparable with Ribera, all that anticipates Mattia Preti. Even the *Stories of Hercules* from the Louvre, plausibly dear to Géricault and Courbet, elicit from him only a tepid, casual assent.

In *The Giving of the Keys* from Perpignan he surprisingly rejects the composition though he finds some kind words for the upper section where the angels are delicately blurred in the diaphanous light of the clouds. At this point I begin to get

30

"The World House Galleries' large exhibition of Morandi's landscapes and still lifes offered accustomed pleasure and gave one the increasing feeling that this rarified artist was not so much looking for formulas for picture-making as he was determined to wrest from subject matter some secret that it jealously guarded."[17]

As already noted from Rewald's introduction, Albert Loeb & Krugier Gallery held a major New York show in 1967. In 1969 Odyssia Skoros included Morandi prints with Paul Klee in an opening show of her new gallery. The next year she gave Morandi a full exhibition and has become, as a collector herself and enthusiast, a principal force in the continuing American enthusiasm for this artist.

Museum exhibitions were more sparse. A coming of age as a completely cosmopolitan artist—taken at formal modernist values, all issues of "Italianess" left aside—was a large show (some 150 works) in 1958 at the Museum of Modern Art of three major print makers: Miró, Braque and Morandi.[18] That same year Thomas Leavitt organized an exhibition for the Pasadena (California) Art Museum entitled *The New Renaissance in Italy*.[19] In many ways it was a historical reflection on the ground-breaking MOMA show of 1949, organized by Soby and Barr, and almost equally ambitious. Morandi featured large and had his first major American museum showing outside of New York. Meanwhile in the English-speaking world shows were held in Edinburgh during the summer of 1965[20] and in London at the Royal Academy in 1970.[21]

A plateau had, perhaps, been reached by the seventies with Morandi, often compared now to Chardin as well as Cézanne, merging into a world of refined

The article by Francesco Arcangeli which appeared in *Art News* in February 1955.

Giorgio Morandi's "flawed, muted" bottles stand in warm brown space infused with the same palpable light that floods the Italian landscape: *Still-life, 1939, 23 inches high.*

Morandi
the metaphysician
of Bologna

The camera sees what the public does not: backstage of Morandi's Bologna studio, paper roses, earthenware bottles, jugs and bowls wait in orderly array their turn to pose.

From *Art News*, February 1955: the article on Morandi by John Berger.

acceptance reserved for "modern old masters." In terms of reception in the United States, one can cite that the 1977 edition of Lamberto Vitali's catalogue raisonné lists sixty-five works in this country, without including drawings and watercolors.[22]

The 1981 exhibition organized by James Demetrion at the Museum of Modern Art in San Francisco, which then traveled to the Guggenheim Museum in New York and Des Moines Art Center, brought the artist to a kind of high receptive point for many, although, as Jane Bell noted in *Art News*, many may have said: "I remember liking his work enormously fifteen years ago."[23] More importantly it brought a large body of work to a new, and not always receptive, generation of American critics and artists. Hilton Kramer, one of the most powerful voices, felt that the work had "an almost niggling refusal to extend itself."[24] One critic, the artist Janet Abramowicz, who had been Morandi's teaching assistant at the Accademia in Bologna in the late fifties, stages an aggressive rally which reappraises the artist in quite new terms. Her Morandi was singularly not a figure of retired seclusion and formalist balancing. He was on the very edge of life and art: "Often deceptively calm and simple on the surface, Morandi's work also reveals the fears and uncertainties he experienced daily in his work."[25] She is particularly vigorous in her defense of his late work which she finds "twisted and tormented, evoke a strange, desolate feeling," and then promptly quotes Giorgio Bassani's characters in *The Garden of the Finzi-Contini*: "Even the poet, in the last analysis has to fight against the hostility of Nature and Death . . . . That's what Morandi's famous paintings of bottles and those sweet little flowers are all about . . . . It's the *fear* of reality."[26]

The modernist Morandi of James Soby's still serenity is brought to a truly Post-Modern fraughtness. One of the things which most bothered Abramowicz in attempts to explain the failure, both of the making and the reception, of the 1981 exhibition was a long, scholarly introduction to the catalog by Joan M. Lukach who was herself to become another new voice about the artist, having done a doctoral dissertation on the artist in the seventies at Harvard University. Abramowicz's concern was the casting of Morandi into an academic camp. However, Lukach concludes her essay with a bid for tolerance of various views, formalistic or expressive: "Indubitably, there are many valid responses to the paintings of Giorgio Morandi, but the one quality upon which most have agreed is that his works are ultimately poetic. But it is poetry of form and structure rather than content. If for a time Morandi looked with an appraising eye at ordinary domestic accoutrements, at a different time he selected extraordinary, even magical things like shadow boxes and floating balls for his compositions."[27]

Lukach first became interested in Italian Modernism through the great futurist scholar, Joshua Taylor, at the University of Chicago in the sixties . . . and if I remember correctly, may well have been in the class in 1964 when John Rewald held us all by the tales of his visit to the Via Fondazza.

[1] J. Rewald, "Visit with Morandi," in *Morandi*, exh. cat., Albert Loeb & Krugier Gallery, New York, 18 May–17 June 1967.
[2] Ibid.
[3] Ibid.
[4] J.Th. Soby, "Painting and Sculpture since 1920. Later Work of de Chirico, Carrà and Morandi," in *Twentieth-Century Italian Art*, ed. by A.H. Barr and J.Th. Soby, exh. cat., The Museum of Modern Art, New York, 28 June–12 September 1949, p. 26.
[5] J.Th. Soby, "A Visit to Morandi," in *Giorgio*

Different color combinations in four studies for Josef Albers' *Homage to the Square*, completed between 1960 and 1967. Private collection.

movement he is usually classified with. Josef Albers's last works were all centered around the theme of the *Homage to the Square*, giving rise to a series of pictures in which the geometric compositional parameters remained unvaried while the chromatic combinations varied. Four squares are inserted each inside the other, with clear mathematical relationships. The numerous variations are generated by their changing color relationships, and the structure of the white support can be seen through the strokes of the palette knife. For more than twenty years, till the day he died, Albers methodically and tenaciously and obsessively pursued this research. This seriality of combinations also appears in the work of Ad Reinhardt who, even before Johns, questioned to the utmost the essence of painting and its possibilities of survival, and painted many times what he considered to be "the last possible painting:" a checker-board of brown violet, and bluish squares that create the illusion of a black monochrome.

Precisely because the object seems so irrelevant in Morandi's late paintings, Barilli's previously mentioned comparison with Claes Oldenburg becomes highly improbable.[13] The American artist employs a whole series of rhetorical devices, from enlargement to the repetition, in soft or different materials, of objects that evoke the domestic landscape. These objects reflect an everyday context characterized by consumerism and mass distribution in the post-industrial era. But Morandi's pots show no particular affinity with this universe of production, and nothing in his work testifies to a desire for social comment. This is proved by the introduction into his compositions of boxes and unrecognizable

Tony Cragg, *Five Bottles on a Shelf*, 1982.
Private collection.

geometric volumes, selected because they represent planes of light that are interesting from the pictorial point of view, as well as symmetries and cadences; they function as pictorial elements that alternately both rupture and obey the two-dimensional grid.

It is true that César, the new realist sculptor who was among the earlier European practitioners of Pop, dedicated a series of large pictures to Morandi in 1990 (though there were precedents in his work in the seventies). In these, decanters are placed like toy soldiers on a white support and are then crushed, provoking an explosion of randomly scattered glass fragments. The result has a *pointilliste* effect, like a Seurat, but it is poles apart from Morandi's paintings. Did César understand Morandi? Or did he consider him, as was habitual in the late fifties and sixties, the humble painter of household pots and pans? Perhaps César wanted only to draw attention to a problem that was all his own, that of urban refuse, or at least to the symbolic content of objects of daily consumption.

The same problem of interpretation underlies Morandi's more recent critical fortunes. There are clear references to him in certain object-based sculptures which are rooted in mediations on Pop Art and Nouveau Réalisme. The reference is there when Tony Cragg spreads out a series of used plastic bottles on a shelf, or when he places sanded, white and luminous bottles on a table. It is there again in the shelves with objects of Haim Steinbach, and in his checker-board in which the pieces are replaced by jugs. It is to be found in the series of vase-urns called *Perfect Vehicles* that Allan McCollum lays out across the floors of galleries and museums, as though they were on tables. But in recent art it is not so much these examples that betray a correspondence with the lessons of Morandi's mature work as it is abstract painting and sculpture, centered on compositional values, by such artists as Sean Scully or Lawrence Carroll.

Certain paintings by Morandi decisively reveal how little he was interested in social problems and how much he was interested in systems for constructing figurative space. A still life of 1956 (Vitali no. 986) shows three parallelepipeds and a low cylinder in the foreground, aligned along their upper edges in order to dramatize a horizontal break in the space, and with the clear intention of creating

Haim Steinbach, *Crisscross*, 1992.
Private collection.

a contrast with the vertical movement of the slender bottles behind. A 1959 still life (Vitali no. 1138) sets up an obvious symmetry of two identical bottles separated by a small vase and a dark cuboid. Again, a 1960 still life (Vitali no. 1181) brings the base line of the vases to the center of the painting and thus sabotages the recognizability of the two jugs in the background. A still life of 1963 (Vitali no. 1300) and a landscape of the same year (Vitali no. 1334) seem constructed according to the same compositional scheme, with a dark mass at the center and two lighter blocks on each side: whether we are looking at houses or boxes becomes a matter of indifference.

It is interesting that Morandi always, and quite contentedly, remained a genre painter, of landscape and above all, as his titles obdurately declare, of still life. Genre painting has a precise history and undeniable roots in the past, which Morandi seemed determined to contradict, digest and annul by working within the genre itself rather than by rejecting it. The seventeenth-century fruit basket had definite realistic connotations but it was also a vehicle for religious symbolism. A spot of mold could be a metaphor for sin. For Morandi such values lost their relevance. At the same time he corroded the genre by undermining its strongest formal aspect, that of the difference between the figure and its background, and thus demonstrated his ability to detach himself from tradition in a way that was as innovative as it was a challenge to the burden of the past.

The process of fusing the object and the space that surrounds it can be seen in numerous instances. In a still life of 1957 (Vitali no. 1066) the strip of background that functions as a support for the figures is treated as a surface in its own right, painted in rectangles, as can be clearly seen from the movements of the artist's brush. In a still life of 1958 (Vitali no. 1100) the two squares of space that scan the volumes between them are so highly defined at a geometric level and so similar in size that they attain exactly the same pictorial value as the volumes. This happens again in a still life of 1960 (Vitali no. 1216). In this way Morandi tackled problems that originate from the history of painting, but which were not posed by history as such.

We have established that any relationship with the poetics of Pop is most

Allan McCollum, *Perfect Vehicles*, 1988. Installation at the Brooke Alexander Gallery, New York.

Donald Judd, *Untitled*, 1987. Private collection.

improbable unless, as in the case of Warhol, there is a shared interest in the compositional aspects of the image. Nevertheless it is possible to place Morandi's late works in relation to much later developments in western art, and in particular with what Filiberto Menna has called, in the title of an essay, "the analytical tendency of modern art." This is offered as an extension of the modernist movement. The paintings by Morandi that go furthest in this direction are the very ones that led Arcangeli to compare them to the elements of repetition and disregard of plot (analogous to the subject in painting) in the French "nouveau roman," and Robbe-Grillet in particular.[14]

The simplicity of Morandi's compositions, his attentiveness to the logic of differentiated repetition, the increasing emphasis on geometry, and the placement of objects in series through the late fifties, all suggest a parallel with certain masters of Minimalism. The painted volumes take on ever more the characteristics of mere "presences," denoted by colors, by the play of light, and by movement dictated by logic. However far-fetched such a comparison may seem, one may plausibly refer to the proliferation of cubes in the early works of Sol LeWitt, to the rhythmic combinations of parallelepipeds in Donald Judd's *Specific Objects*, to the covering of the floor with opaque and shiny metal squares and wooden blocks by Carl Andre, or to the austere watercolors of James Bishop. Morandi's obsession with light and color, rendered with brush strokes that are at times minute and at others generous, might even bring to mind the way Robert Ryman treats his white monochromes—series of apparently identical squares which are actually very different if one looks at the density of the paint, the texture of the brush strokes, the diverse shades of white, and the overall luminosity of the surface.

A case for further investigation is the organization in series of Morandi's late work, which is examined in this catalog by Laura Mattioli. On the one hand this was also a feature of early twentieth-century production of artists such as Monet, Cézanne, and Picasso, and so ought not to come as a surprise in Morandi's work. But it is also true that the production of works in series has grown through the second half of the century and has gone hand in hand with the crisis of painting and more generally of representation in the visual arts. Leaving aside any facile comparisons with serial production in industry (especially the reproduction of images), this is pertinent to one aspect of the crisis: the loss of faith in the "masterpiece"—the work that in itself sums up a career, and is perceived as somehow final and unique. With his relentless attachment to the act of painting, Morandi seems to be aware that the works only function as episodes in a continuum, that it is necessary to disperse them around the world, so that quantity also becomes a factor; that their worth as signs depends, not so much on the representativeness of the best, as on the coherence of the totality. The only possible masterpiece, even the only possible work, is conceived as an onward path and not as a stop on the way.

In these terms we can look again at some of the comparisons suggested by Pasini and particularly the references to the work of On Kawara and Roman Opalka. The former consists of a series of dates, taken from newspapers that the artist bought on specific days, arranged on the canvas and painted in typographical fonts. In each work the date changes but the compositional system does not, with both theoretic and social implications that cannot be explored here. Roman Opalka's work consists of painting a progressive series of numbers from zero to "infinity", with a brush and black color on white canvas. Year by year, however, the black loses its intensity due to a periodic addition of white, a process which leads the paintings gradually to a condition of monochrome. Both of these processes share an autobiographical dimension, and by means of a few codified signs they capture the whole existence of the artist. In other words it could be argued that Morandi too intended to keep a kind of minimal diary by way of the few marks he made on his repetitive canvases. But beyond this aspect of content, it is clear that each work by Kawara and Opalka exists only as a part of the whole. Finally it is interesting to observe how, from the sixties to the beginning of the eighties and again recently, art's most innovative processes are becoming more rational, less emotional: both Minimalism and Conceptual art have bequeathed to the nineties a preference for the negation of individual experience in favor of a cooler posture. Even the genre of monochrome, which could be considered a successor to the still life, has lost the mystic valence that it had for Ad Reinhardt and Yves Klein and offers itself instead as the greatest simplification of reality. Thanks to this our taste at the end of the century is closer to Morandi's late work than to the Expressionist and Informel painters to which Morandi was opposed, and even to the more classic and disturbing Morandi of the pre-war period. One could deduce that the post-war Morandi not only understood his times but also knew how to navigate the Modernist route himself, stayed abreast of an art that is continually re-thinking its own internal logic. Because of this recent shift in taste, surely the outcome of a change in the spirit of the times, we look at Morandi now in a fresh light.

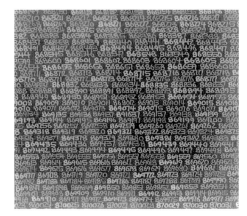

Roman Opalka, *1965/1* (detail), 1965. Private collection.

[1] See "Postilla," *Rinascita*, Rome, no. 12, December 1948, p. 470.

[2] Interview with Giorgio Morandi, recorded 25 April 1957, for "Voice of America," text published in L. Vitali, *Giorgio Morandi pittore*, 2nd expanded edition, 1965, p. 86; 3rd expanded edition, 1970, p. 97.

[3] G.C. Argan, *L'arte moderna 1770–1970*, Sansoni, Florence, 1970, p. 598.

[4] Interview cited in note 2.

[5] See S. Grandini, *Ben Nicholson, opere dal 1921 al 1981*, exh. cat., Museo d'Arte, Mendrisio, 4 April–20 June 1993, p. 42.

[6] S. Grandini interviewed by N. Locarnini in "L'astrattista che si ispirava a Morandi," *Arte*, Milan, no. 239, April 1993, p. 89.

[7] See R. Barilli, "Morandi e il secondo Novecento," in *Morandi e il suo tempo*, ed. by various authors, exh. cat., Galleria Comunale d'Arte Moderna, Bologna, 9 November 1986, pp. 77–78.

[8] See C. Pozzati, "Il tempo 'autre' di Morandi," in ibid., pp. 89–97.

[9] R. Pasini, *Morandi*, CLUEB, Bologna, 1989, pp. 115–116.

[10] Harrison & Wood, *Art in Theory 1900–1990*, Blackwell, Oxford (UK) and Cambridge (USA), 1990.

[11] Stiles & Selz, *Theories and Documents of Contemporary Art*, University of California Press, Berkeley-Los Angeles-London, 1996.

[12] C. Brandi, *Morandi*, Le Monnier, Florence, 1942, p. 51.

[13] See Barilli, p. 84.

[14] See F. Arcangeli, *Giorgio Morandi*, Edizioni del Milione, Milan, 1964, p. 320.

Contributions

Franz Armin Morat
Giuseppe Panza di Biumo

of his later work: even though there is still only a very limited range of earth colors, typical of the twenties and thirties, the painting anticipates that new relationship between objects and background that was to become one of the substantial characteristics of the later works. Already in this canvas we can also see how the background colors tend increasingly to fill the spaces between the objects causing their outlines to lose definition and the sharpness and contrasts typical of earlier paintings. In this way the empty space between the objects acquires an outline, a dimension, and a value equivalent to those of the objects themselves. Attention is given to forms not found on the artist's table but born and developed in a wholly pictorial environment characterized by its own laws. Thanks to the artist's choices and to his "picture making" we are able to appreciate figures that do not exist in reality and we become aware of just how obsolete the distinction between abstract and figurative art is. It could even be said that one of the aims of the later work of Morandi was a demonstration of the absurdity of such a distinction. Without a doubt, though, one of the characteristics of his paintings after 1960 is the increasing "abstraction" of the forms of the objects, at times taken to the point of impeding even the greatest experts of his repertoire from identifying with certainty the objects represented. From the breakdown of real form, Morandi develops the possibility of reconstructing a new one, beyond reality. The antagonism between breakdown and reconstruction, which the viewer experiences simultaneously, is the real theme of these works. As Gottfried Boehm has written, the "objects disintegrate in the same way in which they recompose."[4] We could also say that they dematerialize in order to then take on form, to re-materialize.

The viewer should try to decipher the relationship between the objects shown in a watercolor still life of 1958;[5] if you cannot do so then consider the painting of 1956 (Vitali no. 1005), and you will be surprised to observe the non-verbal explicative force which makes it possible to decipher the objects shown in the watercolor. In fact, by comparing the watercolor and the oil painting, vision suddenly acquires a meaning. Analogously a composition of 1960 (Vitali no. 1187) gives us the key for understanding the object that appears to the left, a clock, which is seen again in a still life of 1962 (Vitali no. 1272). In this case we find ourselves in the field of the "reine Anschauung," that is of pure vision, quite beyond significant language and concepts.

As I have already said, from 1950 onward Morandi's language evolved gradually so that a definition of "later Morandi" might have various meanings and refer to

Still Life, 1941 (Vitali no. 291). Freiburg, Morat-Institut für Kunst und Kunstwissenschaft.

A still life in watercolor of 1958 not present in Pasquali's catalog. Freiburg, Morat-Institut für Kunst und Kunstwissenschaft.

Still Life, 1956 (Vitali no. 1005). Florence, Banca Toscana.

works that stylistically are not totally homogeneous. If, for example, we compare the still life of 1960 just mentioned (Vitali no. 1187) with the one with a similar subject of three years later (Vitali no. 1308), we note at once a substantial difference in the way the objects are represented. The later picture, in fact, has been painted with an attitude that we could call careless, almost with a deliberate awkwardness, as though the painter wanted to forgo any form of pleasantry. His way of working is well-known: he observed, even for many days, his subject, the effects of light on it and on the surrounding space. During this long period of observation at times he moved the objects very slightly. The painting of the work, instead, happened at an ever quicker rate. It almost seems that in such paintings as the last one referred to, Morandi, at the moment he managed to grasp the vision of the subject with his "inner eye" (or, to quote Cesare Brandi, when he caught a glimpse of "painterly ghost"), executed the work with an amazing creative impetus.[6]

We can better understand this process by verifying the *ductus* of the brush on the canvas, where the background color shows through the forms represented: a method we might almost call "gestural painting." His research in his last years, aimed increasingly in this direction, confirms that death did not signify for Morandi the natural completion of an artistic career already finished, but was something that interrupted a development still full of possibilities.

It can be said that the new course of painting, the one that earns it the epithet of "modern," began halfway through the nineteenth century following the invention of photography. This allowed painting to free itself from the burden of reproducing reality and forced it to legitimize its existence with its own means. It was then that Carl Schuch coined the phrase "reine Malerei," or pure painting, which he developed both in his work and in what we might call his theoretic writings, that is his letters and jottings in his diary.[7]

The two still lifes with a clock of 1960 and 1963 (from the left, Vitali nos. 1187 and 1308, both in private collection).

73

The catalog provides essential profiles (title, year, medium, measurements, publication number in the catalogue raisonné of the paintings compiled by Lamberto Vitali, collection) for the paintings exhibited. The information on the medium and measurements has been gathered by means of direct observation. For an analytical description of each painting's history of ownership, exhibition and publication, please consult the Technical Index of the Works *compiled by Laura Lorenzoni. The critical profiles are illustrated with images for comparison with other paintings, watercolors and drawings by Morandi, as well as photographic documentation, historical sources and iconographic parallels.*

Flavio Fergonzi would like to thank: Giacomo Agosti, Luisa Arrigoni, Matteo Ceriana, Graziano Ghiringhelli, Maria Mimita Lamberti, Laura Lorenzoni, Ferruccio Marchiori, Laura Mattioli Rossi, Marilena Pasquali, Francesco Sandroni, Lorenza Selleri, Dario Trento, Francesca Valli.
He would also like to thank the directors and personnel of the following archives and libraries: Archivio Storico delle Arti Contemporanee della Biennale (ASAC), Venice; Biblioteca dell'Accademia di Brera, Milan; Biblioteca d'Arte del Castello Sforzesco, Milan; Biblioteca della Galleria Nazionale d'Arte Moderna, Rome; Biblioteca Nazionale Braidense, Milan; Istituto Germanico di Storia dell'Arte, Florence; Biblioteca Nazionale Centrale, Florence.

Introduction

Morandi's Series and Problems of Chronological Interpretation

Though this exhibition covers the period from the paintings of implacable ranks of objects of 1948–50 to the hovering, larval still lifes of the artist's last year, the paintings have not been arranged in a rigid chronological order. Instead, they have been grouped in smaller and larger sequences, ranging from two to six units. The relationship linking the works in each sequence varies. Some belong to a clearly evident series (as in the case of the paintings with the yellow cloth from 1952, or those with the pitcher and the cylindrical cans from 1960–62). Others are linked by their iconographic motif (the presence of a particular object, like the tall white bottle in the fifth series and the cardboard boxes in the tenth). The unifying element may be a particular color or a question of technique (the veiled shadings of some of the works of 1958–59, the fluid, zig-zag strokes of the last few series). There are groupings based on the arrangement of the objects in the painting (like the "square layouts" of the still lifes of 1953–55); on a particular format (the horizontal works in the eighth sequence); or on questions of collection, when such considerations can shed light on the context in which they were made and enjoyed (as in the case of the grouping of the two paintings that belonged, respectively, to Roberto Longhi and Lionello Venturi).

In an exhibition of the works of one artist, focusing on a single genre (the still life) and a limited time span (about fifteen years), it may be useful to concentrate on the visual and pictorial mechanisms that have made this genre a field of pure research on form. The reconstruction of Morandi's way of working, by means of an analysis of sequences over the years, provides a more informative overview, as opposed to a rigid chronological presentation; we can come into closer contact with obsessions of ways of seeing, recurring elements, continuations, things left "on hold", others brusquely left by the wayside.

Recomposing groups of works spanning a period of a number of years has meant carefully picking through a mass of photographic materials (some five hundred still lifes in the period from 1950 to 1964) in the second volume of Lamberto Vitali's complete catalog, that unsurpassed philological monument to Morandi's work. Here the problem of dating works, of putting the sequences in order remains necessarily unresolved. Marilena Pasquali has confirmed that among the Morandi papers kept in the Bologna museum there is no list of works compiled by the artist himself. Those to which Morandi gave a date, whether on the front or the back, represent a very small percentage of the total output. Apart from

2.

3.

4. *Still Life*, 1951.
Oil on canvas, 40.5 × 45.5 cm.
Vitali no. 763.
Trento, Museo d'Arte Moderna e
Contemporanea di Trento e Rovereto,
deposito Giovanardi.

5. *Still Life*, 1951.
Oil on canvas, 34.8 × 37.9 cm.
Vitali no. 767.
Private collection.

6. *Still Life*, 1951–1953.
Oil on canvas, 30 × 50 cm.
Vitali no. 766.
Private collection.
(Courtesy Claudia Gian Ferrari.)

Toward 1951 Morandi interrupted the series of still lifes bathed in zenithal light and began to represent objects with overtly chiaroscuro modeling; once again the shadows began to be elongated transversely across the table top. This habit of finishing a period of research and suddenly beginning a new series that seems in some way to contradict its predecessor (in this case, after the luminous geometry of a highly modernist cycle, there was a return to the schemes and atmosphere already employed in the thirties and forties) was discussed by Francesco Arcangeli in 1946 in the Florentine magazine *Il Mondo*: Morandi's way of working in series was "rather like that of Petrarch when, in a particular group of sonnets, he seems to vary a sentimental theme just slightly; then, having made the most of these necessary variations, a sudden, thoughtful, but still unexpected move changes the theme; a new cycle begins. And so the bottles are placed in depth rather than in a row; the row is in a pearl white shade and modeled in pure color; now, instead, it has shadows. These are the simple but fundamental events in Morandi's world: based on variation, not that of the seasons, but of that suave, severe season that has, for many years now, shifted colors in the eyes and the spirit of Morandi" (Arcangeli, 1946).
The three pictures of this sequence, whose protagonist is always the white fluted bottle, the fulcrum for a meagre grouping of objects in a precisely identified spatial container (the table top once again shows its corner, after numerous experiments with an absolute frontal view), show three different lighting possibilities and, therefore, options for chromatic construction:

the strong contrasts of the first painting (the ochre-white of the bottle and the ceramic jars is etched on the background which, in a procedure typical of the thirties, concentrates the darkness around the objects) is replaced by a cooler, metallic

light in the second (over the gray-green background are painted the teapot's white decorated with dull blue and the celluloid ball, whose yellow veers toward an earth tone, and the green toward blue) and in the third, the lightest one, which elimi-

Morandi with a still life from the same series as painting no. 4.

92

4.

5.

6.

7.

8.

"Se nestes últimos anos o público e a crítica vão dando atenção a Morandi, isto não é certamente um fenômeno de exumação do século passado. A história do gôsto ignora retrocessos de tal gênero, e também pertence à lei duma gôsto rico e atual descobrirmos novamente um mestre antigo. O interêsse que despertam as pinturas e as gravuras de Morandi denota a compreensão de tudo o que há rico e atual na sua visão artística, aparentemente tradicional, mas efetivamente atual e moderna, muito mais moderna do que tantas outras modas efêmeras e passageiras."

Giorgio Morandi, "Duas naturezas mortas".

"O milagre conseguido por todo artista é o de fazer concordar o seu sentimento com a expressão que foi escolhendo mediante sua livre vontade."

"No panorama caótico da cultura artística dêste século, o processo de sistematização de valores ainda não está definido com segurança: mas desde já se pode prever fàcilmente que Giorgio Morandi há de ficar como um dos grandes poetas do nosso tempo."

Rodolfo Pallucchini

Desde 1951 a crítica brasileira pode ver trabalhos de Morandi sem precisar bater na porta dos colecionadores de Florença, Milão, Veneza e Bolonha. Os trinta quadros que atualmente constituem um dos ápices da IV Bienal de São Paulo constam de um trabalho de 1918, da era metafísica de De Chirico e Carrà e seis paisagens, o resto sendo naturezas mortas.

Diz bem Pallucchini que sua fase metafísica foi um pródomo para a futura constante das naturezas mortas "onde o espaço é medido numa tensão de efeitos nem formais nem plásticos, mas decididamente tonais e luminosos".

As paisagens, das cercanias de Grizzana, ou dos muros e árvores de subúrbios de Bolonha, já apresentam um rigor cezanneano de visão integral e de testemunho contemplativo. O antigo pintor metafísico dos espaços ocupados por manequins e formas, vira poeta da evocação ante a natureza; um poeta circunspecto com senso anti-romântico de crítica. Mas o mundo empoeirado e cinerio de Morandi, é interior, de ambiente, tendo como personagens não criaturas (parece que só pintou duas figuras humanas até agora...) mas de objetos companheiros do seu solipsismo. Tais objetos, garrafas, potes, xícaras, bules, caixas, estojos, nunca deixam sua inércia pacífica e melancólica, mesmo quando certas côres-luzes lhes impregnam a matéria e lhes definem a geometria orgânica. A comparação de ambiência com as telas de Vermeer não acode ao espectador, pois não há opulência, não há reflexos, e sim persiste pobreza, velharia doméstica. Mas a luz onisciente de Morandi, uma luz que não é tropical nem meridiana, mas de gamas filtradas entre o cinza e o branco, dá inflexões, gradações, nessa limitação proposital de tema.

O grande solitário da Via Fondazza, em Bolonha, está desde muito com aquele beavorismo pacífico e experimentado da sabedoria e ao invés dos gatos e netos dos burgueses dos impasses de Paris, tem nesse mundo de vidros, louças, madeiras e papelões, e às vezes de flores fanadas, o seu devaneio taciturno. Ama aqueles objetos e vivifica-os. Vivifica-os com uma coerência de côr e luz, volume e tenuidade, em rigorosas correlações de inércia e tempo, de horas e estações. De forma que tudo assume, nesses paradigmas estáticos e estatísticos de potes, jarras e garrafas, uma existência ascética de cela e de aposento a que as cambiantes das visitas da luz dão ensejo para a contemplação, o silêncio, o devaneio, a tristeza, a alegria, o confôrto, a espera, o efêmero e o eterno.

The painting featured here as no. 7, reproduced in *Habitat*, 16 September 1957, for the solo show of Morandi's works at the 4th São Paulo Biennial in Brazil.

meditations on relationships of form and color, where the form is the simplest possible and the color has the lowest, most neutral tone possible. Yet with a sense of tonal relationships, that reveals the greatness of the artist, each of Morandi's browns contains infinite allusions of chromatic life" (Venturi, 1947, p. 48). But in 1950 the same characteristics inspired a highly polemical page written by a Marxist critic, Raffaele De Grada: "Every room of works by Morandi makes us think of those painters who during their life have never met anybody and have only seen the life of other men and of things through the windows. Morandi is the painter for intellectuals, isolated and cold; he is the holy image hung on the wall to which we turn in moments of crisis; he is the small god of critics who do not want to observe and serve, but who claim to create and to feel themselves artists for their own drama which could well be that of their own inability to narrate or to stay in the company of other men. And so Morandi is the painter who will always be preferred by intellectuals and who will never be understood by the workers, neither today nor in the future" (De Grada, 1951). This passage put a negative spin on a series of observations (the gaze filtered as if through a window, sentimental coldness which becomes visual intelligence) previously put into focus in 1940 by Mario Tobino in an article published in that *Corrente di Vita Giovanile*, which had contained writings by young left-wing Milanese before the war, (Tobino, 1940), and was vigorously attacked by Giuseppe Raimondi in Brandi's *L'Immagine* (G.R., 1950, pp. 460–461); it marked the end of five years of debate on Morandi conducted by writers connected with the Italian Communist Party. The debate had ranged from the rude anti-formalist attacks of De Grada himself after visiting the show in Rome in 1945 ("Continuous rummaging about inside himself and his own formalist sensibility," De Grada, 1945, p. 82), to the ideological overtures of Antonello Trombadori in *Rinascita* ("Like all the other men of bourgeois culture and art, he has no direct, living link with his country and the problems of its people. But . . . in his dignified, serious work we can feel the weight and the condemnation of that bitter detachment, that impotence," Trombadori, 1945, p. 158), to the definitive anathema pronounced by Mario De Micheli, based on an aesthetic that rejected the idea of "poetry as distance" (in the *pars costruens* of *Realismo e poesia* it was easy to identify Morandi among those who use "the resources of a courtly vocabulary, of a sterilized or arduous word, almost uprooted, reduced to a fossil," De Micheli, 1946, p. 43).

9. *Still Life*, 1951.
Oil on canvas, 35 × 45 cm.
Vitali no. 1365.
Private collection.

10. *Still Life*, 1952.
Oil on canvas, 36.2 × 46.4 cm.
Vitali no. 816.
Private collection.

11. *Still Life*, 1960.
Oil on canvas, 30 × 40 cm.
Vitali no. 1188.
Trento, Museo d'Arte Moderna e
Contemporanea di Trento e Rovereto,
deposito Giovanardi.

"In Bologna, as everyone knows, lives the most mystical and lyrical of contemporary painters, Morandi. He paints in his bedroom; on a table his bottles raptly wait for him to draw from them and the spaces between them the music of serene melancholy in which they will appear in his luminous and genteel pictures" (de Giorgi, 1992, p. 190). This was how, in an autobiographical novel published in 1955 and referring to the events in Rome in 1944, Elsa de Giorgio represented the meeting between Sandrino Contini Bonacossi and Giorgio Morandi in Bologna a few months before the Liberation. In the fifties the identification of Morandi's painting with the objects they depicted was virtually complete. In 1957 Lionello Venturi warned the American public, on the occasion of an important Morandi retrospective, against this kind of stereotyping. The public at large, he said, sees a limitation in Morandi's insistence upon representing small bottles and in his refusal to paint a human figure: he is called "il pittore delle bottigliette" (in Italian in the original, Venturi[1], 1957).

Venturi, of course, interpreted Morandi as a strict formalist and he saw in his choice of painting bottles the innocent self-deception of continuing in the figurative tradition ("The task of the bottles in Morandi's paintings is to assure him that the tradition is safe; that he may live, even when he is painting, in the old tradition"). But, though the American public was completely ignorant of the discussions that developed regarding Morandi after the 1939 Quadrennial, to ask what was the meaning of the objects filling his paintings was none the less an overwhelming temptation:

"One suspects that the bottles only contain a little water for sprinkling on the floor or eau-de-cologne for cooling one's brow, certainly nothing as strong as wine," John Berger noted, struck by the extreme delicacy of the tonal passages, in the first article to be published on the artist in the United States (Berger, 1955, p. 67). And, reviewing the new show in the World House Galleries five years later, such a neo-figurative painter as Sidney Tillim po-

lemically overturned Venturi's interpretation and gave a completely content-orientated one of his own: to restore nobility to subject matter, to forcefully declare the factual existence of things was seen as part of a conscious project for the potential rehumanization of art (Tillim, 1960, p. 45). Beginning in 1951–52 Morandi returned, in his still lifes, to the tall narrow bottles of the Bolognese wine-sellers and trattorias, which he had already begun to use in 1929

The city of Bologna held in the hands of St. Petronius, from the altarpiece by Lorenzo Costa
Madonna with Child, St. Petronius and St. Tecla, 1496. Bologna, Pinacoteca Nazionale.

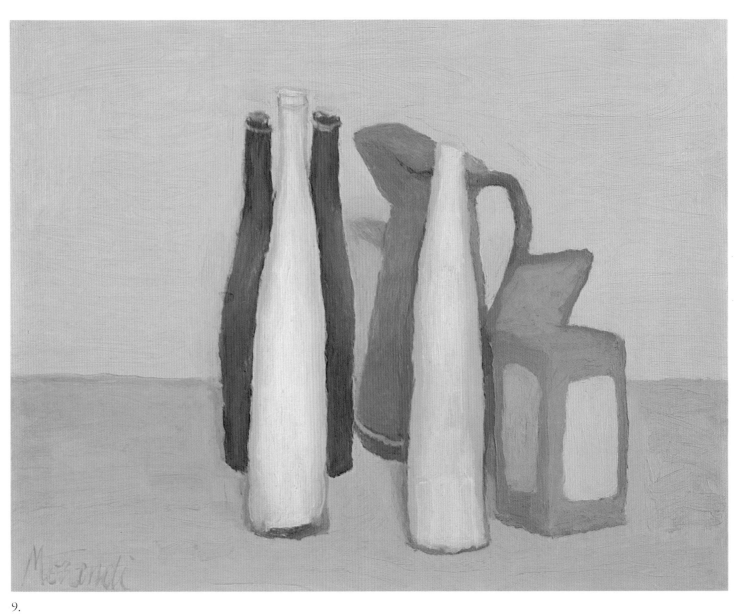

9.

10.

(Vitali no. 138) and that, colored white (with his usual aim of avoiding luminous reflections), from 1932 on, throughout the thirties, were to become a constant presence: their task was to give the still lifes a vertical thrust and, at the same time, give them a strong graphic pattern, with profiles etched against the emptiness of the background.

The three still lifes shown in this sequence reveal very different aspects of this return to the bottles in the post-war period. In the first painting, a continuation of the 1950–51 period of warm amber tones, the bottles become the basic spatial reference point for the picture for which they also supply the extremes of the chromatic range, with a violent difference between the velvety brown of the bottles in the background and the compact white of those in the foreground. In the second, stylistically quite different but close to the first in time (the Milione label no. 6647 allows us, with the help of the gallery archives, to establish that the picture was bought in 1952, directly from the artist), we can see an unexpected reutilization of solutions tried out at the end of the thirties and the beginning of the forties: the objects are lined up in an almost obsessive frontal manner, the application of the paint becomes richer in color (over the plum-brown colored bottle a range of colors extends from the light strokes of the central reflection to blackish shadings), while a strong light from the left lengthens the shadows across the table.

The long bottles return again to Morandi's paintings dating from the fifties, in limited but crucial episodes: especially in cases when, in the arrangement of the group of main objects, it became necessary to emphasize, or even to contradict, the format of the picture. For example, in a beautiful series from 1957 (one of the most significant pictures, Vitali no. 1033, was seen in the two exhibitions at the World House Galleries in 1957 and 1960, and was reproduced in *Art News*) the black and white bottles, painted with vibrant brushstrokes, with a velvety finish, are superimposed over a rectangle developed vertically on a horizontal format. In two paintings from 1959 (one is no. 37 in this show) the long bottles close the back of a composition that, though having a squarish format, seems subjected to a strong centripe-

Still Life, 1957 (Vitali no. 1033). Whereabouts unknown. Reproduced in the catalog of the exhibition *Giorgio Morandi. Retrospective. Paintings, Drawings, Etchings 1912–1957*, World House Galleries, New York, 1957.

tal force. The last time the tall bottle appears in the list of Morandi's works is in the picture exhibited here as no. 11: in this case too the Galleria Il Milione label (no. 8474) permits a precise dating of this acquisition by Ghiringhelli from the artist (14 April 1960), allowing us to date its execution to the previous month. This information is fundamental because the stylistic quality of the picture (which has no chiaroscuro construction at all and is immersed in a clear and cold light that emphasizes the blue-yellow-green juxtaposition of the three objects, from which the chalky white bottle stands out) is unique in Morandi's production and also, it seems to me, in relationship to the two paintings (Vitali nos. 1089 and 1090) which are placed together with it in the artist's catalogue raisonné.

In 1953, in his presentation in Florence of the Mattioli collection, Carlo Ludovico Ragghianti, who had admired Morandi for many years, reversed the intimist-tonal interpretation which still held sway in Morandi criticism and hailed the painter as a lucid architect of space. His still lifes "are not rhythms and atmospheres and tones, or they are these things only in an organization and artistic image that can ideally be reconstructed in plan—and Morandi, as everyone knows, draws, trying out the plans of his compositions, calculating in this way the occupation of the planes and the volumes, establishing the right distance, stepping back or zooming in on the background, the sides, the top and the

bottom with respect to the dimensions, evaluating the orientation and the correlations of the objects, creating a pattern of shadows and light—and can be reconstructed in different elevations and horizontal or oblique cutaways, in a synthesis which, once critically explained, gives the viewer an idea of the immense value of a construction that is, as I said, wholly architectural, so much so that it should prompt us to speak of cathedrals rather than of bottles" (Ragghianti, 1953, p. 16). More recently a Bolognese painter, Concetto Pozzati, has asked himself how much the tension found in the arrangement of the objects might be derived from the academic practice of using a trestle on which to place a model: "Morandi made this boring academic routine an emotional process. . . . The composition is in itself creation, the construction is already a formal certainty in which there is a ritual magical balance" (Pozzati, 1985, p. 70).

In a 1955 issue of *La Fiera Letteraria* on Morandi (in that period certainly the artist most admired by writers and poets), Libero De Libero developed an idea contained in the passage by Ragghianti quoted above, declaring that the still lifes seemed like "little cathedrals held in the arms of new saints" (De Libero, 1955). I must thank Francesca Valli for the suggestion that De Libero was, perhaps at Morandi's suggestion, referring to the traditional images of the city of Bologna, encircled by its walls and towers, held in the arms of St. Petronius. In particular, in an altarpiece depicting the *Madonna with Child, St. Petronius and St. Tecla* by Lorenzo Costa kept in the Pinacoteca Nazionale di Bologna (obviously a museum often visited by Morandi), St. Petronius holds a miniature Bologna that seems to be referred to in the painting shown here as no. 10: the walls and bastions in the foreground that lead to the vertical elements of the towers and houses seem to be repeated in the sequence of bottles and boxes, reflecting the same pursuit of a three-dimensional effect (on the subject of Morandi's ability to isolate analogous details in complex pictures, such as the view of Bologna in the *Madonna del Rosario* by Guido Reni, a text of fundamental importance is the narration by Francesco Arcangeli of a visit with the painter to the exhibition of Reni in 1954, Arcangeli, 1955, pp. 30–32 and 69).

11.

12. *Still Life*, 1952.
Oil on canvas, 32 × 48 cm.
Vitali no. 823.
Bologna, Museo Morandi.

13. *Still Life*, 1952.
Oil on canvas, 40.6 × 40 cm.
Vitali no. 824.
Private collection.

14. *Still Life*, 1952.
Oil on canvas, 35.8 × 45.8 cm.
Vitali no. 826.
Private collection.

15. *Still Life*, 1952.
Oil on canvas, 40.5 × 46 cm.
Vitali no. 828.
Milan, Mattioli Rossi collection.

16. *Still Life*, 1952.
Oil on canvas, 35 × 40 cm.
Vitali no. 831.
Milan, Civiche Raccolte d'Arte.

17. *Still Life*, 1952.
Oil on canvas, 40.5 × 45.9 cm.
Vitali no. 830.
Private collection.

In 1952 Morandi worked on an extremely compact series of ten still lifes featuring a folded cloth at the center of the foreground. The minimum variations from one painting to another have deceived even the compilers of Morandi's catalogue raisonné in which, due to two photographs which seem to be quite different as a result of the lighting and the focus of details, the same picture is reproduced twice as nos. 823 and 829 (this is the work once belonging to the Ingrao collection and now in the Museo Morandi, reproduced here as no. 12).

In the years between the two wars this representation of a cloth on the table had been frequently attempted by Morandi, and the cloth, theatrically placed, alluded directly to the great still life tradition stretching from the seventeenth century to Cézanne. In the period following the Second World War, on the other hand, and for the only time in this series, the artist represented the cloth as being soft and without a previously fixed form (as are the bottles, boxes, and vases) but one decided on by him. In the arrangement of the objects to be represented on the table top, this involves a gesture that goes beyond mere positioning, to also involve the actual modeling of one of the elements. Despite the fact that the folded cloth, as Marilena Pasquali has noted, tends to take on the compactness of the surrounding objects (Pasquali, 1996, p. 116), the particular quality of the paint, one in search of a soft *ductus*, and an unusual tonal complexity that extends from straw-color to violet, underline the exceptional character of this intrusion. The fact that we are looking at a sequence in which there seems to be a

Still Life, 1929 (Vitali n. 137). Private collection.

breaking up of the implacable architecture of the objects displayed in the still lifes of the previous two years, is shown in part by the strange and, until now, unidentified presence seen behind the cloth in the paintings reproduced here as nos. 12, 13, and 17. This is the bread basket already seen in an etching of 1921 (Vitali etchings no. 15) but which has lost its handle and, in this state, is still to be found among the objects in the studio of the Museo Morandi. The same object, no longer subject to the minute examination of the etching, is to be seen in a picture evidently inspired by Cézanne, of 1929 (and which should be compared with painting no. 13 in this catalog). Here the basket is seen together with a cloth placed on the edge of the table, and it cannot be ruled out that, after a break of

over twenty years, Morandi might have taken up the subject again on purpose: for the 1952 series the painter probably roughly covered the basket with paper so as to eliminate the texture of the wicker and, as with the cloth, he seems interested in a painterly effect resulting from an unusual, irregular, mat surface.

The presentation together in this show of six still lifes from the series of ten permits us to reflect on the meaning and modes of Morandi's way of working in series. Apart from the paintings, four drawings have survived that document part of the studies for this series of still lifes. This unified sequence (all the sheets are taken from a single notebook, 23.5 × 32.5 cm) provides some important information on the development of the cycle. In three of the drawings (Pasquali-Tavoni nos. 1952/2, 7, and 9) the objects shown are the same as in the series Vitali nos. 830–833, though the vantage point is at the same level as the objects, which are therefore seen as profiles against a neutral background. In the first, a brief sketch placed together with two other sketches (for a different still life of 1952 and for a vase of flowers) the theme is rendered by a quick outline. In the second the object is emphatically shadowed against the background: this is the starting point for the strong, unique chromatic contrast seen in all the pictures of the series. In the third, today in the Museo Morandi, a light from the left creates a marked chiaroscuro effect on the vase, cup, and bottle; the bottle casts a decisive shadow on the table to the right. At this point the artist must have realized that the folded cloth, penalized by too low a vantage point, would appear flat, nearly

12.

13.

14.

16.

17.

18.

19.

From *Il Giorno*, 16 September 1958: Morandi with a *Still Life* from 1955 (Vitali no. 970). The article discusses the exclusion of Morandi from a group show on the "twentieth-century Renaissance" held in 1958 at the Municipal Museum of Amsterdam.

Still Life, 1954 (Vitali no. 919). The Hague, Gemeentemuseum. The painting was displayed at Morandi's solo exhibition of 1954 at the Hague, though it is not listed in the catalog. It is one of the few in this series in which one object set on the diagonal (the Persian bottle) upsets the equilibrium of the orthogonal construction.

pure geometry (thanks in part, in Italy, two major exhibitions like the one on "De Stijl" at the 1952 Biennial and the Mondrian exhibition in 1956 at the Galleria Nazionale d'Arte Moderna), these paintings by Morandi appeared to represent his closest approach to the poetics of abstraction.

In spite of the fact that the artist denied any involvement in anti-figurative research ("I don't think I have anything in common with Mondrian," he said firmly in an interview with Edouard Roditi, in Roditi, 1960, p. 55), the interpretation of this cycle of paintings winds up on just this ground. Werner Haftmann, author of a major work, in 1954, on twentieth-century art in which Morandi is credited with an important role, focused on the implications of an utterly mental construction in this new phase: "The resulting painting is a rigorously structured architectural whole. Closed in its frame, well-enclosed between the foreground and an ideal ordering and bordering of the the depth created by the volumes of the objects and their colors, the motif is posed as an ideal cube. In terms of

content, these humble objects in their mute grouping achieve an extraordinary force of lyrical expression . . . . The form is pure and without literary associations. It might be called 'abstract' if it were not so dependent on the object" (Haftmann, 1955, p. 292). Heinz Keller, who wrote the preface for the Winterthur show in 1956 saw a musical intent, on the other hand, in an increasingly geometric approach in which "only the bottles and boxes survive:" "Morandi achieves, through the simple rhythm of the forms, and his subtle value relationships, a sublime musicality. By continually softening the object, he makes a spiritual atmosphere become the content of the painting. As a result of such an austere simplification, the work of Giogio Morandi's maturity and old age has, although without showing the human figure, reached an extremely high level of human intensity that, in its palpitating calm, is the exemplary expression of knowledge and of harmony" (Keller, 1956, p. 4). But in both these passages we can still sense a grappling with the problem

that permeated all artistic discussion in the mid-fifties, that of going beyond figuration.

It became difficult for Francesco Arcangeli, in his 1964 monograph, to come to grips with cycle that was certainly of less interest to him than others and where the lyrical abandon of the painter seems to be held in check by constructive intentions. Arcangeli's approach begins with the luminosity of these pictures, in an attempt to link them to the Metaphysical period: "Meanwhile the frontal light abolishes shadows so that the objects appear to be suspended in a time and in a space that, intuitively seen in three dimensions, is then abstracted into a 'suspended vision' with a two-dimensional effect. Moreover, the objects are placed in such a way that their external borders form a square: not a perfect square, Morandi is not Mondrian, but a kind of rectangular fortress of things, whose internal rhythm is established by the light necks of the bottles, and where even the dust . . . . acts as a free geometric caesura" (Arcangeli, 1964, pp. 318–319).

20.

22.

23.

29.

30.

Still Life, watercolor, 1956 (Pasquali no. 1956/5). Turin, Galleria Civica d'Arte Moderna, Fondazione De Fornaris.

Still Life, watercolor, 1956 (Pasquali no. 1956/7). Private collection.

vision of the dark interiors of the objects themselves, clearly seen due to the high position of the vantage point. But the tonal balance, as often occurs in the works of 1957, is interrupted by violent chromatic touches, in this case produced by red tones of the object in the background and, above all, by the bluish shading of the vase in the foreground.

In the second half of the fifties, at the same time as the execution and exhibition of such paintings as these, in which the objects appear to be isolated and dominated by a mysterious (and, in the opinion of many, anguishing) silence, it becomes very tempting to interpret Morandi in the light of the poetics of existentialism. This was a common key for understanding the works, reflected in their use in the sets of two crucial films of the sixties, in the studios of two intellectuals going through an identity crisis (Steiner and Pontano): Federico Fellini's *La dolce vita* and Michelangelo Anto-

nioni's *La notte*. But before the filmmakers decided to use Morandi's work as a symbol, in the world of literature this interpretation was already widespread. Lorenzo Montano, in the first article on Morandi to appear in the *Corriere della Sera*, linked the significance of the paintings to a theatrical work much in vogue at the time ("A few hours earlier [before seeing the Morandi exhibition at Winterthur] I had seen that masterpiece of the theater of desperation *Waiting for Godot* by Samuel Beckett, then being performed in Paris. In the calm canvases of the Italian painter I saw the reflection of the existential lament of the Franco-Irish Job," Montano, 1956). Two years later another writer, Leonida Répaci, faced with the structural breakdown of the objects in the still lifes of Morandi's final period, paintings, seen on a visit to his studio and described in *Tempo*, Milan, rejected any formalist interpretation ("His painting is perhaps the supreme testimon-

ial of dismay. The dismay of a form that fears losing its consistency, its cohesion in the shadows," Répaci, 1958, p. 34). Art historians were obliged to soften the tone, bringing the existential interpretation back into the area of "sentiment" (Rodolfo Pallucchini put it this way for the audience at the São Paulo Biennial, "One is aware . . . . of how his feelings, in all the infinite changes and vibrations that a man undergoes in his journey through time, are concentrated in the world of images he evokes. In the poverty of the theme, an almost adventurous richness is concentrated and taken to its full potential, leading to a poetry that is refined contemplation, but demanding the vibration of every fiber of our being" (Pallucchini[1], 1957, p. 280), or concentrating attention on the moment of the execution of the painting ("an experience, not of the normal control of life, but of an evident and calm tension within life's normality," Arcangeli, 1964, p. 335).

31. *Still Life*, 1955.
Oil on canvas, 26 × 40 cm.
Vitali no. 944.
Freiburg, Morat-Institut für Kunst und
Kunstwissenschaft.

32. *Still Life,* 1955.
Oil on canvas, 30.4 × 35.2 cm.
Vitali no. 972.
Private collection.

33. *Still Life*, 1956.
Oil on canvas, 40.5 × 35.5 cm.
Vitali no. 986.
Trento, Museo d'Arte Moderna e
Contemporanea di Trento e Rovereto,
deposito Giovanardi.

34. *Still Life*, 1956.
Oil on canvas, 35.7 × 45.7 cm.
Vitali no. 1012.
Milan, Mattioli Rossi collection.

35. *Still Life*, 1956.
Oil on canvas, 35.5 × 35 cm.
Vitali no. 1013.
Bologna, Museo Morandi.

From 1946 onward Morandi had attempted to combine simple geometric objects (the parallelepipeds of two coffee boxes and a cigar box), showing them frontally and moving them close to the edge of the table and thus nearer to the viewer. He had not tried this solution since his metaphysical period: the coffee boxes in the pictures from 1942–44, in fact, were either seen by a glimpse of one of their side-facets, or their rectangular geometry was neutralized by the mass of bottles and vases. With the passing of time, in order to make the compositions more compact and their profiles more regular, this strategy was repeated, either by re-using the same objects (though, from 1949 on, with the cigar box mostly seen from the larger rectangle thus making the most of the flattening effect of the colored central band), or from 1950 onwards by using the square facet of the Persian bottle which supplied a harsher light. Starting with the backgrounds of certain "square-based" still lifes of 1953 (Vitali nos. 852 and 853 for instance) Morandi began to use other simple paper boxes: the vibrato of the brushstrokes eliminated the risk of the solids being too inert, their corners resulting irregular, as though the light-filled surfaces were etched, with a slight over-exposure, on a background which could not support the flood of light. As early as 1946 Francesco Arcangeli had understood this phenomenon: "The clarity of the objects vibrates, slightly but visibly, at the edges as a result of the brush work, as though an effect of a subtle but corrugated modulation; the handling is sure and, from a distance, is absorbed into the overall effect of the work" (Arcangeli, 1946). In the series

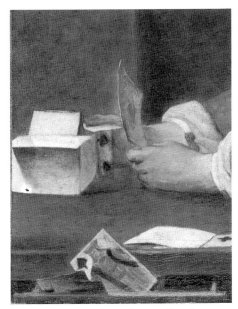

Detail from Jean-Baptiste-Siméon Chardin,
Jeune homme construisant un château de cartes,
1735 ca. Winterthur, Sammlung Oskar Reinhart.

seen here, this trembling at the edges is so marked as to make us think of boxes constructed by the artist himself that have maintained the irregularity of the folds of the paper from which they are made: I think a significant precedent (variously illuminated facets of a fragile and empty solid) is to be found in a detail of the *Jeune homme construisant un château de cartes* by Chardin, a picture long loved by Morandi and admired in the monograph that he owned (published by André de Ridder in 1932; plate LXXVIII). The original was eventually seen by him at the Sammlung Oskar Reinhart in Winterthur on the occasion of his show with Giacomo Manzù

held in 1956 in the Kunstmuseum of the same city.
Used at the beginning as objects for balancing a composition full of other objects (as happens in the first two still lifes exhibited here) these boxes, with the growth of the series were to become the protagonists of a combination game. In the still life here, no. 33, they take over the foreground by themselves and, in the following two, they are what mainly determines the construction and luminous quality of the picture. These two works represent one of the high points of Morandi's spatial research: only in very rare cases (the cigar box in the horizontal still lifes of 1954 for example) did an object arrive at the edge of the table nearest the painter (and viewer) and line up with it. The result is completely new: in this way the two spatial systems of Morandi's still lifes, the stage-like one (the table and the visible portion of the studio hidden by the well-known paper covers) and those of the objects placed in a setting, are forced to be compared directly and find a difficult equilibrium.
For this operation the first priority was obviously that of finding the best vantage point. In what seems to have been a preceding series of pictures (Vitali nos. 944–948) it was already strongly angled from above: in this way there was not only accentuated the tonal contrast between the two faces of the parallelepipeds (the strongly illuminated frontal one and the dust-veiled one higher up) but above all they were aligned with the corners of the boxes in the foreground. The next step, that of placing the objects on two distinct and non-communicating planes (as can be seen in the still life reproduced here as no.

31.

32.

33) is first studied graphically and is very obvious, for example, in the drawing Pasquali-Tavoni no. 1956/6. In still lifes nos. 34 and 35 that conclude our series, the device of displacing two of the three boxes to the point nearest the viewer permits, even while leaving the viewpoint unchanged, the full occupation of the space from the edge of the table to the horizon line.

The desire to balance the composition further can be felt in what I believe to be the last picture in the series, today kept in the Museo Morandi, and characterized by a square format that eliminates the voids at the sides. This painting which, with respect to the preceding one, reduces the chromatic complexity of the ivory-green-peach harmonies, is one of the most surprising and ambiguous of Morandi's output. If it is in fact true that the earth color common to the background, the upper face of the boxes and the areas of bottles in the background can be interpreted as "dust that, deposited on all the horizontal surfaces, becomes chromatically half-toned and a unifying element of the various forms" (Pasquali, 1996, p. 112), it also seems to me that here too Morandi wanted to play openly with the spatial ambiguities that an unfinished state allowed him: the neck of the blue bottle is, in fact, the only part colored, and the green box has its upper facet left unpainted (the profile of the bottle is, though, marked by an almost imperceptible dark line and the brushstrokes hint at the circular closure of the box). In this state the picture was left by an artist notoriously difficult to be convinced that a work was finished and given to Francesco Paolo Ingrao.

That this is the last picture of the series is, for me, proved by the fact that Morandi repeats it in two watercolors (Pasquali nos. 1956/1–2) with a similar composition and coloring. The inquiry into space, in fact, does not seem to continue coherently, as it has done so far, but to be eliminated: the picture Vitali no. 1014 with the bottle flanked by two boxes, one that, according to the order of the catalogue raisonné, follows the one kept today in the Museo Morandi, is evidently united to the homologous and preceding series, Vitali nos. 1005–1007, while Vitali no. 1031 (dated 1957 and perhaps to be back-dated a year as in the 1964 monograph: Vitali, 1964, no. 213) is a minimum variant of the 1956 painting reproduced as no. 33. Morandi, instead, suddenly made an interruption and eliminated the foreground boxes and

Still Life, 1956 (Vitali no. 1031). Private collection. The resemblance to the painting reproduced here as no. 33 indicates that the usual 1957 date of this painting should be changed to 1956.

recuperated the long bottles that had been seen in two pictures from 1956. These bottles were kept well back, exactly in the place they had when they were in the background: now they could be introduced by a low horizontal box, a teapot or by nothing (as in the pictures Vitali nos. 1022–1023 and 1026). In this way the pictures radically change in appearance and in meaning: the image, even while having an analogous format, becomes vertical. The perspectival space between objects and spatial container in the paintings of 1956 is eliminated while the pictorial texture reintroduces rich coloring veined with chiaroscuro. And so the still life again becomes a suspended apparition of presences against the stage-like table.

In one of Morandi's most intellectual series of paintings, then, the artist stops when the basic problems of representation (the relationship between the arranged objects and pictorial fiction, between tonal truth and spatial ambiguity) seem to have arrived at a point of no return. In 1960

Still Life, watercolor, 1956 (Pasquali no. 1956/1). Private collection.

Sidney Tillim, one of the protagonists of new American figurative art, when reviewing the second Morandi solo show at the World House Galleries, clearly saw the paradoxes of Morandi's painting from the second half of the fifties: "The purity of their mass and the subtle gradations of exquisite color further augment the impression that their physical identity is relative. Yet one of the conclusions that can be drawn from this exhibition is that as his works have increased in austerity and formality in recent years, the literal content has become more realistic. The ambiguity, in fact, intensifies the corporeal actuality of the models" (Tillim, 1960, p. 44). Twenty years later, at the time of the Morandi retrospective in San Francisco, Kenneth Baker attempted a reading starting from the picture here shown as no. 31; he reconstructed the optical and mental tour de force (the spatial autonomy of each object, the unnaturalness of the shadows, the ambiguity between the horizon of the table and the real horizon) which Morandi's paintings of this period force us to be aware of (Baker, 1981, pp. 41–45): the outcome of this ambiguity, which Paolo Fossati sees as typical of Morandi from the time of his most experimental Metaphysical phase (Fossati, 1995, pp. 161–167), is his choice of leaving the picture incomplete.

Together with other contemporary series of still lifes, this one caused Italian critics of the fifties and sixties to discuss whether plastic construction rather than color was Morandi's main contribution to art. The question, one that now seems to be boringly abstract, at the time touched on crucial ideological problems in figurative art. The two interpretations were, in the main, considered in parallel. In his presentation of the Morandi anthological show at the World House Galleries in 1957 Lionello Venturi was quite clear and referred to an interpretation first touched on in his *Gusto dei primitivi* in 1926: "Morandi feels that a geometrical form has a sense in painting if an abstract color dresses it . . . . A still life by Morandi is most beautiful when it is most simple; when few objects of common shape are offered on the canvas. In recent years Morandi has become aware of this and his simplifications of motifs are more and more emphasized in order to let the color harmony speak by itself" (Venturi[1], 1957). In his review of the same show James Thrall Soby was similarly struck by the unexpected chromatic richness of many of the pictures on view: "Morandi's

33.

34.

35.

36.

37.

39.

40. *Still Life,* 1957.
Oil on canvas, 28 × 35 cm.
Vitali no. 1049.
Bologna, Museo Morandi.

41. *Still Life,* 1959.
Oil on canvas, 25.7 × 35.7 cm.
Vitali no. 1138.
Private collection.

In the period 1957–58 a favorite constructional procedure of Morandi was to individuate a strong vertical axis around which a still life could be structured. Often the objects are placed mirror-fashion around this axis: the correspondence between the two halves can be underlined by two strong presences equidistant from the center, as in the case of the funnel-shaped bottle and the Persian bottle in no. 40; or the artist can paint the two halves of the canvas perfectly mirrored, as in the case of the Persian bottles in no. 41. This strategy is mostly confined to the period before he began to paint, the moment in which there was decided the layout of the objects. Morandi would then procede altering the view point and above all, and with a freedom previously unknown, the image frame. Once he had decided on the objects in his still lifes and established their position, the artist would daringly cut the rectangle of the horizontal format and transform it into a vertical composition as in the still life Vitali no. 1066; and, in sequence (Vitali nos. 1064 and 1065), he alters the angles between the objects and, above all, the importance of the shadows.

The new layout governing the works of this period is the result of a long process of questioning the compositional criteria of the still lifes that had been valid for Morandi until this time. The acme of frontality, stereometry, and luminous abstraction that can be seen in the picture with two Persian bottles begins with a still life (Vitali no. 1050) dated 1957 in the artist's catalogue raisonné: the frontal surface of the bottle emerges as a sharp luminous plane and the deep space is suggested only by the dust tone that covers the surface of

Still Life, 1957 (Vitali no. 1066).
Private collection.

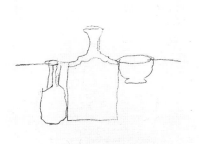

Still Life, drawing, 1957 (Pasquali-Tavoni no. 1957/1). Private collection.

Still Life, 1957 (Vitali no. 1050).
Private collection.

the stopper. In the drawing, that evidently followed the picture, the depth is completely eliminated and the individuation of the three objects (bottle, small bottle, and cup) is entrusted simply to the profile. The next year, in a series of pictures (Vitali nos. 1091–1096 and 1099–1100, one of which is dated) Morandi attempts to redouble the Persian bottle specularly, always, however, rotating the one to the right in order to suggest a perspectival gradation. In four contemporary drawings (Pasquali-Tavoni nos. 1958/29–32, the last two dated) the absolute frontality of the two bottles side by side is attempted for the first time but without exaggerating the solution: the art-

ist makes use of a dark background plane or, having eliminated all spatial references, he places a light source to the left in order to elongate the shadow of the bottles on the right (and obviously the shadow causes us to assume the existence of a volume and a plane on which it is projected).

Only in the watercolors of 1959 (Pasquali

40.

41.

42.

43.

44.

45.

46.

47.

163

Technical Index of the Works

edited by Laura Lorenzoni

The Technical Index of the Works *give title, date, technique, support, measurements, inscriptions, number of publication in the catalogue raisonné edited by Lamberto Vitali and published in 1977 by Electa (or in the updated second edition of 1983), whereabouts, provenance, exhibitions, and bibliography. Next to the title appears the date thought to be the most likely after studies undertaken for the present exhibition. It might, then, sometimes be in disagreement with the date proposed by Vitali in the above-mentioned catalogue raisonné. Any differences of titles or dates are noted between parentheses.*
The measurements have been checked directly against the paintings, so it is possible they are different from those found in other publications. The indication "Vitali no." refers to the publication number in the catalogue raisonné. The provenance has always been checked. Traveling exhibitions are mentioned specifying successive venues between parentheses. Single catalogs accompanying traveling shows are indicated after the information about the city and the year.
When a catalog was unavailable or nonexistent, exhibitions are indicated in the entries only by the place and year in which they were held. When the picture's presence in an exhibition is doubtful, this is pointed out with a question mark after the city and the year. A question mark after the catalog number means it has been impossible to give an exact reference of the work as a result of the vagueness of the catalog information.
The bibliography lists monographs, general studies, articles, and reviews in newspapers, magazines, and periodicals.

We would like to thank the following for their help: Flavio Fergonzi, Marta and Paola Giovanardi, Bruno Grossetti, Laura Mattioli Rossi, Francesco Sandroni, Lorenza Selleri.

1. *Still Life*, 1948–1950.
Oil on canvas, 38 × 45.2 cm.
Signed on reverse at the center: *Morandi*.
Vitali no. 754.
Private collection.

Prov.: Galleria Il Milione, Milan, no. 5852; Nino Levi collection, Turin; Galleria Gissi, Turin, no. 1952.

Exh.: Ancona, 1964, p. 87, and p. 93, repr. (dated 1950); Milan, 1971, p. 21, no. 69, and p. 69, repr. (dated 1950).

Bibl.: Vitali, 1977 (2nd ed. 1983), no. 754, repr. (dated 1950).

2. *Still Life*, 1950 ca.
Oil on canvas, 30 × 46 cm.
Signed lower right: *Morandi*.
Vitali no. 1363.
Private collection.

Prov.: Galleria del Cavallino, Venice; Galleria dello Scudo, Verona; Galleria Forni, Bologna.

Exh.: Madrid, 1984–1985, no. 28, repr. (dated 1950); Kamakura, 1989 (then Okada, 1990; Fukuyama, 1990; Tokyo, 1990; Kyoto, 1990), p. 87, no. 63, repr. (dated 1950).

Bibl.: Vitali (1977), 2nd ed. 1983, no. 1363, repr. (dated 1950).

3. *Still Life*, 1950–1952.
Oil on canvas, 44 × 44.3 cm.
Signed lower center: *Morandi*.
Vitali no. 1364.
Private collection.

Prov.: Galleria Il Milione, Milan, no. 5992; S. Tofanelli collection, Milan.

Exh.: Milan, 1990–1991, p. 152, no. 64, repr., and p. 175, no. 64 (dated 1950).

Bibl.: Vitali (1977), 2nd ed. 1983, no. 1364, repr. (dated 1950 ca.).

4. *Still Life*, 1951.
Oil on canvas, 40.5 × 45.5 cm.

Signed lower right: *Morandi*.
Vitali no. 763.
Trento, Museo d'Arte Moderna e Contemporanea di Trento e Rovereto, deposito Giovanardi.

Prov.: Galleria Il Milione, Milan, no. 6148.

Exh.: The Hague, 1954, no. 61 (*Stilleven met zoutvat*, dated 1950–1951); Turin, 1959, p. 51, no. 44, and pl. 59 (dated 1954); Lucerne, 1960, no. 3 (dated 1950); Venice, 1966, p. 28, no. 64 (dated 1950); Bologna, 1966, p. 76, no. 87, and pl. 87 (dated 1950); Turin, 1968, p. 45, no. 6, and p. 125, repr. (dated 1950); Kamakura, 1989 (then Okada, 1990; Fukuyama, 1990; Tokyo, 1990; Kyoto, 1990), p. 89, no. 65, repr.; Milan, 1990–1991, p. 155, no. 67, repr., and p. 175, no. 67.

Bibl.: Giuffrè, 1970, p. 29, fig. 21 (dated 1950); Vitali, 1977 (2nd ed. 1983), no. 763, repr.

5. *Still Life*, 1951.
Oil on canvas, 34.8 × 37.9 cm.
Signed lower right: *Morandi*.
Vitali no. 767.
Private collection.

Prov.: Galleria Il Milione, Milan; A. Montalto collection, Milan; Carla Montalto Cocorocchia collection, Milan; Galleria dello Scudo, Verona.

Exh.: New York, 1990 (?); Budapest, 1991, p. 76, and p. 77, repr.; Paris, 1992, p. 61, no. 24, repr., p. 85, no. 24, and cover; Brussels, 1992, p. 97, no. 61, repr., and p. 160, no. 61; San Marino, 1997, p. 30, repr.

Bibl.: Vitali, 1964 (2nd ed. 1965; 3rd ed. 1970), pl. 200; Vitali, 1977 (2nd ed. 1983), no. 767, repr.

6. *Still Life*, 1951–1953.
Oil on canvas, 30 × 50 cm.
Signed lower towards the left: *Morandi*.
Vitali no. 766.
Private collection.
(Courtesy Claudia Gian Ferrari).

Prov.: Gisella Levi Cesana collection, Rome; Galleria Gian Ferrari, Milan.

Exh.: Kamakura, 1989 (then Okada, 1990; Fukuyama, 1990; Tokyo, 1990; Kyoto, 1990), p. 90, no. 66, repr. (dated 1951); Milan, 1990–1991, p. 153, no. 65, repr., and p. 175, no. 65 (dated 1951); Paris, 1996–1997, p. 148, repr., and p. 234 (dated 1951); São Paulo, 1997, p. 144, repr., and p. 250 (dated 1951).

Bibl.: Vitali, 1977 (2nd ed. 1983), no. 766, repr. (dated 1951).

7. *Still Life*, 1950.
Oil on canvas, 43.5 × 60.3 cm.
Signed lower center: *Morandi*.
Dedication on back of mount, top: *A Lina, Natale 1953 Pietro*.
Vitali no. 779.
Private collection.

Prov.: Galleria Il Milione, Milan, no. 5941; Pier Maria Bardi collection, São Paulo; Da Silva collection, Rio de Janeiro; Galleria Gissi, Turin, no. 2694.

Exh.: Milan, 1954–1955, p. 67, no. 104, and pl. 114 (dated 1951); Turin, 1967, no. 23, repr. (dated 1951); Milan, 1970–1971, no. 13, repr.; Milan, 1971, p. 21, no. 72, and p. 69, repr. (dated 1951).

Bibl.: "Itália. Sala Giorgio Morandi," 1957, p. 52, repr.; Vitali, 1977 (2nd ed. 1983), no. 779, repr. (dated 1951).

8. *Still Life*, 1951 ca.
Oil on canvas, 35.8 × 43 cm.
Signed lower left: *Morandi*.
Vitali no. 775.
Private collection.

Prov.: Galleria Il Milione, Milan, no. 6111; Pier Maria Bardi collection, São Paulo; Gullicsen collection, Helsinki; Galleria Il Milione, Milan; Cesare Tosi collection, Milan; Galleria d'Arte Zanini, Rome, no. 873; Galleria Levi, Milan; Nicola Mobilio collection, Florence; Galleria d'Arte Falsetti, Prato, no. 8260; Galleria Medea, Milan.

Exh.: Focette, 1989 (then Cortina d'Ampezzo, 1989; Milan, 1989), pl. XIX (dated 1951); Kamakura, 1989 (then Okada, 1990; Fukuyama, 1990; Tokyo, 1990; Kyoto, 1990), p. 91, no. 67, repr. (dated 1951); Rome, 1990, p. 20, repr. (dated 1951); Sydney, 1997, p. 53, no. 23, repr. (dated 1951).

Bibl.: Bardi, 1957, pl. XIII (dated 1947); Vitali, 1964 (2nd ed. 1965; 3rd ed. 1970), pl. 173 (dated 1947); Vitali, 1977 (2nd ed. 1983), no. 775, repr. (dated 1951).

9. *Still Life*, 1951.
Oil on canvas, 35 × 45 cm.
Signed lower left: *Morandi*.
Vitali no. 1365.
Private collection.

Prov.: Alberta Ulrich Frua collection, Milan; Galleria dell'Oca, Rome; Galleria dello Scudo, Verona.

Bibl.: Vitali (1977), 2nd ed. 1983, no. 1365, repr.

10. *Still Life*, 1952.
Oil on canvas, 36.2 × 46.4 cm.
Signed lower towards the left: *Morandi*.
Vitali no. 816.
Private collection.

Prov.: Galleria Il Milione, Milan, no. 6647; Gianni Mattioli collection, Milan.

Exh.: Turin, 1959, no. 39 (?); Bern, 1965, no. 87 (dated 1953); Milan, 1971, p. 21, no. 74, and p. 69, repr.; Kamakura, 1989 (then Okada, 1990; Fukuyama, 1990; Tokyo, 1990; Kyoto, 1990), p. 93, no. 69, repr.; Milan, 1990–1991, p. 157, no. 69, repr., and p. 175, no. 69.

Bibl.: Arcangeli, 1964 (2nd ed. 1968), between p. 240 and p. 241, fig. 49 (dated 1953), and 3rd ed. 1981, between p. 120 and p. 121, fig. 48 (dated 1953); Vitali, 1977 (2nd ed. 1983), no. 816, repr.; Arcangeli, 1987, between p. 240 and p. 241, fig. 48 (dated 1953).

11. *Still Life*, 1960.
Oil on canvas, 30 × 40 cm.
Signed lower left: *Morandi*.
Vitali no. 1188.
Trento, Museo d'Arte Moderna e Contemporanea di Trento e Rovereto, deposito Giovanardi.

Prov.: Galleria Il Milione, Milan, no. 8474.

Exh.: Lucerne, 1960, p. 7, no. 16; Bern, 1965, no. 97; Venice, 1966, p. 28, no. 78; Bologna, 1966, p. 77, no. 102, and pl. 102; Milan, 1971, p. 21, no. 85, and p. 71, repr.; Tübingen, 1989 (then Düsseldorf, 1990), no. 127, repr., and p. 299, no. 127; Bologna, 1990, p. 220, no. 154, repr., and p. 412, no. 154.

Bibl.: Carrà, 1967, p. 109, repr.; Giuffrè, 1970, p. 34, fig. 27 (dated 1957); Vitali, 1977 (2nd ed. 1983), no. 1188, repr.

12. *Still Life*, 1952.
Oil on canvas, 32 × 48 cm.
Signed lower left: *Morandi*.
Vitali no. 823.
Bologna, Museo Morandi.

Prov.: Francesco Paolo Ingrao collection, Rome.

Exh.: Rome, 1966, p. 9, no. 11, and p. 23, no. 11, repr. (dated 1951); Ferrara, 1978, "Collezione F.P. Ingrao, Roma" section, no. 9, repr. (dated 1951); Bologna, 1985–1986, p. 207, no. 92, repr., and p. 257, no. 92; Paris, 1987, p. 76, no. 40, repr., and p. 170, no. 40; Bologna, 1990, p. 192, no. 126, repr., and p. 411, no. 126; Budapest, 1991, p. 78, and p. 79, repr.

Bibl.: Vitali, 1977 (2nd ed. 1983), no. 823, repr., and no. 829, repr. (wrong cataloging); Pasquali-Solmi-Vitali, 1988, p. 64, no. 41, repr., and p. 156, no. 41; Eco, 1993, repr.; Pasquali, 1993, p. 116, no. 38, and p. 117, no. 38, repr.; Pasquali, 1996, p. 102, no. 44, and p. 103, no. 44, repr.

13. *Still Life*, 1952.
Oil on canvas, 40.6 × 40 cm.
Signed lower left: *Morandi*.
Vitali no. 824.
Private collection.

Prov.: Galleria Il Milione, Milan, no. 6438; Augusto Giovanardi collection, Milan; Gianni Mattioli collection, Milan.

Exh.: Florence, 1953, no. 39 (*Natura morta con panno giallo*).

Bibl.: Valsecchi, 1953; Giani, 1958, no. 59, repr. (*Natura morta con panno giallo*); Ballo, 1960, p. 26, repr.; Valsecchi, 1964 (2nd ed. 1966), p. 32, and p. 33, pl. XIII; Siblík, 1965, pl. 52 (dated 1957); Raini, 1966; Bortolon, 1968, p. 57, repr.; Vitali, 1977 (2nd ed. 1983), no. 824, repr.; Brolatti, 1985, repr.

14. *Still Life*, 1952.
Oil on canvas, 35.8 × 45.8 cm.
Signed lower left: *Morandi*.
Dedication on back of mount, top: *A Lauro ora Marco con infiniti auguri, Lionello. Roma, 2 ottobre 1952*.
Vitali no. 826.
Private collection.

Prov.: Lionello Venturi collection, Rome; Lauro Venturi collection, Geneva; Galleria Internazionale, Milan; Galleria Medea, Milan; Galleria dello Scudo, Verona.

Exh.: Verona, 1976–1977, p. 25, repr.; Ferrara, 1978, no. 55, repr.

Bibl.: Vitali, 1977 (2nd ed. 1983), no. 826, repr.

15. *Still Life*, 1952.
Oil on canvas, 40.5 × 46 cm.
Signed lower left: *Morandi*.
Vitali no. 828.
Milan, Mattioli Rossi collection.

Prov.: Galleria Il Milione, Milan, no. 6536; Ferrante Farneti collection, Forlì; Galleria Il Milione, Milan; Augusto Giovanardi collection, Milan.

Bibl.: Vitali, 1977 (2nd ed. 1983), no. 828, repr.

16. *Still Life*, 1952.
Oil on canvas, 35 × 40 cm.
Signed lower left: *Morandi*.
Vitali no. 831.
Milan, Civiche Raccolte d'Arte.

Prov.: Galleria Il Milione, Milan; Giuseppe Vismara collection, Montecarlo.

Exh.: Milan, 1990–1991, p. 159, no. 71, repr., and p. 175, no. 71 [*Natura morta (Lo straccio giallo)*].

Bibl.: Vitali, 1977 (2nd ed. 1983), no. 831, repr.

17. *Still Life*, 1952.
Oil on canvas, 40.5 × 45.9 cm.
Signed lower towards the left: *Morandi*.
Vitali no. 830.
Private collection.

Prov.: Emilio Jesi collection, Milan; Curt Valentin Gallery, New York, no. 14460; H.

Troy collection, New York; C. Gorham collection, New York; Staempfli Gallery, New York; Robert M. Benjamin collection, New York.

Exh.: New York, 1966, no. 248; New Haven, 1967; San Francisco, 1981 (then New York, 1981–1982; Des Moines, 1982), p. 113, no. 43, repr., and p. 171, no. 43.

Bibl.: Vitali, 1977 (2nd ed. 1983), no. 830, repr.

18. *Still Life*, 1952.
Oil on canvas, 43.3 × 56.3 cm.
Signed on reverse, at the center towards the right: *Morandi.*
Vitali no. 817.
Bologna, private collection.

Prov.: World House Galleries, New York; José Luis and Beatriz Plaza collection, Caracas; Galleria Annunciata, Milan, no. 5242; E. Rossi collection, Turin; Gianni Tinto collection, Turin.

Exh.: Caracas, 1959, no. 33; Caracas, 1965, no. 11; Innsbruck, 1982; Freiburg, 1984, p. 7, pl. III, and p. 24, no. 8; Budapest, 1991, p. 80, and p. 81, repr.; Paris, 1992, p. 65, no. 26, repr., and p. 85, no. 26; Brussels, 1992, p. 99, no. 63, repr., and p. 160, no. 63; San Marino, 1997, p. 31, repr.

Bibl.: Vitali, 1977 (2nd ed. 1983), no. 817, repr.

19. *Still Life*, 1953.
Oil on canvas, 30 × 35 cm.
Signed lower left: *Morandi.*
Vitali no. 848.
Cuneo, private collection.

Prov.: Rodolfo Pallucchini collection, Venice; Galleria Gian Ferrari, Milan.

Exh.: Munich, 1981, pl. 58, and p. 245, no. 58; Racconigi, 1996, p. 52, repr. (dated 1956).

Bibl.: Vitali, 1977 (2nd ed. 1983), no. 848, repr., between no. 849 and no. 850, repr. detail; 2nd ed. reprint, 1994, jacket, detail.

20. *Still Life*, 1954.
Oil on canvas, 35.6 × 45.5 cm.
Signed lower center: *Morandi.*
Vitali no. 920.
Rome, private collection.

Prov.: Galleria Il Milione, Milan, no. 6922; Valerio Zurlini collection, Rome; Alvaro Marchini collection, Rome.

Exh.: Kamakura, 1989 (then Okada, 1990; Fukuyama, 1990; Tokyo, 1990; Kyoto, 1990), p. 96, no. 72, repr.

Bibl.: Vitali, 1977 (2nd ed. 1983), no. 920, repr.

21. *Still Life*, 1954.
Oil on canvas, 30 × 35 cm.
Signed lower left: *Morandi.*
Vitali no. 906.
Private collection.

Prov.: Roberto Longhi collection, Florence.

Bibl.: Boschetto, 1971, pl. 149; Vitali, 1977 (2nd ed. 1983), no. 906, repr.; Gregori, 1980, pp. 323–324, no. 203, and pl. 231.

22. *Still Life*, 1953.
Oil on canvas, 40.6 × 40.6 cm.
Signed lower left: *Morandi.*
Vitali no. 874.
Private collection.

Prov.: Galleria Il Milione, Milan, no. 6908; Cesare Tosi collection, Milan; Augusto Giovanardi collection, Milan.

Exh.: Turin, 1959, p. 51, no. 42; Bern, 1965, no. 86, repr.; Rome, 1973, p. 118, no. 85, and p. 121, repr.; Sydney, 1997, p. 55, no. 25, repr.

Bibl.: Vitali, 1964 (2nd ed. 1965; 3rd ed. 1970), pl. 206; Vitali, 1977 (2nd ed. 1983), no. 874, repr.

23. *Still Life*, 1953.
Oil on canvas, 30.5 × 45.5 cm.
Signed lower left: *Morandi.*
Vitali no. 870.
Private collection.

Prov.: Lionello Venturi collection, Rome; Maria Venturi collection, Rome; Galerie Marie-Louise Jeanneret, Geneva.

Exh.: Sydney, 1997, p. 52, no. 22, repr.

Bibl.: Vitali, 1977 (2nd ed. 1983), no. 870, repr.

24. *Still Life*, 1953.
Oil on canvas, 30.5 × 45.5 cm.
Signed lower center: *Morandi.*
Vitali no. 873.
Albinea, Achille and Ida Maramotti collection.

Prov.: Galleria Il Milione, Milan; Henry R. Luce collection, New York; Clare Booth Luce collection, New York; Curt Valentin Gallery, New York; Delius Gallery, New York; Acquavella Galleries, New York; Galerie Krugier, Geneva, no. 5414; Galleria Medea, Milan.

Exh.: New York, 1955, no. 6; Ferrara, 1978, no. 59, repr.

Bibl.: Vitali, 1977 (2nd ed. 1983), no. 873, repr.

25. *Still Life*, 1953–1954.
Oil on canvas, 35.5 × 40.4 cm.
Signed lower center: *Morandi.*
Vitali no. 895.
Private collection.

Prov.: Federico Leumann collection, Turin.

Exh.: Milan, 1963, pl. 3 (dated 1954); Rome, 1965–1966, p. 164, no. 9 (*Natura morta con scodelle*); Venice, 1966, p. 28, no. 75 (*Natura morta con tazzina*, dated 1958); Bologna, 1966, p. 77, no. 98, and pl. 98 (*Natura morta con tazzine*, dated 1958); Kamakura, 1989 (then Okada, 1990; Fukuyama, 1990; Tokyo, 1990; Kyoto, 1990), p. 95, no. 71, repr. (dated 1954); Milan, 1990–1991, p. 163, no. 75, repr., and p. 175, no. 75 (dated 1954).

Bibl.: Arcangeli, 1964 (2nd ed. 1968), between p. 240 and p. 241, fig. 47 (dated 1953), and 3rd ed. 1981, between p. 120 and p. 121, fig. 47 (dated 1953); Giuffrè, 1970, pl. 38 (*Natura morta con tazzine*, dated 1953), and jacket, repr. detail; Vitali, 1977 (2nd ed. 1983), no.

895, repr. (dated 1954); Arcangeli, 1987, between p. 240 and p. 241, fig. 47 (dated 1953); Pasini, 1989, fig. 62 (dated 1954).

26. *Still Life*, 1953–1954.
Oil on canvas, 26 × 70 cm.
Signed towards the bottom towards the left: *Morandi.*
Vitali no. 896.
Trento, Museo d'Arte Moderna e Contemporanea di Trento e Rovereto, deposito Giovanardi.

Prov.: Galleria Il Milione, Milan.

Exh.: Turin, 1959, p. 51, no. 43 (dated 1953); Lucerne, 1960, no. 5 (dated 1953); Rome, 1973, p. 118, no. 84, repr. (dated 1953); Tübingen, 1989 (then Düsseldorf, 1990), no. 101, repr., and p. 298, no. 101 (dated 1954); Bologna, 1990, p. 197, no. 131, repr., and p. 411, no. 131 (dated 1954).

Bibl.: Bardi, 1957, p. XI, repr. (dated 1953); Vitali, 1977 (2nd ed. 1983), no. 896, repr. (dated 1954); Pasini, 1989, fig. 63 (dated 1954).

27. *Still Life*, 1953.
Oil on canvas, 26 × 70 cm.
Signed lower towards the left: *Morandi.*
Vitali no. 904.
London, private collection.

Prov.: Giuseppe Raimondi collection, Bologna; Curt Valentin Gallery, New York; Delius Gallery, New York.

Exh.: New York, 1955, no. 10; Ferrara, 1978, no. 62, repr. (dated 1954); Munich, 1981, pl. 63, and p. 246, no. 63 (dated 1954); San Francisco, 1981 (then New York, 1981–1982; Des Moines, 1982), p. 114, no. 46, repr., and p. 171, no. 46 (dated 1954); Madrid, 1984–1985, no. 49, repr. (dated 1954); Marseilles, 1985, no. 45, repr. (dated 1954); New York, 1990, pl. X (dated 1954).

Bibl.: Vitali, 1977 (2nd ed. 1983), no. 904, repr. (dated 1954).

28. *Still Life*, 1955.
Oil on canvas, 35.6 × 40.5 cm.
Signed lower right: *Morandi.*
Vitali no. 949.
Private collection.

Prov.: Gianni Mattioli collection, Milan.

Exh.: Bologna, 1966, p. 77, no. 91, and pl. 91 (*Natura morta con bottiglia bianca e piccola bottiglia bleu*); Copenhagen, 1968, no. 14, repr. (*Nature morte med hvid flaske og lille blå flaske*); London, 1970–1971, p. 18, no. 66, and p. 55, no. 60, repr. (*Still life with white bottle and small blue bottle*) [then Paris, 1971, p. 16, no. 66, and p. 55, no. 60, repr. (*Nature morte à la bouteille blanche et à la petite bouteille bleue*)]; Milan, 1971, p. 21, no. 77, and p. 68, repr.; Paris, 1987, p. 77, no. 41, repr., and p. 170, no. 41.

Bibl.: Giani, 1958, no. 58, repr. (*Natura morta con bottiglia bianca e blu*); Ballo, 1960, p. 26, repr.; Siblík, 1965, pl. 53; Vitali, 1977 (2nd ed. 1983), no. 949, repr.; Pasquali-Solmi-Vitali, 1988, p. 65, no. 42, repr., and p. 156, no. 42.

29. *Still Life*, 1956.
Oil on canvas, 30.7 × 35.7 cm.
Signed on reverse, at the center towards the top: *Morandi*.
Vitali no. 1004.
Busto Arsizio, private collection.

Prov.: Galleria Il Milione, Milan, no. 7239; Riccardo and Magda Jucker collection, Milan; Galleria dello Scudo, Verona.

Bibl.: Vitali, 1977 (2nd ed. 1983), no. 1004, repr.

30. *Still Life*, 1957.
Oil on canvas, 30.5 × 35.5 cm.
Signed lower towards the left: *Morandi*.
Vitali no. 1059.
Private collection.

Prov.: Galleria Il Milione, Milan, no. 7692/2; Antonio Mazzotta collection, Milan; Galleria Farsetti, Prato, no. 7285; Dino Facchini collection, Verona; Luigi Ferro collection, Verona; Galleria Forni, Bologna; Galleria dello Scudo, Verona.

Exh.: Kamakura, 1989 (then Okada, 1990; Fukuyama, 1990; Tokyo, 1990; Kyoto, 1990), p. 102, no. 78, repr. (dated 1957–1959); Milan, 1990–1991, p. 165, no. 77, repr., and p. 175, no. 77; Ischia, 1996, p. 52, and p. 53, repr., and cover; San Marino, 1997, p. 33, repr.

Bibl.: Siblík, 1965, pl. 55; Vitali, 1977 (2nd ed. 1983), no. 1059, repr.

31. *Still Life*, 1955.
Oil on canvas, 26 × 40 cm.
Signed lower left: *Morandi*.
Vitali no. 944.
Freiburg, Morat-Institut für Kunst und Kunstwissenschaft.

Prov.: Battista Pero collection, Milan; G. David Thompson collection, Pittsburgh; Galerie Beyeler, Basel; Galerie Marie-Louise Jeanneret, Geneva, no. 614; Charlotte Morat collection, Freiburg.

Exh.: Zurich, 1960, no. 154; Turin, 1963, pl. 33, and no. 48 (*Composizione con bottiglia bianca*, dated 1956); Geneva, 1977–1978 (then Paris, 1978; Frankfurt, 1978), no. 12, repr.; Munich, 1981, no. 66, repr., and p. 246, no. 66; San Francisco, 1981 (then New York, 1981–1982; Des Moines, 1982), p. 118, no. 50, repr., and p. 171, no. 50; Nijmegen, 1982, no. 6; Innsbruck, 1982; Saarbrücken, 1993 (then Dresden, 1993; Cheb, 1993; Salzburg, 1993; Frankfurt, 1993–1994), p. 85, no. 2, repr., and p. 233, no. 2; Rolandseck, 1997–1998, p. 45, repr., p. 63, no. 5, and cover.

Bibl.: Morat, 1979, p. 17 no. 6, repr., and p. 28, no. 6; Vitali, 1977 (2nd ed. 1983), no. 944, repr.; Strauss, 1983, p. 251, pl. 8.

32. *Still Life*, 1955.
Oil on canvas, 30.4 × 35.2 cm.
Signed top center: *Morandi*.
Vitali no. 972.
Private collection.

Prov.: Mario Andreis collection, Rome; Galleria De' Foscherari, Bologna; Galleria dello Scudo, Verona.

Exh.: Ferrara, 1978, no. 64, repr.; Kamakura, 1989 (then Okada, 1990; Fukuyama, 1990; Tokyo, 1990; Kyoto, 1990), p. 98, no. 74, repr.

Bibl.: Vitali, 1977 (2nd ed. 1983), no. 972, repr.

33. *Still Life*, 1956.
Oil on canvas, 40.5 × 35.5 cm.
Signed lower center: *Morandi*.
Vitali no. 986.
Trento, Museo d'Arte Moderna e Contemporanea di Trento e Rovereto, deposito Giovanardi.

Prov.: Galleria Il Milione, Milan, no. 7540/2; L. Pisani collection, Milan.

Exh.: Turin, 1959, p. 51, no. 48, and pl. 61; Turin, 1968, p. 45, no. 9, and p. 127, repr.; Tübingen, 1989 (then Düsseldorf, 1990), no. 106, repr., and p. 298, no. 106; Bologna, 1990, p. 200, no. 134, repr., and p. 411, no. 134.

Bibl.: Valsecchi, 1964 (2nd ed. 1966), p. 34, repr.; Vitali, 1977 (2nd ed. 1983), no. 986, repr.

34. *Still Life*, 1956.
Oil on canvas, 35.7 × 45.7 cm.
Signed lower center: *Morandi*.
Vitali no. 1012.
Milan, Mattioli Rossi collection.

Prov.: Galleria Il Milione, Milan, no. 7442; H. Mayer collection, New York; Augusto Giovanardi collection, Milan.

Exh.: Venice, 1966, p. 28, no. 71; Bologna, 1966, p. 77, no. 92, and pl. 92; Milan, 1971, p. 21, no. 78, and p. 70, repr.

Bibl.: Giuffrè, 1970, p. 33, fig. 25; Vitali, 1977 (2nd ed. 1983), no. 1012, repr., between no. 1012 and no. 1013, repr. detail, 2nd ed. 1983, cover.

35. *Still Life*, 1956.
Oil on canvas, 35.5 × 35 cm.
Signed lower left: *Morandi*.
Vitali no. 1013.
Bologna, Museo Morandi.

Prov.: Francesco Paolo Ingrao collection, Rome.

Exh.: Rome, 1966, p. 9, no. 13, and p. 25, no. 13, repr.; Venice, 1966, p. 28, no. 70; Bologna, 1966, p. 77, no. 93, and pl. 93; Ferrara, 1978, "Collezione F.P. Ingrao, Roma" section, no. 11, repr.; Bologna, 1985–1986, p. 208, no. 95, repr., and p. 257, no. 95; Siena, 1989, p. 62, repr.; Bologna, 1990, p. 201, no. 135, repr., and p. 411, no. 135; Budapest, 1991, p. 86, and p. 87, repr.; London, 1993.

Bibl.: Ragghianti, 1964, p. 12, repr.; Vitali, 1964 (2nd ed. 1965; 3rd ed. 1970), pl. 215; Giuffrè, 1970, pl. 39; Vitali, 1977 (2nd ed.

1983), no. 1013, repr.; Marti, 1980, pl. 25; Ragghianti, 1982, no. 351, repr.; Pasquali, 1990, p. 41, repr., and cover detail; Graham-Dixon, 1993, repr.; Pasquali, 1993, p. 124, no. 42, and p. 125, no. 42, repr.; Pasquali, 1996, p. 112, no. 49, p. 113, no. 49, repr., and cover.

36. *Still Life*, 1958.
Oil on canvas, 20.7 × 30.5 cm.
Signed lower left: *Morandi*.
Vitali no. 1104.
Milan, private collection.

Prov.: Galleria Il Milione, Milan, no. 7946; Emilio Jesi collection, Milan; Galleria Annunciata, Milan, no. 5291 bis; R. Giacosa collection, Milan; Galerie Marie-Louise Jeanneret, Geneva; Galleria Medea, Milan; Silvano Lodi collection, Campione d'Italia; Maurizio Danieli collection, Vestenanuova; Luigi Ferro collection, Verona; Galleria dello Scudo, Verona; Galleria Tega, Milan.

Exh.: Turin, 1970, no. 18, repr.; Bologna, 1976, no. 13, repr.; Tübingen, 1989 (then Düsseldorf, 1990), no. 112, repr., and p. 298, no. 112.

Bibl.: Vitali, 1964 (2nd ed. 1965; 3rd ed. 1970), pl. 238; Siblík, 1965, pl. 57; Borsini, 1971, p. 5, repr.; Vitali, 1977 (2nd ed. 1983), no. 1104, repr.

37. *Still Life*, 1959.
Oil on canvas, 25 × 28 cm.
Signed lower right: *Morandi*.
Vitali no. 1133.
Private collection.

Prov.: Galleria Il Milione, Milan, no. 8134/2; Gianni Mattioli collection, Milan; Galleria dello Scudo, Verona.

Exh.: Turin, 1959, p. 43, no. 42, and pl. 14.

Bibl.: Siblík, 1965, pl. 59; Vitali, 1977 (2nd ed. 1983), no. 1133, repr.

38. *Still Life*, 1960.
Oil on canvas, 30.1 × 45.3 cm.
Signed lower left: *Morandi*.
Vitali no. 1198.
Private collection.

Prov.: Galleria Il Milione, Milan, no. 8772; Cesare Tosi collection, Milan; Galleria Il Milione, Milan; Antonio Mazzotta collection, Milan; M. Nobili collection, Milan; Galleria Falsetti, Prato, no. 6845.

Exh.: Ancona, 1964, p. 87, and p. 95, repr.; Focette, 1980 (then Cortina d'Ampezzo, 1980), no. 22, repr.; Sydney, 1997, p. 60, no. 30, repr.

Bibl.: Siblík, 1965, pl. 60; Vitali, 1977 (2nd ed. 1983), no. 1198, repr.

39. *Still Life*, 1962.
Oil on canvas, 31.4 × 36 cm.
Signed and dated on reverse, at the center towards the right: *Morandi 1962*.
Vitali no. 1263.
Private collection.

Prov.: Galleria Il Milione, Milan, no. 9676; Gianni Mattioli collection, Milan.

Exh.: Milan, 1971, p. 21, no. 90, and p. 72, repr.; Rome, 1973, p. 142, repr., and p. 146, no. 114.

Bibl.: Vitali, 1977 (2nd ed. 1983), no. 1263, repr.; Skira, 1989, p. 167, repr.

40. *Still Life*, 1957.
Oil on canvas, 28 × 35 cm.
Signed top center: *Morandi*.
Vitali no. 1049.
Bologna, Museo Morandi.

Prov.: Francesco Paolo Ingrao collection, Rome.

Exh.: Rome, 1966, p. 9, no. 17, and 29, no. 17, repr.; Ferrara, 1978, "Collezione F.P. Ingrao, Roma" section, no. 15, repr.; Bologna, 1985–1986, p. 211, no. 101, repr., and p. 257, no. 101; Locarno, 1989, p. 111, no. 62, repr., and p. 201, no. 62; Rio de Janeiro, 1989 (then São Paulo, 1989), no. 2, repr.; Tübingen, 1989 (then Düsseldorf, 1990), no. 110, repr., and p. 298, no. 110; Bologna, 1990, p. 207, no. 141, repr., and p. 412, no. 141; Budapest, 1991, p. 88, and p. 89, repr.; Madrid, 1993; Dublin, 1997, p. 41, repr., and p. 124, no. 59 (dated 1960).

Bibl.: Vitali, 1977 (2nd ed. 1983), no. 1049, repr.; Brolatti, 1985, repr.; *Quaderni*, 1985, p. 50, repr.; Pasquali, 1993, p. 132, no. 46, and p. 133, no. 46, repr.; Pasquali, 1996, p. 120, no. 53, and p. 121, no. 53, repr.

41. *Still Life*, 1959.
Oil on canvas, 25.7 × 35.7 cm.
Signed lower left: *Morandi*.
Vitali no. 1138.
Private collection.

Prov.: Galleria Il Milione, Milan, no. 8125; Ernesto Bestagini collection, Milan; Galerie Krugier, Geneva; Leone Polacco collection, Milan; Galleria Annunciata, Milan; Ernesto Bestagini collection, Milan; Galleria Medea, Milan; Galleria Falsetti, Prato, no. 6809.

Exh.: Geneva, 1968, p. 20, repr., and no. 36 (dated 1954); Paris, 1968–1969, no. 31, repr. (dated 1954); Ferrara, 1978, no. 69, repr.; Munich, 1981, pl. 85, and p. 248, no. 85; Madrid, 1984–1985, no. 57, repr.; Marseilles, 1985, no. 53, repr.; Paris, 1987, p. 82, no. 46, repr., and p. 170, no. 46; Tampere, 1988–1989, p. 118, no. 52, repr., and p. 246, no. 52; Leningrad, 1989 (then Moscow, 1989), p. 88, no. 50, repr., and p. 208, no. 50; Locarno, 1989, p. 115, no. 65, repr., and p. 201, no. 65 (dated 1960); Tübingen, 1989 (then Düsseldorf, 1990), no. 114, repr., and p. 298, no. 114; Bologna, 1990, p. 211, no. 145, repr., and p. 412, no. 145; Paris, 1992, p. 73, no. 31, repr., and p. 86, no. 31; Brussels, 1992, p. 109, no. 73, repr., and p. 161, no. 73; Haarlem, 1996, p. 104, and p. 105, repr.; Modena, 1997, p. 62, p. 64, and p. 65, repr.

Bibl.: Vitali, 1977 (2nd ed. 1983), no. 1138, repr.; Pasquali-Solmi-Vitali, 1988, p. 71, no. 50, repr., and pp. 156–157, no. 50.

42. *Still Life*, 1960.
Oil on canvas, 30 × 35 cm.
Signed lower right: *Morandi*.

Vitali no. 1176.
Bologna, Museo Morandi.

Prov.: Francesco Paolo Ingrao collection, Rome.

Exh.: Rome, 1966, p. 9, no. 20, and p. 32, no. 20, repr. (dated 1959); Ferrara, 1978, "Collezione F.P. Ingrao, Roma" section, no. 18, repr. (dated 1959); Bologna, 1985–1986, p. 214, no. 106, repr., and p. 258, no. 106; Bologna, 1990, p. 217, no. 151, repr., and p. 412, no. 151; Charleroi, 1991, p. 50, repr.

Bibl.: Vitali, 1977 (2nd ed. 1983), no. 1176, repr.; Pasquali, 1993, p. 142, no. 51, and p. 143, no. 51, repr.; Pasquali, 1996, p. 130, no. 58, and p. 131, no. 58, repr.

43. *Still Life*, 1962.
Oil on canvas, 30 × 30 cm.
Signed on reverse, center: *Morandi*.
Vitali no. 1272.
Albinea, Achille and Ida Maramotti collection.

Prov.: Galleria Il Milione, Milan; Nathan Cummings collection, Chicago; Morat-Institut für Kunst und Kunstwissenschaft, Freiburg.

Exh.: Freiburg, 1984, p. 11, pl. V, and p. 25, no. 20; Brussels, 1992, p. 115, no. 79, repr., and p. 161, no. 79; Saarbrücken, 1993 (then Dresden, 1993; Cheb, 1993; Salzburg, 1993; Frankfurt, 1993–1994), p. 90, no. 7, repr., and p. 233, no. 7.

Bibl.: Vitali (1964), 2nd ed. 1965, pl. 254, and 3rd ed. 1970, pl. 256; Vitali, 1977 (2nd ed. 1983), no. 1272, repr.

44. *Still Life*, 1963.
Oil on canvas, 25 × 30 cm.
Signed lower right: *Morandi*.
Vitali no. 1324.
Paola Ghiringhelli collection.

Prov.: Galleria Il Milione, Milan, no. 10213; H.C. Goldsmith collection, New York; Albert Loeb & Krugier Gallery, New York.

Exh.: Ringenberg, 1964 (then Stuttgart, 1964), no. 6, repr.; Bielefeld, 1964, no. 6, repr.; Karlsruhe, 1964, no. 25 or no. 26 (?); Braunschweig, 1965, no. 6, repr.; Wuppertal, 1965, no. 6, repr.; New York, 1967, no. 36, repr.; Milan, 1970–1971, no. 20, repr.; Madrid, 1984–1985, no. 65, repr.; Marseilles, 1985, no. 60, repr.; Bologna, 1990, p. 235, no. 169, repr., and p. 413, no. 169; Brescia, 1996–1997, p. 114, no. X.7, repr.

Bibl.: Vitali (1964), 3rd ed. 1970, pl. 255; Vitali, 1977 (2nd ed. 1983), no. 1324, repr.

45. *Still Life*, 1963.
Oil on canvas, 30 × 35 cm.
Signed lower left: *Morandi*.
Vitali no. 1323.
Bologna, Museo Morandi.

Prov.: from the artist.

Exh.: Bern, 1965, no. 102; Venice, 1966, p. 28, no. 83; Bologna, 1966, p. 77, no. 107 and pl. 107; Copenhagen, 1968, no. 17, repr.; London, 1970–1971, p. 18, no. 78, and p. 43, no. 23,

repr. (then Paris, 1971, p. 16, no. 78, and p. 43, no. 23, repr.); Milan, 1971, p. 21, no. 91, and p. 57, repr.; Leningrad, 1973 (then Moscow, 1973), no. 24, repr.; Bologna, 1975, no. 39, repr.; Ferrara, 1978, no. 78, repr.; Munich, 1981, pl. 102, and p. 250, no. 102; San Francisco, 1981 (then New York, 1981–1982; Des Moines, 1982), p. 125, no. 63, repr., and p. 172, no. 63; Sasso Marconi, 1984, p. 95, repr.; Madrid, 1984–1985, no. 66, repr.; Bologna, 1985–1986, p. 218, no. 115, repr., and p. 258, no. 115; Marseilles, 1985, no. 61, repr.; Paris, 1987, p. 89, no. 53, repr., and pp. 170–171, no. 53; Tampere, 1988–1989, p. 127, no. 61, repr., and p. 246, no. 61; Leningrad, 1989 (then Moscow, 1989), p. 97, no. 59, repr., and p. 208, no. 59; Locarno, 1989, p. 126, no. 73, repr., and pp. 201–202, no. 73; Tübingen, 1989 (then Düsseldorf, 1990), no. 134, repr., and p. 299, no. 134; Bologna, 1990, p. 234, no. 168, repr., and p. 413, no. 168; Grizzana Morandi, 1990, p. 53, repr.

Bibl.: Vitali (1964), 2nd ed. 1965 and 3rd ed. 1970, pl. 260; Giuffrè, 1970, pl. 44; Vitali, 1977 (2nd ed. 1983), no. 1323, repr.; Jouvet-Schmied, 1982, no. 82, repr.; *Quaderni*, 1985, p. 72, repr.; Pasquali-Solmi-Vitali, 1988, p. 78, no. 57, repr., and p. 157, no. 57; Brandi, 1990, between p. 128 and p. 129, repr.; Pasquali, 1993, p. 158, no. 59, and p. 159, no. 59, repr., and cover; Pasquali, 1996, p. 148, no. 67, and p. 149, no. 67, repr.

46. *Still Life*, 1963.
Oil on canvas, 30.5 × 30.4 cm.
Signed lower left: *Morandi*.
Vitali no. 1307.
Private collection.

Prov.: Giuseppe Marchiori collection, Lendinara.

Exh.: Verona, 1976–1977, p. 25, repr. (dated 1964); Sasso Marconi, 1977, p. 31, repr.; Ischia, 1996, p. 62, and p. 63, repr.; Brescia, 1996–1997, p. 115, no. X.8, repr.

Bibl.: Vitali, 1977 (2nd ed. 1983), no. 1307, repr.

47. *Still Life*, 1963–1964.
Oil on canvas, 30.7 × 30.9 cm.
Signed lower right: *Morandi*.
Vitali no. 1340.
Rome, private collection.

Prov.: Galleria Il Milione, Milan, no. 10337; Alvaro Marchini collection, Rome.

Exh.: Tübingen, 1989 (then Düsseldorf, 1990), no. 135, repr., and p. 299, no. 135 (dated 1964); Bologna, 1990, p. 241, no. 175, repr., and p. 414, no. 175 (dated 1964); Budapest, 1991, p. 102 and p. 103, repr. (dated 1964); Brussels, 1992, p. 118, no. 82, repr., and p. 161, no. 82 (dated 1964); Haarlem, 1996, p. 128, and p. 129, repr. (dated 1964).

Bibl.: Vitali (1964), 2nd ed. 1965 and 3rd ed. 1970, pl. 263 (dated 1964); Vitali, 1977 (2nd ed. 1983), no. 1340, repr. (dated 1964); Pasini, 1989, fig. 72 (dated 1963).

Exhibitions and Bibliography Cited in the Technical Index of the Works

Exhibitions

Florence, Palazzo Strozzi, *Arte moderna in una raccolta italiana*, April-May 1953, catalog, text by C.L. Ragghianti.

The Hague, Gemeentemuseum, *Giorgio Morandi*, 14 April–6 June 1954, catalog, texts by V. Bloch and L. Vitali.

Milan, Palazzo Reale, *Dipinti del Museo d'Arte di San Paolo del Brasile*, November 1954–February 1955, catalog, text by P.M. Bardi.

New York, Delius Gallery, *Giorgio Morandi*, 5 October–5 November 1955, catalog, text by L. Deuel.

Turin, Civica Galleria d'Arte Moderna, *Capolavori d'arte moderna nelle raccolte private*, 31 October–8 December 1959, catalog ed. by M. Valsecchi.

Caracas, Fundación Eugenio Mendoza, *La evolución de la pintura moderna*, 1959, catalog.

Lucerne, Kunstmuseum, *Italienische Maler der Gegenwart*, 6 August–18 September 1960, catalog, text by P.F. Althaus.

Zurich, Kunsthaus, *Thompson Pittsburgh: Aus einer Amerikanischen Privatsammlung*, 15 October–27 November 1960, catalog, texts by A.H. Barr Jr, G. David Thompson and R. Wehrli.

Turin, Galleria Narciso, *Italian Still-Life Paintings XXth Century*, 20 January–24 February 1963, catalog.

Milan, Galleria Sianesi, *Maestri moderni*, from 29 March 1963, catalog.

Ringenberg, Galerie Schloss Ringenberg, *Giorgio Morandi. Gemälde, Aquarelle, Druck-Grafik*, 14 March–5 April 1964, catalog, texts by G. de Chirico and W. Haftmann (then Stuttgart, Galerie Lutz & Meyer, 16 May–13 June 1964, catalog, texts by G. de Chirico and W. Haftmann).

Bielefeld, Städtisches Kunsthaus, *Giorgio Morandi. Gemälde, Aquarelle, Druckgraphik*, exhibition organized in collaboration with the Galerie Schloss Ringenberg of Ringenberg, 19 April–10 May 1964, catalog, texts by G. de Chirico and W. Haftmann.

Karlsruhe, Badischer Kunstverein, *Giorgio Morandi. Gemälde, Aquarelle. Zeichnungen, Radierungen*, 22 June–26 July 1964, catalog, text by W. Haftmann.

Ancona, Palazzo del Liceo Scientifico, *Premio Marche 1964. 8a Mostra nazionale di arti figurative*, 6–29 September 1964, catalog, text by G. Marchiori, special exhibition *Omaggio a Giorgio Morandi*, text by G. Marchiori.

Braunschweig, Kunstverein, *Giorgio Morandi. Gemälde, Aquarelle, Druck-Grafik*, January 1965, catalog, texts by G. de Chirico and W. Haftmann.

Wuppertal, Kunst- und Museumsverein, *Giorgio Morandi. Gemälde, Aquarelle, Druck-Grafik*, 12 February–14 March 1965, catalog, texts by G. de Chirico and W. Haftmann.

Bern, Kunsthalle, *Giorgio Morandi*, 23 October–5 December 1965, catalog, texts by G. de Chirico and W. Haftmann.

Rome, Palazzo delle Esposizioni, *IX Quadriennale nazionale d'arte*, October 1965–March 1966, catalog, texts by various authors.

Caracas, Fundación Eugenio Mendoza, *Exposicion homenaje a Giorgio Morandi*, November 1965, catalog, text by J.L. Plaza.

Rome, Galleria Nazionale d'Arte Moderna, *Giorgio Morandi, opere della Collezione Ingrao*, 27 March–25 April 1966, catalog, text by P. Bucarelli.

New York, Public Education Association, *Seven Decades 1895–1965*, 26 April–21 May 1966.

Venice, Giardini di Castello, *XXXIII Esposizione biennale internazionale d'arte*, 18 June–16 October 1966, catalog, texts by various authors, rooms XII–XIX, retrospective dedicated to Giorgio Morandi, curated by G.A. Dell'Acqua, R. Longhi and L. Vitali.

Bologna, Palazzo dell'Archiginnasio, *L'opera di Giorgio Morandi*, curated by G.A. Dell'Acqua, R. Longhi and L. Vitali, 30 October–15 December 1966, catalog, texts by R. Bacchelli and L. Vitali.

New Haven, Yale University Art Gallery, *The Helen and Robert M. Benjamin Collection*, 4 May–18 June 1967.

New York, Albert Loeb & Krugier Gallery, *Morandi*, 18 May–17 June 1967, catalog, text by J. Rewald.

Turin, Galleria Gissi, *Una scelta da museo*, June-July 1967, catalog.

Turin, Galleria Civica d'Arte Moderna, *I pittori italiani dell'associazione internazionale arti plastiche UNESCO*, 1 February–17 March 1968, catalog ed. by L. Mallé, text by E. Paulucci.

Copenhagen, Kunstforeningen, *Giorgio Morandi*, 6-29 September 1968, catalog, text by G. Købke Sutton.

Geneva, Galerie Krugier, *Giorgio Morandi*, October 1968, catalog, texts by C. Brandi and G. Marchiori.

Paris, Galerie Villand & Galanis, *Morandi*, exhibition organized in collaboration with the Galerie Krugier, Geneva, December 1968–January 1969, catalog, texts by C. Brandi, A.P. de Mandiargues and C. Esteban.

Turin, Galleria La Bussola, *Antologia internazionale*, from 14 March 1970, catalog.

London, Royal Academy of Arts, *Giorgio Morandi*, curated by J. Leymarie, L. Vitali and G. White, exhibition organized by The Arts Council of Great Britain, 5 December 1970–17 January 1971, catalog, texts by G. de Chirico, A. Forge and J.Th. Soby (then Paris, Musée National d'Art Moderne, 9 February–12 April 1971, catalog, texts by J. Leymarie and J.Th. Soby).

Milan, Galleria Il Milione, *Morandi Morlotti*, 12 December 1970–12 January 1971, catalog, text by R. Tassi.

Milan, Rotonda della Besana, *Giorgio Morandi*, May-June 1971, texts by F. Arcangeli, A. Forge and J. Leymarie.

Leningrad, The State Hermitage Museum, *Giorgio Morandi*, curated by L. Vitali, 17 April–10 May 1973 (then Moscow, Pushkin Museum of Applied Arts, 18 May–16 June 1973), single catalog, texts by I. Antonova and L. Vitali.

Rome, Galleria Nazionale d'Arte Moderna, *Giorgio Morandi*, 18 May–22 July 1973, catalog, texts by C. Brandi, P. Bucarelli and G. de Marchis, catalog entries by A. del Monte.

Bologna, Galleria d'Arte Moderna, *Giorgio Morandi*, curated by L. Vitali, 1 May–2 June 1975, catalog, texts by various authors.

Bologna, Galleria Marescalchi, *Omaggio a Morandi*, May 1976, text by G. Ruggeri.

Verona, Galleria dello Scudo, *Giorgio Morandi*, 20 November 1976–6 January 1977, catalog, texts by C. Brandi, N. Finotti, L. Magagnato, G. Marchiori, M. Valsecchi and G.L. Verzellesi.

Sasso Marconi, Galleria La Casa dell'Arte, *Omaggio a Giorgio Morandi*, curated by E. Tavoni, 22 October–30 November 1977, catalog, texts by various authors.

Geneva, Galerie Marie-Louise Jeanneret, *Giorgio Morandi*, 10 November 1977–15 January 1978, catalog, texts by C. Brandi and G. Marchiori (then Paris, Grand Palais, exhibition organized on occasion of the FIAC, 20–29 October 1978, catalog, texts by C. Brandi and G. Marchiori; Frankfurt, Deutsch-Italienische Vereinigung, 23 September–20 November 1978).

Ferrara, Galleria Civica d'Arte Moderna, Palazzo dei Diamanti, *Giorgio Morandi*, 1 July–8 October 1978, catalog, text by F. Solmi.

Focette, Galleria d'Arte Moderna Farsetti, *Giorgio Morandi*, 12 July–3 August 1980 (then Cortina d'Ampezzo, Galleria d'Arte Moderna Farsetti, 6–31 August 1980), single catalog.

Munich, Haus der Kunst, *Giorgio Morandi. Ölbilder, Aquarelle, Zeichnungen, Radierungen*, curated by F.A. Morat, 18 July–6 September 1981, catalog, texts by various authors.

San Francisco, San Francisco Museum of Modern Art, *Giorgio Morandi*, curated by J.T. Demetrion, 24 September–1 November 1981 (then New York, The Solomon R. Guggenheim Museum, 19 November 1981–17 January 1982; Des Moines, Des Moines Art Center, 1 February–14 March 1982), single catalog, texts by K. Baker, J.T. Demetrion, J.M. Lukach, L. Magnani and A. Namovitz Worthen.

Nijmegen, Nijmeegs Museum, Commanderie van St. Jan, *Giorgio Morandi 1890–1964. Schilderijen, Aquarellen, Tekeningen en Etsen*, 17 April–31 May 1982, catalog, text by H. van der Grinten.

Innsbruck, Kunstpavillon im Kleinen Hofgarten, *Giorgio Morandi 104 Werke aus der Sammlung F.A. Morat, Freiburg im Breisgau*, 3 June–18 July 1982.

Sasso Marconi, Galleria La Casa dell'Arte, *Omaggio a Giorgio Morandi nel ventennale della morte. Oli, acquarelli, disegni, grafiche*, from 28 January 1984, catalog, texts by various authors.

Freiburg, Morat-Institut für Kunst und Kunstwissenschaft, *Morandi in Freiburg*, May 1984, catalog ed. by F.A. Morat, texts by C. Brandi and F.A. Morat.

Madrid, Sala de Exposiciones de la Caja de Pensiones, *Giorgio Morandi*, curated by M. Corral, 11 December 1984–28 January 1985, catalog, texts by C. Bertelli, C. Brandi, J. Gallego, M. Pasquali and F. Solmi.

Marseilles, Musée Cantini, *Giorgio Morandi*, curated by N. Cendo, 13 April–18 June 1985, catalog, texts by C. Bertelli, C. Brandi, C. Esteban and M. Pasquali.

Bologna, Galleria Comunale d'Arte Moderna, *Morandi e il suo tempo*, curated by various authors, 9 November 1985–10 February 1986, catalog, texts by R. Barilli, F. Caroli, S. Evangelisti, M. Pasquali, C. Pozzati, E. Riccòmini and F. Solmi.

Paris, Hôtel de Ville, *Morandi*, 12 June–20 August 1987, catalog, texts by J. Clair, F. Solmi and L. Vitali.

Tampere, Sara Hildénin Taidemuseo, *Giorgio Morandi*, exhibition organized in collaboration with the Civico Museo d'Arte Contemporanea, Milan, the Pinacoteca Nazionale, Bologna, and the Fondazione Magnani Rocca, Parma, 4 November 1988–8 January 1989, catalog ed. by M. Pasquali and R. Valorinta, texts by G. Briganti, P.G. Castagnoli, F. D'Amico, F. Gualdoni and M. Pasquali.

Leningrad, The State Museum of the Hermitage, *Giorgio Morandi*, exhibition organized in collaboration with the Pinacoteca Nazionale, Bologna, and the Fondazione Magnani Rocca, Parma, 21 January–19 February 1989 (then Moscow, Central Gallery of Painters, 1-26 March 1989), single catalog ed. by M. Pasquali, texts by various authors.

Locarno, Pinacoteca Comunale Casa Rusca, *Giorgio Morandi*, exhibition organized in collaboration with the Pinacoteca Nazionale, Bologna, and the Fondazione Magnani Rocca, Parma, 4 June–20 August 1989, catalog, texts by G. Briganti, P.G. Castagnoli, F. D'Amico, F. Gualdoni and M. Pasquali.

Rio de Janeiro, Museu de Bellas Artes, *Aspectos da pintura italiana do após-guerra aos nossos dias*, 14 June–2 July 1989 (then São Paulo, Museu de Arte de São Paulo, 11-30 July 1989), single catalog.

Siena, Magazzini del Sale di Palazzo Pubblico, *L'immagine dell'arte. Omaggio a Cesare Brandi*, 21 July–1 October 1989, catalog ed. by V. Rubiu, texts by G.C. Argan, A. Bonito Oliva, M. Calvesi, G. Carandente, L. Piccioni and M. Volpi.

Focette, Galleria d'Arte Modena Farsetti, *"A Prato per vedere i Corot." Corrispondenza Morandi-Soffici per un'antologica di Morandi*, curated by L. Cavallo with the collaboration of O. Nicolini, July 1989 (then Cortina d'Ampezzo, Galleria d'Arte Moderna Farsetti, August 1989; Milan, Galleria d'Arte Moderna Farsetti, September 1989), single catalog.

Tübingen, Kunsthalle, *Giorgio Morandi 1890–1964. Gemälde, Aquarelle, Zeichnungen, Radierungen*, 23 September–26 November 1989 (then Düsseldorf, Kunstsammlung Nordrhein-Westfalen, 20 January–18 March 1990), single catalog, texts by G. Briganti, P.G. Castagnoli, F. D'Amico, F. Gualdoni, W. Haftmann, M. Pasquali and M. Semff.

Kamakura, The Museum of Modern Art, *Giorgio Morandi*, curated by M. Garberi, 18 November–24 December 1989 (then Okada, Mie Prefectural Art Museum, 4 January–4 February 1990; Fukuyama, Fukuyama Museum of Art, 10 February–11 March 1990; Tokyo, Yurakucho Art Forum, 16 March–3 April 1990; Kyoto, The National Museum of Modern Art, 10 April–13 May 1990), single catalog, texts by L. Arrigoni, M. Calvesi, M. Cordaro, M. Garberi, E. Pontiggia, R. Tardito and G. Verzotti.

New York, Philippe Daverio Gallery, *Giorgio Morandi. Nature morte*, 7 February–10 March 1990, catalog, text by P. Baldacci and P. Daverio.

Bologna, Galleria Comunale d'Arte Moderna, *Giorgio Morandi 1890–1990. Mostra del centenario*, curated by M. Pasquali, 12 May–2 September 1990, catalog, texts by P.G. Castagnoli, F. D'Amico, F. Gualdoni, W. Haftmann, M. Pasquali and M. Semff.

Grizzana Morandi, Sala Mostre Municipale, *Giorgio Morandi. L'immagine di Grizzana*, curated by M. Pasquali, 20 July–30 September 1990, catalog, text by M. Pasquali.

Milan, Palazzo Reale, *Morandi e Milano*, 22 November 1990–6 January 1991, catalog, texts by M. Calvesi, G.A. Dell'Acqua, M. Garberi, E. Pontiggia, R. Tardito and L. Vitali.

Rome, Galleria Il Gabbiano, *Realtà e visione*, December 1990, catalog.

Charleroi, Palais des Beaux-Arts, *Un détail immense*, 16 March–5 May 1991, catalog, text by L. Busine.

Budapest, Szépmüvészeti Múzeum, *Giorgio Morandi*, curated by P.G. Castagnoli and S. Evangelisti, exhibition organized in collaboration with the Galleria Comunale d'Arte Moderna, Bologna, 10 May–16 June 1991, catalog.

Paris, Galerie Claude Bernard, *Giorgio Morandi. Peintures et aquarelles*, 17 March–2 May 1992, catalog, text by M. Pasquali.

Brussels, Le Botanique, *Giorgio Morandi artista d'Europa*, curated by M. Pasquali, 12 June–9 August 1992, catalog, texts by M.R. Bourge, M. Pasquali, V. Scheiwiller and R. Tassi.

Saarbrücken, Saarland-Museum, *Giorgio Morandi. Gemälde, Aquarelle, Zeichnungen, Radierungen*, curated by E.G. Güse and F.A. Morat,

31 January–21 March 1993 (then Dresden, Gemäldegalerie Neue Meister and Kupferstich-Kabinett der Staatlichen Kunstsammlungen Dresden, 4 April–6 June 1993; Cheb, Státm Galerie Vytvarnéno Umęní, 24 June–26 August 1993; Salzburg, Rupertinum, 23 October–5 December 1993; Frankfurt, Jahrhunderthalle Hoechst, 13 December 1993–30 January 1994), single catalog, texts by various authors.

London, Accademia Italiana delle Arti, *Giorgio Morandi. Five Paintings for Contemplation*, 10 May–30 June 1993.

Madrid, Academia San Fernando, *Seis pinturas de Giorgio Morandi para contemplación*, 29 June–31 July 1993.

Haarlem, Teylers Museum, *Giorgio Morandi. La maturità*, curated by M. Pasquali, 1 March–12 May 1996, catalog, texts by M. Pasquali and J. van Geest.

Racconigi, Castello di Racconigi, *Morandi e morandiani*, curated by M. Vescovo, April

1996, catalog, texts by M. Macera, M. Pasquali and M. Vescovo.

Ischia, Castello Aragonese, *Giorgio Morandi e la luce del Mediterraneo*, curated by M. Pasquali, 29 June–29 September 1996, catalog ed. by M. Pasquali, text by M. Pasquali, critical anthology by L. Selleri.

Paris, Fondation Dina Vierny, Musée Maillol, *Giorgio Morandi*, 6 December 1996–15 February 1997, catalog, texts by A. Bertolucci, J. Clair, P. Fossati, C. Gian Ferrari and M. Scolaro.

Brescia, Palazzo Martinengo, *Giorgio Morandi. Oggetti e stati d'animo*, 7 December 1996–28 February 1997, curated by M. Pasquali, texts by E. Cassa Salvi, G. Giudici, M. Luzi, M. Pasquali and E. Tadini.

São Paulo, Museu de Arte de São Paulo, *Morandi*, 27 February–13 March 1997, catalog, texts by A. Bertolucci, J. Clair, C. Gian Ferrari, P. Fossati and M. Scolaro.

Sydney, The Art Gallery of New South Wales, *Giorgio Morandi. The Dimension of Inner Space*, curated by L. Klepac, 9 May–13 July 1997, catalog, texts by L. Ficacci, J. Herman, L. Klepac, P. Mandelli and M. Pasquali.

Modena, Palazzo Santa Margherita, *Maestri del Novecento nelle collezioni private modenesi*, curated by G. Roganti and C. Zanfi, 18 May–13 July 1997, catalog, texts by W. Guadagnini, G. Roganti and C. Zanfi.

Dublin, Irish Museum of Modern Art, *The Pursuit of Painting*, curated by S. McKenna, 26 June–2 November 1997, catalog.

San Marino, Galleria d'Arte Moderna and Pinacoteca San Francesco, *Segno e colore. Morandi, Manaresi, De Vita*, curated by F. Basile, 12 July–12 October 1997, catalog, texts by F. Basile, P. Bellini and E. Raimondi.

Rolandseck, Bahnhof, *Giorgio Morandi. Gemälde, Aquarelle, Zeichnungen, Radierungen*, 31 October 1997–11 January 1998, catalog, texts by S. Gon and F.A. Morat.

Bibliography

Arcangeli F., *Giorgio Morandi*, Edizioni del Milione, Milan, 1964 (2nd ed., 1968; 3rd ed., Einaudi, Turin, 1981).

Arcangeli F., *Giorgio Morandi*, Editura Meridiane, Bucarest, 1987.

Ballo G., "Chiarezza di Morandi," in *Ideal Standard Rivista*, Milan, April-June 1960.

Bardi P.M., *16 dipinti di Giorgio Morandi*, Edizioni del Milione, Milan, 1957.

Borsini O.C., "Bottiglie nell'arte. 'Gli umili vetri' di Morandi," in *Notiziario CE.T.IM.*, Milan, October 1971.

Bortolon L., "Il pittore del silenzio," in *Grazia*, no. 1418, Milan, 21 April 1968.

Boschetto A., *La collezione Roberto Longhi*, Sansoni, Florence, 1971.

Brandi C., *Morandi*, introduction by V. Rubiu, *Carteggio Brandi-Morandi 1938–1963*, ed. by M. Pasquali, Editori Riuniti, Rome, 1990.

Brolatti G., "Morandi, è fatta," in *Carlino*, Bologna, 18 April 1985.

Carrà M., "Carrà e Morandi," in *L'Arte Moderna*, vol. IX, no. 75, Fabbri, Milan, 1967.

Eco U., "Morandi, l'arte della variazione infinita," in *Corriere della Sera*, Milan, 5 October 1993.

Giani G., *Pittori del Novecento*, Edizioni della Conchiglia, Milan, 1958.

Giuffrè G., *Giorgio Morandi*, series *I Maestri del Novecento*, Sansoni, Florence, 1970.

Graham-Dixon A., "The Still, Small Voice of Turmoil," in *The Independent*, London, 1 June 1993.

Gregori M., *La Fondazione Roberto Longhi a Florence*, Electa, Milan, 1980.

"Itália. Sala Giorgio Morandi," in *Habitat*, no. 44, São Paulo, September 1957.

Jouvet J., Schmied W., *Giorgio Morandi. Ölbilder, Aquarelle, Zeichnungen, Radierungen*, Diogenes, Zurich, 1982.

Marti L., *Morandi*, series *I Classici della Pittura*, Armando Curcio, Milan, 1980.

Morat F.A., *Giorgio Morandi. Ölbilder, Aquarelle, Zeichnungen, Radierungen*, F.A. Morat, Freiburg, 1979.

Pasini R., *Morandi*, Cooperativa Libraria Universitaria Editrice, Bologna, 1989.

Pasquali M., "Morandi," in *Art e Dossier*, supplement to no. 50, Florence, October 1990.

Pasquali M., *Museo Morandi Bologna, il catalogo*, texts by various authors, Charta, Milan, 1993.

Pasquali M., *Museo Morandi. Catalogo generale*, texts by various authors, Grafis, Bologna, 1996.

Pasquali M., Solmi F., Vitali L., *Morandi*, Riz-

zoli International Publications, New York, 1988.

Quaderni morandiani n. 1. I Incontro internazionale di studi su Giorgio Morandi: Morandi e il suo tempo, Mazzotta, Milan, 1985.

Ragghianti C.L., "Una antologia di Morandi," in *Critica d'Arte*, no. 62, Florence, May 1964.

Ragghianti C.L., *Bologna cruciale 1914 e saggi su Morandi, Gorni, Saetti*, Calderini, Bologna, 1982.

Raini A., "Retrospettiva di Giorgio Morandi," in *Le Arti*, no. 7–8, Milan, July-August 1966.

Siblík J., *Giorgio Morandi*, Současné Svętové Umęní, Prague, 1965.

Skira P., *La nature morte*, Skira, Geneva, 1989.

Strauss E., *Koloritgeschichtliche Untersuchungen zur Malerei seit Giotto und andere Studien*, Deutsch Kunstverlag, Berlin and Munich, 1983.

Valsecchi M., "Mezzo secolo a Firenze," in *Tempo*, Milan, 23 May 1953.

Valsecchi M., *Morandi*, Garzanti, Milan, 1964 (2nd ed. 1966).

Vitali L., *Giorgio Morandi pittore*, Edizioni del Milione, Milan, 1964 (2nd expanded ed., 1965; 3rd expanded ed., 1970).

Vitali L., *Morandi. Catalogo generale*, Electa, Milan, 1977, 2 vols. (2nd expanded ed., 1983).

Giorgio Morandi
Life and Work 1950–1964
Exhibitions 1950–1964
Bibliography 1950–1964
Select Bibliography

Morandi in photograph by Ugo Mulas, 1964.

Giorgio Morandi
Life and Work 1950–1964

edited by Lorenza Selleri

Giorgio Morandi was born on 20 July 1890 in Bologna, the city where he was to study at the academy of fine arts, obtaining his diploma in 1913.

Even though he was never part of any movement, in his first years as a painter he felt attracted to Futurism, Metaphysics, and the Valori Plastici movement. He took part in the Italian Novecento show as well as in various editions of the Venice Biennial (where, in 1948, he won the main prize for painting), the Rome Quadrennial, and some exhibitions at the Carnegie Institute in Pittsburgh.

In 1950 Morandi turned sixty and had by then reached his creative prime. He occasionally opened his home in Via Fondazza, where he lived his whole life, to art critics and intellectuals from all over the world. In his last fifteen years he painted many of his best works and he became known at an international level.[1]

In 1950, the year of his solo show in January at the Galleria Annunciata in Milan, he also took part in a series of shows abroad, in Brussels, Amsterdam, Paris, and London. His works were constantly on show—the mark of growing recognition, not only in Europe but also in the United States. In fact, in Boston one of his still lifes of 1940 (Vitali no. 263), was included in a show dedicated to twentieth-century Italian painting that Mr. and Mrs. Markson, together with the Galleria del Cavallino in Venice, presented in the rooms of their collection.

For the twenty-fifth anniversary of the prestigious Parisian magazine *Cahiers d'Art*, a special 276-page issue dedicated to *Un demi-siècle d'art italien* was published. Gian Alberto Dell'Acqua wrote a text some forty pages long on "La peinture 'métaphysique'" dedicating to Morandi a critical essay in which he underlined "his inflexible coherence. . . and his subtle conception of space which is transformed into a free play of imagination."

At the *Mostra internazionale di bianco e nero*, held from April to May at the Villa Ciani in Lugano, besides the main prize awarded to Jacques Villon, the jury assigned other awards to nine artists, one of whom was Morandi. In June the painter was on the jury for the 25th Venice Biennial together with Longhi, Barbantini, Pallucchini, Manzù, Carrà, and Casorati. He was not, however, among the exhibitors, and critics noted that he was "one of the great absences."[2]

On 8 July Maria Maccaferri Morandi, the artist's mother, died. In a few words brimming with emotion, Morandi was to announce to Cesare Brandi ten days later, "My mother left us on the 8th. I will say no more, dear Brandi."[3]

On 19 October the international painting show at the Carnegie Institute in Pittsburgh opened and the artist was again present after his participation from 1929 to 1939. Among the works chosen to represent Italian art, were paintings by de Pisis, Carrà, Saetti, and Guidi as well as one of Morandi. In the same month a group of Italian critics, amongst whom Ragghianti, Marchiori, Argan, and Rai-

mondi, together with their German colleagues, Werner Haftmann, Bernhard Degenhart and others organized a show of contemporary Italian painting that included 9 of Morandi's works. Opening in Florence, it went on to tour in the major German cities. For the occasion the president of the Tuscan tourist board bought one of Morandi's paintings and donated it to the Florentine gallery of modern art (from which it was stolen ten years later). In November Morandi exhibited 14 can-

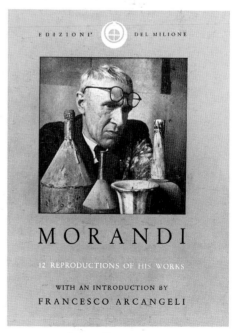

Cover of the English edition of the monograph edited by Francesco Arcangeli for Edizioni del Milione in 1950. (Courtesy Mattioli archive, Milan.)

The commission of the 26th Venice Biennial during the meeting on 3 December 1951: from left Lucio Fontana (with his back to camera), Giuseppe Montanarini, Enrico Paulucci, Giuseppe Santomaso, Enrico Prampolini, Roberto Longhi (center), Rodolfo Pallucchini, Paolo Ricci, Publio Morbiducci, Mario Novello, Pericle Fazzini and Umbrio Apollonio. (Courtesy ASAC, Venice.)

Venice, Giardini della Biennale, June 1952: from right Morandi, Marco Valsecchi (with his back to camera), Giuseppe Ungaretti, Fernand Léger and his wife Nadia. (Courtesy Museo Morandi, Bologna.)

vases dating from 1913 to 1919 at the show dedicated to Futurism and Metaphysics held at the Zurich Kunsthaus. The catalog reproduced the 1918 *Still Life*, at that time in the Riccardo Jucker collection (Vitali no. 39).

The Edizioni del Milione published a small monograph, *12 opere di Giorgio Morandi*, edited by Francesco Arcangeli: the paintings that were reproduced, dating from 1946 to 1949, testified—according to the author—how "after almost forty years of work, the painter's art, even if isolated in its own kind of withdrawal, has not suffered any decline and shows no sign of tiredness" but on the contrary "is in harmony . . . with the boldest formal experiences of the painting of our century."

Between February and May of 1951 Morandi's works were included in an itinerant show of Italian art in Scandinavia. From 29 March a show of graphic art was held in Antwerp in which the artist exhibited together with Jacques Villon, Mario Prassinos, Edgard Tytgat, and Fritz Pauli. In the spring, the exhibition *I Mostra nazionale d'arte moderna della città di Firenze* was held in the ex-convent of the Oblates in Florence. The curatorial committee consisted of, among others, Argan, Brandi, Marchiori, Gnudi, and Parronchi. Morandi was invited to take part with a solo

show. Above all in these highly creative years, the artist did not want to be involved in any premature summing up of his career. The catalogue raisonné of his paintings shows, in fact, for 1951, 36 works, a number which increased further in the following years (52 paintings in 1952, 58 in 1953, 44 in 1954, 43 in 1955). In October he was represented by 10 paintings and 10 etchings at the first Biennial of São Paulo, in the section dedicated to Italian art and presented by Pallucchini. Most of these works came from the collections of Roberto Longhi and Arturo Deana. In the meantime he was invited by Luigi Carluccio to the first presentation of *Peintres d'aujourd'hui. France-Italie / Pittori d'oggi. Francia-Italia* held in Palazzo Belle Arti in Turin, where other exhibiting Italians were Carrà, Licini, and Sironi and among the French were Braque, Chagall, Dufy, and Léger. In the catalog's introductory essay Raymond Cogniat, curator at the Louvre and commissioner for the exhibition, wrote that "the choice has been limited to that of quality, and therefore aimed at establishing certain names we consider to be amongst the greatest in every genre."

During the early fifties his already limited production of watercolors was even further reduced. In the catalogue raisonné

edited by Marilena Pasquali, there are, in fact, only two, dated respectively 1950 and 1953. Despite this, the show that opened in Delft in March 1952, entitled *De aquarel 1800–1950*, displayed, for the first time abroad, watercolors by Morandi. In the meantime, as can be read in the article by Jean-Pierre in *Les Lettres Françaises* of 27 March, the artist exhibited four etchings (among which *The Bridge on the Savena at Bologna* of 1912, no. 1 in Vitali's catalog of graphic works) in the group show *Jeune gravure contemporaine* held at the Musée National d'Art Moderne in Paris.

In a letter Roberto Longhi wrote to the artist on 6 May 1952, the critic referred to another show in Paris held between April and June in the Orangerie, *La nature morte de l'antiquité à nos jours*.[4] The only work by Morandi shown on this occasion was one painted between 1947 and 1948, at the time in the collection of Vitale Bloch. This provided Charles Sterling with the occasion for calling the artist "un Chardin du XXe siècle."

At the 26th Venice Biennial, inaugurated on 14 June, a work Morandi had recently finished stood out among landscapes by de Pisis, Carrà, Tosi and portraits by Balla and Funi, in the section *Antologia di maestri*.

In October his works were shown to an American public, first in Pittsburgh in a new presentation of the exhibition of contemporary painting at the Carnegie Institute, and then in New York at the John Heller Gallery together with works by Campigli and Musič. The weekly magazine *Time* (10 November) briefly reviewed the show.[5] He participated with a landscape and two still lifes, one with shells. In Milan that November he took part in a group show at the Galleria Il Milione. In room V his 3 paintings (amongst which a *Still Life* of 1915, Vitali no. 23) were together with works by Sironi, Modigliani, and Marino Marini.

1953 opened and closed with two very important international exhibitions in which Morandi was included. From March, in the Scandinavian countries, there was a show of Italian art organized by the Venice Biennial and presented in catalog by Umbro Apollonio. In December the Museu de Arte Moderna of São Paulo mounted *Futuristas e artistas italianos de hoje* as part of the 2nd Biennial. The two events had a great success: the Swedish press dedicated a lot of space to positive comments, above all about Morandi, while in Brasil the artist, who participated with a solo exhibition of etchings (as can be seen from the catalog introduction by Pallucchini), received the first prize for engraving.

In Italy the outstanding event was doubtless the exhibition *Arte moderna in una raccolta italiana*, held in Palazzo Strozzi, Florence, from April to May: it contained masterpieces from the Milanese collection of Gianni Mattioli who, on this occasion, wished to remain anonymous. Beside key works by Boccioni, Balla, Carrà, Soffici, and Modigliani, there were 18 paintings by Morandi.

For some time Morandi had stopped producing etchings mainly because of the hard work involved in this technique. In fact the last plate dates from 1947, as confirmed by a letter of 18 October to the director of the Rome Calcografia Nazionale, Carlo Alberto Petrucci, in which Morandi wrote, "Unfortunately I have still not started etching again even though I would really like to."[6]

In November Paolo D'Ancona published for the Edizioni del Milione *I classici della pittura italiana del Novecento*, a brief guide to the art of the twentieth century in which he states: "The essence of Morandi's expression has always been metaphysical, yesterday like today, because he transports us through reality to an absolutely hermetic world that goes beyond reality." In this same year Morandi was also mentioned by Maurice Raynal in the book *Peinture moderne* published by Skira in Geneva.

For the January 1954 issue of *Critica d'Arte* Ragghianti wrote an essay in which he compared Morandi to Frank Lloyd Wright in order "to highlight the architectural substance of Morandi's art as well as to show the analogy that exists between two creative minds that express themselves through a universal alignment and condensation of life and sentiment in a formal language that is both new and complete. . . that makes history but which history cannot explain."

On 14 April an anthological show of Morandi's works opened at the Gemeentemuseum in the Hague (63 paintings and 43 etchings), presented by Vitale Bloch and Lamberto Vitali,[7] and to which the press devoted ample space and many articles.[8] With the help of the Arts Council of Great Britain, the show moved on to the New Burlington Galleries in London, opening on 25 June. The exhibition met with great success and the artist was complimented by Philip James in a letter, now in the archives of the Museo Morandi in Bologna, written on the day of the opening on behalf of the direction of the Arts Council.

From a letter dated 6 May and written to Morandi by Carlo Alberto Petrucci we know that, in the meantime, the artist had once again begun to make etchings, producing the *Still Life with Nine Objects* (Vitali etchings no. 115) for the Associazione Amatori d'Arte, thanks to the interest of Lionello Venturi.[9] The print is comparable to a contemporary painting (Vitali no. 920) formerly in the Valerio Zurlini collection and present in this show.

The next year, from 19 March to 15 May, on the occasion of the "Semaine italienne," the Rome Calcografia Nazionale organized the show *La gravure contemporaine en Italie* held at the Musée Paul Dupuy in Toulouse. No works by Morandi are listed in the catalog even though the cover repro-

Nutida italiensk konst, Liljevalchs Konsthall, Stockholm, 1953: two views of the room dedicated to 18 works by Morandi. (Courtesy ASAC, Venice.)

duces the etching *Flowers in a Small White Vase*, 1928 (Vitali etchings no. 51). However, some prints were included in the show thanks to the generosity of a collector from Toulouse.

Again in March Morandi showed 8 works, amongst which were 3 Metaphysical paintings (Vitali nos. 39, 42, and 46, the latter lent by Roberto Longhi), at the *Exposición de pintura italiana contemporánea* which opened in Barcelona at the Palacio de la Virreina, and was then transferred in May to the Palacio del Retiro in Madrid.

In the meantime Werner Haftmann organized a room dedicated to Morandi with 11 still lifes at the first presentation of Documenta which opened in Kassel on 15 June. This important German exhibition aimed to show the three generations of artists on whom the western tradition in modern art is based.

On 25 September a special issue of *La Fiera Letteraria* was published. It was wholly dedicated to Morandi, with essays by, among others, Apollonio, Arcangeli, Carlo Carrà, Libero De Libero, Marchiori, Parronchi, and Milla Nigro. Meanwhile the frequency of solo shows both in Italy and abroad was on the upswing. On 5 October his first New York exhibition opened at the Delius Gallery, with 11 paintings. This was followed shortly afterward by a show at the Studio d'Arte La Medusa in Rome, where Claudio Bruni put together 11 paintings, 1 watercolor, and 11 etchings despite opposition.[10] At the same time 11 works of his painted between 1949 and 1954 were shown in *Contemporary Italian Art* at the City Art Museum of Saint Louis.

The following month the Nationalmuseum in Stockholm held another show of graphics organized by the Rome Calcografia Nazionale. On this occasion Petrucci managed, with some difficulty, to gather together the etchings *Still Life of Vases, Bottles etc., on a Table*, 1929; *Landscape*, 1930 ca.; *The White Road*, 1933 (respectively Vitali etchings nos. 67, 77 and 104) and *The Farmhouse*, unidentified.[11] The show, which closed on 3 December, then moved on to Göteborg. After having participated in almost all the earlier presentations, Morandi returned to the Rome Quadrennial which opened in November in the Palazzo delle Esposizioni. This anthological show of Italian painting and sculpture from 1910 to 1930, presented in the catalog by Giorgio Castelfranco, included 6 of his paintings, among which were *Landscape*, 1911 (Vitali no. 2) formerly belonging to Mario Broglio, the *Landscape* of 1916 lent by Mino Maccari (Vitali no. 30), and the *Still Life* with spiral-fluted bottle, also of 1916 (Vitali no. 28). The latter had been acquired by Gianni Mattioli in Milan from the Feroldi collection in Brescia. It was on this occasion that Cesare Brandi wrote in a letter to Morandi on 20 December: "On the television, when speaking about the Quadrennial, I really took wing when mentioning your work. Did anyone tell you?"[12] The Edizioni del Milione published *Morandi. Sei tavole a colori* with an introduction by Vitale Bloch.

On 18 February 1956 the artist, through the Bolognese academy of fine arts, asked for a passport "for reasons of study" (there is a record of a previous brief journey to Lugano at the beginning of the fifties to see the masterpieces in the Thyssen-Bornemisza collection in Villa Favorita). On 23 June he left for Winterthur in order to be present, the following day, at the opening of his solo show at the Kunstmuseum which was flanked by a show of bronzes by Giacomo Manzù. He was accompanied by Vitale Bloch and Lamberto Vitali who had lent his whole collection of graphics and a large part of the paintings.[13] The following day, still in the company of Vitali and Bloch, Morandi visited the collection of Oskar Reinhart with its many works by Bruegel, Rubens, Goya, El Greco, Chardin, Poussin, and Cézanne. Heinz Keller, who was then the director of the Kunstmuseum, remembers the visit in this way: "Morandi's attention was always selective... As one might imagine the Chardin paintings in the small salon were the object of his greatest enthusiasm. He paid particular attention to the *Card Players*, examining in detail the layout of the cards... He was highly impressed, as were the other two visitors, by the overall view of the Manet-Cézanne room. Morandi was particularly taken with the three still lifes by Cézanne."[14]

On 18 June, shortly before leaving for Switzerland, the artist had submitted his application for retirement after having acted for over 26 years as professor of engraving at the Bologna academy of fine arts.[15] The request was granted on 11 October despite "the insistent pleas" of the

Documenta, Kassel, 1955: the *Still Life* of 1929 (Vitali no. 143), at the time in the Jesi collection and presently at the Pinacoteca di Brera, is visible to the right. Photograph by Gunther Becker. (Courtesy Documenta Archiv, Kassel.)

Special issue of *La Fiera Letteraria* wholly dedicated to Morandi, 25 September 1956: the front page and a page from the supplement.

head of the institute and his colleagues asking Morandi to "reconsider the decision he has taken. . . not to continue working in the academy next year."[16]

That summer Morandi spent his vacation with his sisters at Levico, Valsugana, as can be read in a letter to his friend Petrucci dated 14 August.[17]

On 21 November, the show *Modern Italian Art from the Estorick Collection*, organized by the Arts Council of Great Britain together with the London branch of the Italian Institute opened at the Tate Gallery in London. In this important collection of over 120 works of Italian art Morandi was represented by 3 paintings (amongst which a *Still Life* of 1931, Vitali no. 167, and a composition with shells of 1943, Vitali no. 441), 5 etchings and 3 drawings. The exhibition included import-

ant works by Boccioni, Balla, Carrà, Modigliani, and Severini. The show, introduced in the catalog by Argan, later moved to Plymouth and Birmingham, where it closed in March of the following year, and then traveled to Newcastle and Cardiff.

In Paris Larousse published a volume by André Chastel, *L'art italien*, in which Morandi was defined as "the most notable of his contemporaries" and "a great example: he represents the awareness of an art that has to discover its real roots, seriously and in depth."

In the large exhibition *Diez años de pintura italiana*, organized by the Venice Biennial at the Museo de Bellas Artes in Caracas from 27 January 1957, Morandi was present with 3 works, one of which, a *Still Life* of 1946 (Vitali no. 516), was chosen for the

cover of the catalog. The show moved on to various South American cities: Bogotà, Lima, Concepción, Buenos Aires, Montevideo, and Rio de Janeiro.

In February Einaudi published the fundamental folio volume by Lamberto Vitali dedicated to the artist's graphic works, with 113 plates printed using the collotype process.

Italy, the New Vision opened on 1 March at the World House Galleries in New York. This was a selection of contemporary paintings and sculptures including 15 works, mainly still lifes, done by Morandi between 1935 and 1956.

On 25 April an interview with Morandi was recorded for "The Voice of America." This, together with the one with Edouard Roditi the following year, is a precious record of the ideas underpinning his painting:

"What we see is, I believe, the artist's creation, invention, whenever he is able to eliminate those diaphragms or conventional images that are interposed between him and things. . . For me nothing is abstract; moreover, I believe that there is nothing more surreal, nothing more abstract, than reality."

From 4 May a solo show was held at the Galleria Galatea in Turin. Curated by Luigi Carluccio it included 9 paintings, 3 watercolors, and 45 etchings. In June the artist sent 12 works to the large show at the Haus der Kunst in Munich for the special section dedicated to Italian art, organized by the Rome Quadrennial.

Morandi again spent that summer at Levico, where he painted 11 watercolor landscapes (Pasquali nos. 1957/12–22), characterized by the easily recognizable "white 'chimney' that emerges from the green of the trees."[18]

In July the Edizioni del Milione published the elegant album *16 dipinti di Giorgio Morandi* with an introduction by Pier Maria Bardi, director of the São Paulo Museu de Arte. Among the color plates are a *Still Life* of 1951, erroneously dated 1947 (Vitali no. 775), and a strongly horizontal composition painted in 1954 part of the Giovanardi collection (Vitali no. 896); both works are in this show.

In September, as part of the Italian section of the 4th Biennial of São Paulo, a "special room" was reserved for him (introduced in the catalog by Pallucchini), where 30 works synthesizing his career since 1918 were displayed. On the 22nd of the same month the president of the organizing body informed Morandi that he had been awarded the Grand Prize for painting, the equivalent of two million Italian Lire, a prize never previously given to an Italian artist. The jury had preferred him to Ben Nicholson and Marc Chagall who had been considered among the favorites. Pallucchini praised him in an article on 17 September in *Il Resto del Carlino*, comparing his production with that of Mondrian: "The civilizations that they have behind them have determined quite different expressive stories; and yet this desire for an abstract space, so differently conveyed, historically defined according to such different figurative traditions, links them both and makes them men of their time. So whoever believes Morandi is an heir to

The publication edited by Vitale Bloch for Edizioni del Milione, 1955. (Courtesy Museo Morandi, Bologna.)

the nineteenth century or a master of a genre which ended with Chardin, is mistaken."

On 5 November an important "retrospective" presented by Lionello Venturi opened at the World House Galleries in New York. This was the second solo show to be

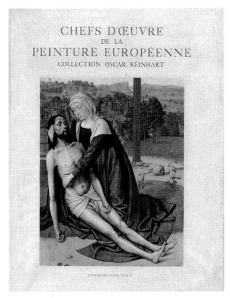

From Morandi's library: a book on the masterpieces of the Oskar Reinhart collection in Winterthur, edited by Librairie Plon, Paris, 1941. (Courtesy Museo Morandi, Bologna.)

dedicated to Morandi after the one held in the Delius Gallery in 1955. James Thrall Soby, American art historian and collector, highly praised the artist in his article for the *Saturday Review* published the following 4 January.

Also in November, the Galleria Il Milione organized a group show with recent works by Marino Marini, Sironi, Tosi, and Morandi. He contributed with 7 still lifes and 1 landscape which, as can be read in the anonymous introduction to the catalog, "constitute almost a year's meditated and attentive work."

1958 began with another appointment in New York: the February exhibition of his works together with those of Manzù at the American Federation of Art, which repeated the experience of two years before at the Kunstmuseum in Winterthur.

In April Morandi sent two still lifes of 1918 and 1957 (respectively Vitali nos. 38 and 1027) to the important group show *50 ans d'art moderne* held at the Palais International des Beaux-Arts for the *Exposition universelle et internationale de Bruxelles*. He was to be present again in August, in the second special show organized in the Italian section with the title *L'homme et l'art*. In June, 7 of his paintings were included in the exhibition *Moderne Italiansk Maleri* at the Statens Museum for Kunst in Copenhagen which, in August, moved to the Galleria Nazionale d'Arte Moderna in Rome.

During the summer months, together with his sister Dina, he went on vacation to Grizzana in the Tuscan-Emilian Apennines near Bologna, where they stayed at the Pensione Italia.

Morandi's presence in shows in the United States was by now a regular occurrence. In fact the whole year was marked by important events underlining his fame overseas: from the shows *A Decade in Review*, April, Lincoln, Massachusetts, and *The New Renaissance in Italy*, October, Pasadena, to the important exhibition *Painting in Post-War Italy 1945–1957*, Columbia University, New York, where a *Still Life* of 1952 (Vitali no. 837) was displayed together with the works of such recent protagonists of abstraction as Afro, Birolli, Fontana, and Vedova.

His fame was already such as to provoke Marco Valsecchi to denounce in an article published in *Il Giorno* on 16 September, the inexplicable exclusion of the artist from a show in Amsterdam centered on the "twentieth-century renaissance."

In this period Morandi received a visit from the Franco-American writer Edouard Roditi, to whom he gave an interview which was included in the volume *Dialogues on Art*, (Secker and Warburg, London, 1960).

In the same year Editions Albin Michel in Paris published an essay by Pierre Courthion, *L'art indépendant. Panorama international de 1900 à nos jours*, in which the French critic wrote of Morandi: "This artist from Bologna has his own place in European art. By trying to express through a balanced style the most subtle nuances of his painterly sensibility, Morandi exists without having had recourse for inspiration to either Paris or to the School of Paris."[19]

From 27 May 1959 the show *Peintres et sculpteurs italiens du futurisme à nos jours*, organized by the Venice Biennial was held in Saint-Etienne. Morandi was represented by 1 landscape and 2 still lifes. There followed, on 4 June, the vast panorama of Futurism at Palazzo Barberini in Rome, where the only work of his was the *Still Life* of 1912 in the Scheiwiller collection (Vitali no. 4). On the same day, the *Birmingham Mail* reported that one of his still lifes painted in that year (Vitali no. 1141) had been bought for one million Lire, about £. 580,000, by the city museum.

Having taken part in the first Documenta in Kassel in 1955, and in confirmation of the fame and appreciation he enjoyed in Germany, Morandi was invited to participate again, in the 1959 presentation of the exhibition.

In Bologna in the meantime work had begun to heighten a building that, by notably reducing the light and the sense of space in the courtyard of Via Fondazza, would cut off the view of the nearby gardens and the distant hills. Morandi was to find in this limitation of "his" landscape the spur to begin constructing a house at Grizzana, in front of Campiaro, that would be simple in form, bathed in light, and immersed in nature. However, this summer he again stayed at the Pensione

Some paintings by Morandi shown on the occasion of the opening exhibition of the Galleria d'Arte Moderna, Turin, 1959. (Courtesy Giovanardi archive, Milan.)

Italia with his sister Dina, where Cesare Brandi, Cesare Gnudi and the painter Sergio Romiti paid a visit to him. The views Brandi saw from his room windows were an unexpected revelation: "Apart from a roofless house next to the Pensione—which in the watercolors was depicted in the most amazing ways depending on how, at the various times of the day, the light and shadow cut it up or put it back together again—his other themes were in the distance," the critic was to say in the *Corriere della Sera* of 21 August. This ruined house was already the recurring subject of numerous watercolors done the previous year (Pasquali nos. 1958/11–18 and nos. 1959/45–47).

From 31 October, to inaugurate their new building the Galleria d'Arte Moderna of Turin held the big exhibition entitled *Capolavori dell'arte moderna nelle raccolte private*. The numerous works exhibited came from the Milanese Giovanardi, Mattioli and Jucker collections and included paintings by such artists as Rousseau, Cézanne, Braque, Picasso, and Matisse. However, a prominent role was also given to the Italian artists, with 54 works by Morandi as well as pictures by Carrà, Casorati, de Chirico, de Pisis and Rosai on show.

In the same period the first Paris Biennial

took place. As Silvio Branzi wrote in *Il Gazzettino* of 4 November, "Morandi is not present. And just because of this we were extremely pleased at Rodolfo Pallucchini's talk on Morandi in the halls of the 'Entretiens culturels franco-italiens'. . . before an auditorium crowded with various artists and art critics."

On 19 December both a solo show at the Galleria Annunciata and a group show at the Galleria Bergamini with such artists as Soldati, Campigli, and Sironi opened in Milan.

That year the art historian John Canaday published the book *Mainstreams of Modern Art* for Thames and Hudson. When speaking of Morandi in the chapter "Other Abstract and Non-objective Isms," he wrote that although both Mondrian and Purism may have left their mark on the reserved and pensive art of Giorgio Morandi, the objects he arranges into abstract relationships—a few ordinary bottles and bowls, combined and recombined in picture after picture, yet without monotony—retain their concrete reality.

L'arte dopo il 1945 by Willy Grohmann, published in Italy by Il Saggiatore, and *Ist die malerei zu Ende?* by Georges Floersheim published by Atlantis in Zurich also contained profiles on Morandi.[20]

In 1960 the famous film by Federico Fellini, *La dolce vita*, introduced Morandi to a wider public. In the drawing-room of the intellectual Steiner, played by the actor Alain Cuny, the host passes in front of a picture saying, "It's a Morandi" (*Still Life* of 1941, Vitali no. 305). The film *La notte* by Michelangelo Antonioni, which came out in the same period, also showed a painting by the artist.

In January *Palatina* published an article by Cesare Brandi, "Appunti per un ritratto di Morandi," which Scheiwiller reprinted soon afterward in the small volume celebrating the artist's seventieth birthday, *Ritratto di Morandi*.

At the end of April the big review *Arte italiana del XX secolo da collezioni americane* opened in Palazzo Reale in Milan. It included 9 paintings by Morandi, among them a *Still Life* of 1916 (Vitali no. 27) and one of 1938 (Vitali no. 225), both belonging to the Museum of Modern Art in New York. James Thrall Soby, who kept various works by the artist in his collection, wrote in his essay for the catalog that Morandi had remained unknown to the greater part of the American public until the end of second World War. He remarked that when he and Alfred Barr had gone to Italy in 1948 to put together the show *Twentieth-Century Italian Art* for the Museum of Modern Art of New York, they knew that many Italian critics and art historians considered Morandi their best living painter and that this seemed at the time an exaggerated opinion. He went on to say that the present show demonstrated how Morandi had found a fervent group of followers in America, and that it would be difficult to think of an artist who was more deserving of the international success achieved by this hermit, whose integrity and perceptive ability in exploring painting's intimate nature transcends any fashionable aesthetic.

Beginning with the summer of this year Morandi and his sisters spent their vacation at Grizzana in the new house with the view of the Case del Campiaro. Here he was to spend more and more of his time, looked after above all by his sister Dina.

After having taken part in the show *Italienische Maler der Gegenwart* from August to September at the Kunstmuseum in Lucerne with 2 landscapes and 14 still lifes, all belonging to Milanese collections,

From *Epoca*, 24 May 1959: Morandi and his sister Dina in Via Santo Stefano, Bologna. (Courtesy Museo Morandi, Bologna.)

from 4 November he was represented in Paris by 5 early works in the vast panorama *Les sources du XXe siècle. Les arts en Europe de 1884 à 1914* at the Musée National d'Art Moderne. At the beginning of 1962, after the Paris exhibition closed, the Ministry for Cultural Affairs bought one of his paintings for the collection of the museum directed by Jean Cassou. With the agreement of the artist they chose the *Still Life* of 1914 (Vitali no. 18) seen in the show together with the *Landscape* of 1911 (Vitali no. 2), and the *Landscape* and the *Still Life* with a silver plate, both of 1914 (Vitali nos. 16 and 19). The work was sold for the token sum of 5,500 New Francs, the equivalent at the time of 500,000 Lire. Meanwhile, in Milan, a *Still Life* of 1946 went for 3,700,000 Lire at an auction by a gallery in Via Brera.

The year ended with the solo show at the World House Galleries in New York which opened on 6 December and presented 43 paintings, 9 watercolors, 8 drawings, and 19 etchings, mostly lent by American collectors.

In February 1961 works by Morandi were to be seen in a show dedicated to the collection of James Thrall Soby at the New York Museum of Modern Art on the occasion of the thirtieth anniversary of its foundation, and, in April, in the group show *The Maremont Collection of Twentieth-Century Art* at the Illinois Institute of Technology in Chicago. In June a *Still Life* of 1918 was included in the group show in Turin organized for the exhibition *Italia '61*, and in July other works of his were chosen for a vast enquiry into the Apollonian and the Dionysian aspects of art from the fifteenth century onward which opened at the Stedelijk Museum in Amsterdam.

In the fall the disagreement between Morandi and Francesco Arcangeli deepened over the 250 pages the scholar had written for the monograph commissioned by the Galleria Il Milione some ten years earlier.[21] In fact the text, fundamental for understanding Morandi's language, contains polemical references to artists and critics the artist admired, amongst whom were Picasso, Brandi, and Argan, and above all it made unwelcome comparisons with contemporary trends, especially the Informel movement. The argument hung in the air all through the winter and saw Morandi and Gino Ghiringhelli holding one position and the author and Cesare Gnudi another. In the spring of 1962 their positions became even more rigid and, despite attempts at mediation by such authoritative figures as Roberto Longhi, a breaking point was arrived at causing great distress on both sides. Morandi rejected the whole of Arcangeli's text and decided to entrust the editing of the monograph to Lamberto Vitali.[22]

In this troubled year, mostly taken up with problems connected with the preparation of the book, Morandi produced 40 paintings, 60 drawings, and 3 watercolors. He also made a last, extraordinary etching. To enrich the forthcoming publication Ghiringhelli had, in fact, persuaded the artist to prepare a new plate. And so he made the *Small Still Life with Three Objects* (Vitali etchings no. 131), which can be related to two contemporary paintings showing the same elements in the foreground (Vitali nos. 1220 and 1223), even though the etching is more compact and intimate, based on strong chiaroscuro contrasts that underline the inner drama of the objects.

In the meantime, Olivetti in Ivrea published a monograph by Vitali with 12 color-plate illustrations.

A *Still Life* of 1959, which had been recently purchased by the Birmingham Museum and Art Gallery, was included in the show *Primitives to Picasso*, held at the Royal Academy in London between January and March 1962. The exhibition, to which the important South American collector José Luis Plaza referred in a letter to the artist on 7 February, gathered together all the works kept in public British collections outside London.[23]

That summer Pallucchini selected 3 of his paintings for the special section of the 31st Venice Biennial dedicated to artists who had won prizes in the post-war presentations (Morandi in fact had won, in 1948, the first prize for painting awarded by the Venice city council). The catalog reproduced the 1946 *Still Life* (Vitali no. 502) shown for the occasion in Ca' Pesaro together with a composition with a shell and fruit bowl of 1931 (Vitali no. 164) and a *Landscape* of 1941.

In the meantime the exhibition *Italienische Meister des XX. Jahrhunderts* opened at the Galerie Welz in Salzburg. It included 4 works by Morandi, amongst them the *Courtyard of Via Fondazza*, 1935 (Vitali no. 203), a *Landscape* of 1943 (Vitali no. 465) and a *Still Life* of 1962 (Vitali no. 1265). Again in Austria the artist participated in the important show *Kunst von 1900 bis heute* held in Vienna between September and November with a painting of 1944 (Vitali no. 476) now in the Musée National d'Art Moderne in Paris.

On 27 October in Siegen, birthplace of Peter Paul Rubens, a solo show opened, organized to coincide with the award to Morandi of the Rubenpreis, which Hans Hartung had won six years earlier. After much urging Morandi accepted the prize of 10,000 Marks which he later gave to charity.[24]

The November issue of *Paragone* published an excerpt from Longhi's inaugural address for the university academic year 1934–35 under the title "Momenti della pittura bolognese (dai Carracci a Morandi)." In it the critic describes Morandi as "one of the best living Italian painters" who "even though navigating in the most dangerous waters of modern painting, has wisely continued his journey with such deliberate slowness and loving study as to seem to be at the beginning of a new journey."

In December the Galleria Galatea in Turin

The 31st Venice Biennial, 1962: one of the rooms in Ca' Pesaro dedicated to the artists who won prizes in the Biennial post-war presentations. Two still lifes by Morandi (to the right, of 1946, Vitali no. 507; to the left, of 1931, Vitali no. 1931) are seen together with paintings by Carrà. (Courtesy ASAC, Venice.)

mounted a solo show of 30 etchings. In the meantime an outstanding show at the Galleria Lorenzelli in Milan placed some Morandi still lifes side by side with those of the eighteenth-century painter Carlo Magini.

Morandi's etchings began to be shown with increasing frequency. In 1963 there were, among others, the exhibitions at the Galleria Il Centro in Naples and at the Galleria Don Chisciotte in Rome between January and February.

That summer, as usual, the artist and his sisters stayed in the house in Grizzana. In the fall he was given the "Archiginnasio d'oro," the prestigious award that the Bologna city council confers on people born in the city or linked to it who have distinguished themselves in a given area of cultural acrivity.

Futurism and Metaphysical painting were the themes of the exhibition held in September at the Hamburg Kunstverein which then went to Frankfurt in November. Morandi's interests at the beginning of the century were documented with a *Still Life* of 1918 from the Jucker collection (Vitali no. 39) and one from 1920 lent by the Milanese collector Antonio Mazzotta (Vitali no. 55).

In November the Galleria L'Obelisco, in

Rome, held a solo show with 14 paintings from 1915 to 1962, 4 watercolors, and 8 drawings; at the same time the Galerie Krugier in Geneva dedicated a show to the artist with a wide selection of works, presented in the catalog by Georges Floersheim, whose essay finished by underlining that for the viewer "the paintings by Morandi. . . give the satisfaction of realizing that the highest aim of his art lies in its moral effect."

Again in November the artist showed his works in two important exhibitions in New York: the Marlborough-Gerson Gallery's homage to the great dealer Curt Valentin, and the show of drawings by the masters of the twentieth century at the Guggenheim Museum which traveled to Minneapolis and Cambridge, Massachusetts. From 17 December, during the temporary closure of the Museum of Modern Art, a part of the museum's collection, including the *Still Life* of 1916 (Vitali no. 27), was exhibited at the National Gallery of Art in Washington.

At the end of his work on Chardin, published by Skira, Pierre Rosenberg analyzes the French master's influence on later artists, such as Cézanne, Matisse, Picasso, Gris, and Braque, and states that "Giorgio Morandi in his 'Metaphysical' still lifes, recreates, with a preciosity resulting from

The "white road" at Grizzana, which often recurs in Morandi's landscapes, in a photograph by Lamberto Vitali. (Courtesy Enrico Vitali.)

Biennial. A *Still Life* of 1955 (Vitali no. 943), lent by the Museu de Arte Moderna of Rio de Janeiro, was on show in Room no. X, dedicated to *Arte d'oggi nei musei.* The press, both in Italy and abroad, gave great attention to his death.

Among the various comments of particular note is that of Roberto Longhi, made on 28 June during the television program "L'Approdo," and published in July in *Paragone* with the title "Exit Morandi."[25] "My dismay at hearing of Giorgio Morandi's death," the scholar said, "was almost not so much for the physical end of the man as for the irrevocable, desperate certainty that his career was interrupted, that it will not continue, and just when there was need of it. There will be no more new paintings by Morandi: this for me is the most agonizing thought. Even more so when I remember that just a few days ago he said to me, 'If you knew, dear Longhi, how much I want to work;' and also, 'I've new ideas I want to develop.' These are words that demonstrate why it is wrong, even if very common, to think of the career of an artist, above all of an older one, as a parabola. With Morandi's constant lucidity it was more of a well-aimed trajectory, a long road; let's hope it remains open. Those few sentences he whispered

his reductive procedure, the magic serenity of the French painter."

In March 1964 a selection of works on paper—27 etchings and 4 drawings—was exhibited at the Galerie Obere Zäune in Zurich, and the month after 11 paintings, mostly from the sixties, together with 4 watercolors and 20 etchings, were seen in a solo show at the Städtisches Kunsthaus in Bielefeld.

Among the shows presenting his work abroad during the year of note were the enquiry into painting and sculpture of the previous decade at London's Tate Gallery from April to June, and *Preferencias de los coleccionistas* at the Fundación Eugenio Mendoza held in Caracas in May.

Meanwhile the Edizioni del Milione published the seminal monograph by Lamberto Vitali, complete with 252 plates and a valuable critical anthology comprising a selection of 36 texts by Italian and foreign authors, ranging from the article by Riccardo Bacchelli published in *Il Tempo* on 29 March 1918 to the essay quoted above by Rosenberg on Chardin.

After suffering for a time from lung cancer, Morandi died on 18 June, two days before the opening of the 32nd Venice

From *Successo*, August 1963: Gino Ghiringhelli (standing) and the poet Antonio Rinaldi with Morandi in the living-room of his home in Via Fondazza, Bologna. (Courtesy Biblioteca Braidense, Milan.)

to me in his last days (his closest friends will certainly relate others) will amaze the many even in Italy who believed he faced his simple 'objects' laid in line, ordered, varied, exchanged with a certain immobile complacency; without understanding that in his long, tireless, solemn 'luminous elegy'. . . he was conducting such a poetical reconnaissance of the world of nature as to have no equal in the fifty years he crossed with his dense shadow like that of a tall, austere wayfarer who, with his 'vox clamantis' reached even the most stony regions of contemporary art. I mean to say that the stature of Morandi can and must grow further, after these last fifty years have been accordingly redimensioned, re-duced to their correct limits and, where necessary, even placed outside a history that is civilized, one, that is, able to understand that part of humanity expressed in the artistic act. A capricious nemesis, though not without meaning, wanted Morandi to leave the stage the very day in which were exhibited in Venice the products of Pop art. His death more than anything else, can stimulate this work of putting into perspective, after which there will be few left to count, perhaps just the number of the fingers of our hand. And Morandi will be second to nobody."

In Bologna, during a meeting of the city council on 30 June, the councillor for cultural affairs, Renato Zangheri, underlined just how "bitter it is to remember the death of Giorgio Morandi; the more so because it has happened too soon. Most of us believed he still had a long career ahead."

On 31 July the Edizioni del Milione's publication of the passionate and disputed essay by Francesco Arcangeli was completed. Neither the artist nor his friend Ghiringhelli, who died at the beginning of August, were able to see the end of this second and equally important study on Morandi, one which extended the field of enquiry to an international level, establishing contacts and comparisons with the protagonists of the artistic stage of the time.

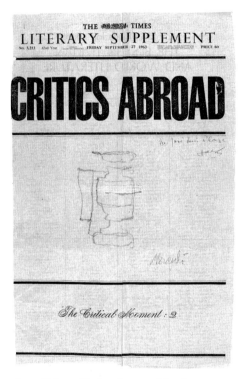

One of Morandi's drawings used for the cover of the literary supplement of the London daily *The Times* of 27 September 1963.
(Courtesy Museo Morandi, Bologna.)

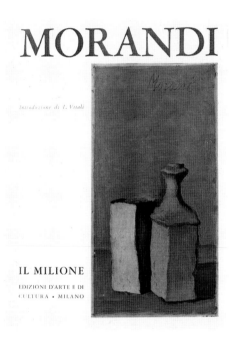

The monograph by Lamberto Vitali published by Edizioni del Milione in January 1964.
The volume is dedicated to Gianni Mattioli and his brother Ferdinando, who in November 1943 helped Vitali to flee to Switzerland.

FRANCESCO ARCANGELI

GIORGIO
MORANDI

EDIZIONI DEL MILIONE
MILANO

The cover of the monograph by Arcangeli published by Edizioni del Milione in July 1964.

[1] For a complete biography see M. Pasquali, *Museo Morandi. Catalogo generale*, Grafis, Bologna, 1996, pp. 429–435. This volume is the amplified version of the earlier *Museo Morandi Bologna, il catalogo*, edited by the same author for Charta, Milan, 1993.

[2] S. Giannelli, "Bottiglie e umanità di Morandi," *Le Carte Parlanti*, Florence, July-September 1950.

[3] "Carteggio Brandi-Morandi 1938–1963," ed. by M. Pasquali, in C. Brandi, *Morandi*, introduction by V. Rubiu, Editori Riuniti, Rome, 1990, p. 227.

[4] This letter is taken from the section published in the Italian version of the present catalog: M. Pasquali, "Morandi e il mondo dell'arte. Lettere 1950–1964," document no. 2.

[5] "Digestible Moderns," *Time*, New York, 10 November 1952.

[6] "Il carteggio Morandi-Petrucci", ed. by L. Ficacci, in *Morandi. L'opera grafica. Rispondenze e variazioni*, ed. by M. Cordaro, exh. cat., Istituto Nazionale per la Grafica, Calcografia, Rome, December 1990–February 1991, p. 173, letter no. 223b.

[7] See letter from K.E. Schuurman to Morandi of 16 August 1954, published in the Italian version of this catalog in the section "Morandi e il mondo dell'arte. Lettere 1950–1964," document no. 6.

[8] Some of these reviews, translated into Italian, were sent to Morandi by Bloch himself. In the cover letter dated 6 May, the scholar asks Morandi to congratulate the translator: "Dear Morandi, here are the translations of the articles published in the Hague. I have sent another example to Ghiringhelli. Please write a line to *Sig. Ottochian, c/o the Italian Embassy, Zeestr. 65, The Hague* thanking him for the translation. I hope to see you soon. Most affectionately, Vitale Bloch. Tomorrow I have to talk about the show on the radio." The document is in the archives of the Museo Morandi in Bologna.

[9] See "Il carteggio Morandi-Petrucci," p. 173, letter no. 224.

[10] See letter from G. Ghiringhelli to Morandi of 2 November 1955, published in the Italian version of this catalog in the section "Morandi e il mondo dell'arte. Lettere 1950–1964," document no. 8.

[11] See "Il carteggio Morandi-Petrucci," pp. 175–176, letters nos. 240 and 241.4. In fact Petrucci wrote to Morandi on 22 September 1955: "Everybody is asking me about your prints, above all in Scandinavia where I am preparing a group show: do you have anything at hand that you can send me at once? The two ministries would be more than happy." The artist replied two days later from Bologna: "Dearest Petrucci. I returned at the end of August . . . Unfortunately I don't have any prints left. Not even the last two we printed last year. And no new plate. I would like to do some more but I think it will remain a wish. Perhaps this winter."

[12] "Carteggio Brandi-Morandi 1938–1963," p. 230.

[13] See letter from L. Vitali to Morandi of 14 October 1955, published in the Italian version of this catalog in the section "Morandi e il mondo dell'arte. Lettere 1950–1964," document no. 7, note 2.

[14] This testimony by Keller, "Relazione sulla visita alla Collezione Oskar Reinhart," is reprinted in *Giorgio Morandi 1890–1990. Mostra del centenario*, ed. by M. Pasquali, exh. cat., Galleria Comunale d'Arte Moderna, Bologna, 12 May–2 September 1990, pp. 350–354.

[15] In this regard see letter to Cesare Brandi of 9 June in which Morandi states, "I feel very tired and I only want a little of the calm necessary for my work. So I have asked to retire." The document is published in "Carteggio Brandi-Morandi 1938–1963," pp. 231–232.

[16] Ibid., note 1.

[17] See "Il carteggio Morandi-Petrucci," p. 177, letter no. 254.

[18] M. Pasquali, "Gli acquerelli di Giorgio Morandi," in M. Pasquali, *Morandi. Acquerelli. Catalogo generale*, Electa, Milan, 1991, p. 11.

[19] See letter from Morandi to L. Vitali, undated [1963], published in the Italian version of this catalog in the section "Morandi e il mondo dell'arte. Lettere 1950–1964," document no. 28, note 1.

[20] See letter from G. Floersheim to Morandi of 1st December 1963, ibid., document no. 30, note 1.

[21] See letter from G. Ghiringhelli to Morandi of 2 November 1955 and from F. Arcangeli to Morandi on 16 August 1960, ibid., documents nos. 8, note 4, and 19, note 5.

[22] See letter from L. Vitali to Morandi of 7 November 1962, ibid., document no. 25.

[23] See letter from J.L. Plaza to Morandi of 7 February 1962, ibid., document no. 21.

[24] See letter from W. Haftmann to Morandi of 3 May 1962 and from Morandi to W. Haftmann, undated [1962], ibid., documents nos. 22 and 23.

[25] See letters from Morandi to L. Vitali, undated [1963], and from R. Longhi to Anna, Dina, and Maria Teresa Morandi of 9 July 1964, ibid., documents no. 28, note 1, and no. 32, note 1.

Exhibitions 1950–1964

edited by Lorenza Selleri
with the collaboration of Laura Lorenzoni

The list includes all of Morandi's solo and group exhibitions during the period covered by the present show (1950–1964). For events of particular significance, the cover of the corresponding catalog is reproduced next to the specific entry.
The traveling exhibitions are described with an indication of the single or various editions of the catalog. Whenever an original exhibition title has been impossible to trace because the catalog and other data are missing, the compiler has attributed a title, indicated by square brackets. Square brackets are also used to show where the exact venue or dates of an exhibition were not available.
For shows without a catalog the information has been derived from reviews and other documentation.

Milan, Galleria Annunciata, *Opere scelte di Morandi*, 31 December 1949–13 January 1950, catalog, text by F. Arcangeli.

Brussels, Palais des Beaux-Arts, *Art italien contemporain*, 28 January–26 February 1950, catalog, text by G. Raimondi.

Amsterdam, Stedelijk Museum, *Figuren uit de Italiaanse Kunst na 1910*, 3 March–3 May 1950, catalog.

Lugano, Villa Ciani, *Mostra internazionale di bianco e nero*, 6 April–31 May 1950, catalog.

Florence, Galleria dell'Accademia, *Mostra Premio del Fiorino*, 22 April–30 May 1950.

Paris, Musée National d'Art Moderne, *Exposition d'art moderne italien*, curated by P. D'Ancona, exhibition organized by the "Amici di Brera," May-June 1950, catalog, texts by J. Cassou and P. D'Ancona.

London, Tate Gallery, *Modern Italian Art*, exhibition organized by The Arts Council of Great Britain, 25 June–31 July 1950, catalog, texts by P. James and P. D'Ancona.

Sassari, Ente Provinciale per il Turismo, *Mostra di incisioni italiane*, exhibition organized by the Calcografia Nazionale, 15–31 August 1950, catalog, text by C.A. Petrucci.

Boston, The Robert T. Markson Collection, *Contemporary Italian Paintings*, exhibition organized in collaboration with the Galleria del Cavallino, Venice, from 14 September 1950, catalog, text by J.S. Plaut.

Pittsburgh, Carnegie Institute, *Pittsburgh International Exhibition of Paintings*, 19 October–21 December 1950, catalog.

Florence, Palazzo Strozzi, [*Exhibition of Italian contemporary art*], from 28 October 1950 (then Munich, Mannheim, Hamburg, Bremen, Berlin, *Italienische Kunst der Gegenwart. Ausstellung 1950–1951*, [dates unknown] 1950–1951, single catalog, texts by B. Degenhart and W. Haftmann).

PITTSBURGH INTERNATIONAL
EXHIBITION OF PAINTINGS
CARNEGIE INSTITUTE
OCTOBER 19 · DECEMBER 21 · 1950

Pittsburgh, *Pittsburgh International Exhibition of Paintings*, 1950.

Asti, [venue not known], *Antologia di disegni italiani dal 1900 al 1950*, autumn 1950, catalog.

Zurich, Kunsthaus, *Futurismo & Pittura Metafisica*, November-December 1950, catalog, texts by various authors.

Cincinnati, Cincinnati Art Museum, *Paintings 1900–1925*, 2 February–4 March 1951.

Palm Beach, Society of the 4 Arts, *Futurism and Later Italian Art*, 9 February–4 March 1951, catalog.

Göteborg, Konsthallen, *Italian Artists of Today. Exhibition of Italian Contemporary Art*, exhibition organized by the Art Club, Rome, February 1951 (then Helsinki, Konsthallen, 14–27 March 1951; Oslo, Kunsternes Hus, April 1951; Copenhagen, Frie Udstilling, May 1951), single catalog, text by G.C. Argan. A separate catalog, containing the text by Argan, accompanies the Finnish edition of the show, presented under the title *Italiensk Nutidskonst*.

Brussels, Galerie Georges Giroux, *Art graphique italien contemporain*, 17 March–3 April 1951, catalog, texts by G. de Angelis d'Ossat and C.A. Petrucci.

Antwerp, Stedelijk Kunstsalon, *Tentoonstellingen gewijd aan Europese Grafiek: Jacques Villon, Mario Prassinos, Edgard Tytgat, Giorgio Morandi, Fritz Pauli*, exhibition organized by the Comité voor Artistieke Werking, 29 March–12 April 1951.

Lordgen, *Grafik av Giorgio Morandi*, from 14 April 1951.

Florence, Galleria dell'Accademia, *Mostra nazionale Premio del Fiorino 1951*, 28 April–31 May 1951.

Salerno, Galleria d'Arte, *[Group show]*, from 9 July 1951.

Torre Pellice, Collegio Valdese, *3ª Mostra d'arte moderna*, exhibition organized by the Art Club, Turin, 25 August–10 September 1951, catalog, text by V. Orengo.

Turin, Palazzo Belle Arti, Parco del Valentino, *Peintres d'aujourd'hui. France-Italie / Pittori d'oggi. Francia-Italia*, October 1951, catalog ed.

by L. Carluccio and J. Lassaigne, text by R. Cogniat.

São Paulo, Museu de Arte Moderna, *I Bienal do Museu de Arte Moderna de São Paulo*, October-December 1951, catalog, texts by various authors, special exhibition *Artistas italianos de hoje* organized by the Venice Biennial, catalog, text by R. Pallucchini.

Buenos Aires, Instituto de Arte Moderno, *21 pintores italianos contemporáneos de la Colección del Senōr Mario Remorino*, November 1951, catalog.

The Hague, Gemeentemuseum, *Drie grafici. Giorgio Morandi, Mario Prassinos, Jacques Villon*, [dates unknown] 1951, catalog.

ORANGERIE DES TUILERIES

La Nature Morte
DE L'ANTIQUITÉ A NOS JOURS

CATALOGUE PAR
CHARLES STERLING

Avril–Juin 1952

Paris, *La nature morte de l'antiquité à nos jours*, 1952.

Paris, Musée National d'Art Moderne, *Jeune gravure contemporaine*, 12 March–20 April 1952.

Delft, Museum Het Prinsenhof, *De aquarel 1800–1950*, 25 March–5 May 1952.

Paris, Orangerie des Tuileries, *La nature morte de l'antiquité à nos jours*, April-June 1952, catalog ed. by C. Sterling, texts by various authors.

Genoa, Galleria Rotta, *Mostra collettiva d'arte contemporanea*, 27 May–8 June 1952, catalog.

Venice, Giardini di Castello, *XXVI Esposizione biennale internazionale d'arte*, 14 June–19 October 1952, catalog, texts by various authors.

Pittsburgh, Carnegie Institute, *The 1952 Pittsburgh International Exhibition of Contemporary Painting*, 16 October–14 December 1952, catalog.

New York, John Heller Gallery, *Massimo Campigli, Giorgio Morandi, Antonio Musič*, 27 October–14 November 1952.

Milan, Galleria Il Milione, *[Group show]*, until 29 November 1952, catalog.

Stockholm, Liljevalchs Konsthall, *Nutida italiensk konst*, exhibition organized by the Venice Biennial, 6 March–12 April 1953, catalog, text by U. Apollonio (then Helsinki, Taidehalli, 8 May–7 June 1953, catalog, text by U. Apollonio).

Athens, Zappeion, *Art italien d'aujourd'hui*, exhibition organized by the Venice Biennial, 20 March–19 April 1953, catalog, text by U. Apollonio (then, but not mentioned in the catalog, Dolmabahce, Istanbul, [venue not known], 26 April–16 May 1953).

Rome, Galleria dello Zodiaco, *[Group show]*, March 1953.

Florence, Palazzo Strozzi, *Arte moderna in una raccolta italiana*, April-May 1953, catalog, text by C.L. Ragghianti.

London, Arcade Gallery, *The Art of Still Life 1600–1950*, 12 June–10 July 1953, catalog, text by V. Bloch.

Genoa, Galleria Rotta, *Mostra d'arte contemporanea*, 1–20 July 1953, catalog.

Prato, Palazzo Pretorio, *Mostra di pittura dell'800 e del '900 nelle collezioni private pratesi*, 6–30 September 1953, catalog.

Biella, La Piccola Galleria, *Mostra collettiva di pittura*, 3–15 October 1953, catalog, text by V. Da Savona.

São Paulo, Museu de Arte Moderna, *II Bienal do Museu de Arte Moderna de São Paulo*, 8 December 1953–8 February 1954, catalog,

PEINTRES D'AUJOURD'HUI
FRANCE - ITALIE

TORINO
1951

PITTORI D'OGGI
FRANCIA - ITALIA

Turin, *Peintres d'aujourd'hui. France-Italie / Pittori d'oggi. Francia-Italia*, 1951.

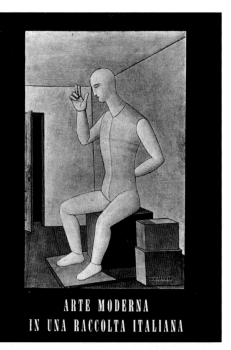

ARTE MODERNA
IN UNA RACCOLTA ITALIANA

Florence, *Arte moderna in una raccolta italiana*, 1953.

São Paulo, II *Bienal do Museu de Arte Moderna de São Paulo*, 1953–1954.

texts by various authors, special exhibition *Futuristas e artistas italiano de hoje* organized by the Venice Biennial, catalog, text by R. Pallucchini.

Rome, Galleria dello Zodiaco, *Campigli, de Pisis, Morandi, Rosai, Sironi, Tosi*, March 1954, catalog.

Wakefield, City Art Gallery, *Contemporary Italian Art*, 3 April–2 May 1954 (then Liverpool, Walker Art Gallery, 8 May–5 June 1954; Salford, City Art Gallery, 12 June–3 July 1954; Huddersfield, City Art Gallery, 10 July–7 August 1954; Scarborough, City Art Gallery, 14 August–11 September 1954; Hull, The Ferens Art Gallery, 18 September–14 October 1954; Newcastle-on-Tyne, The Hatton Gallery, 23 October–20 November 1954; York, City Art Gallery, 27 November–24 December 1954), single catalog, text by R. Melville.

The Hague, Gemeentemuseum, *Giorgio Morandi*, 14 April–6 June 1954, catalog, texts by V. Bloch and L. Vitali.

London, New Burlington Galleries, *Giorgio Morandi. Paintings & Prints*, exhibition organized by The Arts Council of Great Britain, 25 June–24 July 1954, catalog, texts by V. Bloch and L. Vitali.

Verbania, Kursaal, *Capolavori dell'arte italiana contemporanea (1918–1930)*, 25 July–30 September 1954, catalog ed. by M. Valsecchi.

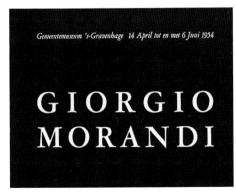

The Hague, *Giorgio Morandi*, 1954.

Modena, Caffè Nazionale, *Dipinti di maestri contemporanei da collezioni modenesi*, 23 October–4 November 1954, catalog.

Milan, Palazzo Reale, *Dipinti del Museo d'Arte di San Paolo del Brasile*, November 1954–February 1955, catalog, text by P.M. Bardi.

Bologna, Galleria La Loggia, *36 dipinti di maestri italiani*, 18 December 1954–8 January 1955, catalog, text by F. Arcangeli.

Toulouse, Musée Paul Dupuy, *La gravure contemporaine en Italie*, curated by C.A. Petrucci, 19 March–15 May 1955, catalog.

Barcelona, Palacio de la Virreina, *Exposición de pintura italiana contemporánea*, exhibition organized on occasion of the *Bienal hispano-americana de arte*, March-April 1955, catalog, text by P. Bucarelli (then Madrid, Palacio del Retiro, May-June 1955, catalog, text by P. Bucarelli).

London, Institute of Contemporary Art, *Twentieth-Century Paintings and Sculptures*, 9 June–2 July 1955.

Kassel, Museum Fridericianum, *Documenta. Kunst des XX. Jahrhunderts. Internationale*

Toulouse, *La gravure contemporaine en Italie*, 1955.

Ausstellung, 15 July–18 September 1955, catalog, text by W. Haftmann.

Cortina d'Ampezzo, Circolo Artistico, Palazzo Ariston, *Pittori contemporanei*, exhibition organized by the Circolo Artistico, Cortina d'Ampezzo, with the collaboration of G. Zanini, from 20 August 1955.

Marseilles, Musée Cantini, *L'art italien contem-*

GIORGIO MORANDI

New York, *Giorgio Morandi*, 1955.

porain, September-October 1955, catalog, text by P. Bucarelli.

New York, Delius Gallery, *Giorgio Morandi*, 5 October–5 November 1955, catalog, text by L. Deuel.

Pittsburgh, Carnegie Institute, *The 1955 Pittsburgh International Exhibition of Contemporary Painting*, 13 October–18 December 1955, catalog.

Saint Louis, City Art Museum, *Contemporary Italian Art*, 13 October–14 November 1955, catalog, text by W.N. Eisendrath Jr.

Los Angeles, County Museum, *Contemporary Italian Prints. A Loan Exhibition*, 14 October–13 November 1955, catalog, text by E. Feinblatt.

Rome, Studio d'Arte La Medusa, *Giorgio Morandi*, from 29 October 1955, catalog.

Stockholm, Nationalmuseum, *Italiensk grafik av idag*, 11 November–3 December 1955, catalog, text by C.A. Petrucci (then Göteborg, venue and dates unknown).

GIORGIO MORANDI

LA MEDUSA
STUDIO D'ARTE
ROMA
1955

Rome, *Giorgio Morandi*, 1955.

Rome, Palazzo delle Esposizioni, *VII Quadriennale nazionale d'arte*, November 1955–April 1956, catalog, texts by various authors.

Milan, Galleria Bergamini, *Mostra di pittura contemporanea italiana*, 17 December 1955–6 January 1956, catalog.

New York, Curt Valentin Gallery, *Closing Exhibition, Sculpture, Paintings and Drawings*, [dates unknown] 1955, catalog, text by R.F. Colin.

New York, John Heller Gallery, *Massimo Campigli, Giorgio Morandi, Antonio Musič*, 24 January–11 February 1956.

New York, Columbus Gallery of Fine Arts, *Italian Design Today*, 9 March–15 April 1956.

Winterthur, Kunstmuseum, *Giorgio Morandi. Giacomo Manzù*, 24 June–29 July 1956, catalog, text by H. Keller.

Leverkusen, Städtisches Museum Morsbroich, *Italienische Malerei heute*, 23 July–9 September 1956, catalog, texts by C. Schweicher and L. Venturi.

Newark (New York), The Newark Museum, *20th-Century Italian Art*, 12 October–18 November 1956, catalog, text by W.H. Gerdts.

Deerfield, Deerfield Academy, *Contemporary Italian Art*, 20 October–10 November 1956.

Zagreb, Udruženja Likovnih Umjetnika Hrvatske, *Savremena Italijanska Umetnost. Slikarstvo i skulptura*, October 1956–January 1957 (then Ljubljana, Moderne Galerije, 1957; Skopje, Umetničke Galerije, 1957; Belgrade, [venue not known], 1957), catalog, text by E. Lavagnino.

KUNSTMUSEUM WINTERTHUR

GIORGIO MORANDI

GIACOMO MANZÙ

24. Juni bis 29. Juli 1956

Winterthur, *Giorgio Morandi. Giacomo Manzù*, 1956.

Modern Italian Art

from the Estorick Collection

The Arts Council of Great Britain

London, *Modern Italian Art from the Estorick Collection*, 1956–1957.

Turin, Palazzo Madama, *La collezione donata da Alberto Rossi alla città di Torino per la Civica Galleria d'Arte Moderna*, October 1956, catalog.

Turin, Galleria La Bussola, *Maestri italiani dell'arte contemporanea*, from 3 November 1956, catalog.

London, Tate Gallery, *Modern Italian Art from the Estorick Collection*, exhibition organized by The Arts Council of Great Britain in collaboration with the Italian Institute of London, 21 November–19 December 1956 (then Plymouth, City Museum and Art Gallery, 26 January–16 February 1957; Birmingham, City Museum and Art Gallery, 23 February–16 March 1957), single catalog, text by G.C. Argan. Other cities the exhibition traveled to, though not listed in the catalog, are on record as: Newcastle, Laing Art Gallery, 23 March–27 April 1957; Cardiff, National Gallery of Wales, 4–25 May 1957.

Milan, Galleria Bergamini, *Mostra di pittura contemporanea italiana*, 15 December 1956–4 January 1957, catalog, text by G. Giani.

Geneva, Galerie Internationale, *30 peintres artistes d'aujourd'hui*, [dates unknown] 1956.

New York, Weyhe Gallery, *Contemporary Italian Graphics*, [dates unknown] 1956.

San Sebastián, Galeria San Sebastián, *20 maestri pintor scelti*, [dates unknown] 1956.

Caracas, Museo de Bellas Artes, *Diez años de pintura italiana*, exhibition organized by the

Venice Biennial, 27 January–17 February 1957 (then Bogotá, venue not known, 7–21 March 1957; Lima, venue not known, 15 April–14 May 1957; Concepción, Escuela de Periodismo, 25–31 July 1957; Buenos Aires, Museo Nacional de Bellas Artes, 27 August–29 September 1957; Montevideo, Comisión Nacional de Bellas Artes, 14–31 October 1957; Rio de Janeiro, Museu Nacional de Belas Artes, 19 November–4 December 1957), single catalog, text by U. Apollonio.

New York, World House Galleries, *Italy, the New Vision*, 1–23 March 1957, catalog, text by A.R. Krakusin.

Ivrea, Centro Culturale Canavesano, *L'opera grafica*, March 1957.

New York, Brooklyn Museum of Art, *Trends in Watercolors Today*, 9 April–26 May 1957, catalog, text by L. Venturi.

Rome, Galleria Nazionale d'Arte Moderna, *Mostra d'arte per gli artisti esuli d'Ungheria*, exhibition organized by the Associazione italiana per la libertà della cultura, 15 April–10 May 1957, catalog.

Rome, Galleria La Bussola, *La pittura italiana fino alla seconda guerra*, from 27 April 1957, catalog.

Turin, Galleria Galatea, *Morandi*, 4–15 May 1957, catalog, text by L. Carluccio.

Munich, Haus der Kunst, *Grosse Kunstausstellung München 1957 und Ausstellung italienischer Kunst von 1910 bis zur Gegenwart*, 7 June–15 September 1957, catalog, text by F. Bellonzi.

Messina, Società Filarmonica Antonio Laudano, *Cento opere di sessantasette "firme" del nostro tempo*, August 1957, exhibition organized by the Galleria d'Arte Cairola, catalog, text by S. Cairola.

São Paulo, Museu de Arte Moderna, *IV Bienal do Museu de Arte Moderna de São Paulo*, September-December 1957, catalog, texts by various authors, special exhibition *Artistas italianos de hoje* organized by the Venice Biennial, catalog, text by R. Pallucchini.

diez años de pintura italiana
por la Bienal de Venecia · 1957

Caracas, *Diez años de pintura italiana*, 1957–1958.

GIORGIO MORANDI

WORLD HOUSE GALLERIES

New York, *Giorgio Morandi. Retrospective. Paintings, Drawings, Etchings 1912–1957*, 1957.

New York, World House Galleries, *Giorgio Morandi. Retrospective. Paintings, Drawings, Etchings 1912–1957*, 5 November–7 December 1957, catalog, text by L. Venturi.

Milan, Galleria Il Milione, *Alcune opere recenti di Marini, Morandi, Sironi e litografie inedite di Arturo Tosi*, 9–23 November 1957, catalog.

Milan, Galleria Bergamini, *Mostra di pittura contemporanea italiana*, 21 December 1957–10 January 1958, catalog, text by G. Giani.

Turin, Galleria Galatea, *Dipinti e sculture dei nostri giorni*, 23 February–4 March 1958, catalog.

New York, The American Federation of Art, *Manzù and Morandi*, February-June 1958.

New York, The Museum of Modern Art, *Three Painters as Printmakers*, March 1958, catalog.

Lugano, Villa Ciani, *V Mostra internazionale di bianco e nero*, 3 April–15 June 1958, catalog, texts by various authors.

Brussels, Palais International des Beaux-Arts, *Exposition universelle et internationale de Bruxelles*, April-October 1958, catalog, special exhibition *50 ans d'art moderne*, 17 April–21 July 1958, catalog, text by E. Langui, and special exhibition *L'homme et l'art*, August-October 1958.

Lincoln (Massachusetts), De Cordoba Museum, *A Decade in Review*, 27 April–1 June 1958.

Milan, Palazzo di Brera, *Incisioni della raccolta Majno*, May 1958, catalog, texts by C.A. Petrucci and L. Vitali.

Copenhagen, Statens Museum for Kunst, *Moderne Italiensk Maleri*, June-July 1958, catalog, text by P. Bucarelli (then Rome, Galleria Na-

50 ANS D'ART MODERNE

Brussels, *Exposition universelle et internationale de Bruxelles*, 1958.

zionale d'Arte Moderna, 10 August–31 October 1958).

Caracas, Galeria de Arte Contemporáneo, *Morandi, Tosi, Marino Marini, Campigli, Sironi, de Pisis*, September 1958.

Prato, Palazzo Pretorio, *Pittura italiana contemporanea nelle collezioni di Prato*, September 1958, catalog, text by L. Carluccio.

Pasadena, Pasadena Art Museum, *The New Renaissance in Italy*, curated by T.W. Leavitt, 7 October–16 November 1958, catalog.

PAINTING IN
POST-WAR ITALY
1945-1957

INTRODUCTION BY LIONELLO VENTURI

COLUMBIA UNIVERSITY · NEW YORK

New York, *Painting in Post-War Italy 1945–1957*, 1958.

Turin, Galleria Galatea, *Disegni e incisioni di Casorati, Morandi, Spazzapan*, 18–31 October 1958, catalog.

Pittsburgh, Carnegie Institute, *The 1958 Pittsburgh Bicentennial International Exhibition of Contemporary Painting and Sculpture*, 5 December 1958–8 February 1959, catalog.

Milan, Galleria Bergamini, *Mostra di pittura contemporanea italiana*, 20 December 1958–9 January 1959, catalog, text by G. Giani.

New York, The Casa Italiana of Columbia University, *Painting in Post-War Italy 1945–1957*, [dates unknown] 1958, catalog, text by L. Venturi.

Padua, Galleria Le Stagioni, *Giorgio Morandi. 30 acqueforti*, 10–27 January 1959, catalog.

Nancy, Musée des Beaux-Arts, *La gravure contemporaine en Italie*, January 1959.

Taranto, Galleria Taras, *Cinquanta pittori figurativi*, 30 April–15 May 1959, catalog, text by R. Biasion.

Modena, Palazzo dei Musei, *Maestri italiani della pittura contemporanea*, 19–31 May 1959, catalog, texts by E. Cecchi and R. Triva.

Saint-Etienne, Musée d'Art et d'Industrie, *Peintres et sculpteurs italiens du futurisme à nos jours*, exhibition organized by the Venice Biennial, from 27 May 1959, catalog, text by G.A. Dell'Acqua (then Dijon, Musée des Beaux-Arts, from 10 July 1959; Blois, Château de Blois, from 15 September 1959; Lyon, Musée des Beaux-Arts, from 22 October 1959, catalog, text by G.A. Dell'Acqua; Charleroi, Palais des Beaux-Arts, from 17 December 1959, catalog, text by G.A. Dell'Acqua).

Florence, Palazzo Strozzi, *La collezione minima di Zavattini*, May 1959, catalog ed. by N. Lo Vullo, texts by C.L. Ragghianti and C. Zavattini.

Rome, Palazzo Barberini, *Il futurismo*, 4 June–6 September 1959, catalog ed. by J. Recupero, texts by G. Castelfranco, A. Palazzeschi and J. Recupero, back matter and bibliography by L. Drudi Gambillo.

New York, World House Galleries, *Summer International*, 17 June–29 August 1959, catalog.

Ascona, Isole di Brissago, *Mostra internazionale di grafica contemporanea*, 27 June–27 September 1959, catalog, text by R. Broggini.

Kassel, Museum Fridericianum, Orangerie, Bellevue-Schloss, *II. Documenta '59. Kunst nach 1945. Internationale Ausstellung*, 11 July–11 October 1959, catalog, text by W. Haftmann.

Prato, Palazzo Pretorio, *Grafica contemporanea nelle collezioni di Prato*, curated by G. Marchiori, September 1959, catalog.

Turin, Civica Galleria d'Arte Moderna, *Capolavori d'arte moderna nelle raccolte private*, 31 October–8 December 1959, catalog ed. by M. Valsecchi.

Turin, *Capolavori d'arte moderna nelle raccolte private*, 1959.

Lima, Museo de Arte Italiano, *Obras de pintura italiana contemporánea*, October 1959, catalog, text by G. del Corso.

New York, World House Galleries, *Drawings, Watercolors, Collages by 20th-Century Masters*, 8 December 1959–9 January 1960, catalog.

Milan, Galleria Annunciata, *Trenta opere di Giorgio Morandi*, 19 December 1959–8 January 1960, catalog, text by M. Fin.

Milan, Galleria Bergamini, *Campigli, Morandi, Sironi, Soldati*, 19 December 1959–8 January 1960, catalog, text by G. Giani.

Macerata, Amici dell'Arte, *Pittori d'oggi*, 20 December 1959–3 January 1960, catalog.

Pisa, Università degli Studi di Pisa, Istituto di Storia dell'Arte, *Gabinetto dei disegni e stampe e raccolta Timpanaro*, December 1959, catalog, text by C.L. Ragghianti.

Caracas, Fundación Eugenio Mendoza, *La evolución de la pintura moderna*, [dates unknown] 1959, catalog.

Alessandria, Camera di Commercio, Industria ed Agricoltura, *Mostra d'arte italiana contemporanea*, 9–21 January 1960, catalog, text by G. Giani.

Milan, Galleria Sacerdoti, *I classici della pittura italiana del Novecento*, 23 January–14 February 1960, catalog.

Amsterdam, Stedelijk Museum, *De Estorick verzameling van moderne italiaanse kunst*, 4 March–4 April 1960 (then Eindhoven, Stedelijk van Abbe Museum, 9 April–21 May 1960), single catalog, text by G.C. Argan.

Milan, Galleria Annunciata, *Opere di M. Campigli, C. Carrà, F. de Pisis, G. Morandi, M. Sironi*, 5 March–April 1960, catalog.

Johannesburg, Johannesburg Fair, Italian Pavilion, *Exhibition of Italian Contemporary Art*, 4–23 April 1960, catalog, texts by G.C. Argan and A. Mezio.

New York, Knoedler Gallery, *The Colin Collection*, 12 April–14 May 1960.

Boston, Boston University Art Gallery, *Works from Private Collections*, 23 April–14 May 1960.

Milan, Palazzo Reale, *Arte italiana del XX secolo da collezioni americane*, 30 April–26 June 1960, catalog, text by J.Th. Soby (then Rome, Galleria Nazionale d'Arte Moderna, 16 July–18 September 1960, catalog, text by J.Th. Soby).

Vienna, Schauräume der Akademie der Bildenden Künste, *Italienische Kunst der Gegenwart. Die Sammlung Estorick*, exhibition organized by the Institut zur Förderung der Künste in Österreich, 17 June–25 July 1960 (then Linz, Neue Galerie der Stadt, 5 August–4 September 1960), single catalog, text by G.C. Argan. Another city the exhibition traveled to, though not listed in the catalog, is Recklinghausen, Städtische Kunsthalle, 17 September–16 October 1960.

Lucerna, Kunstmuseum, *Italienische Maler der Gegenwart*, 6 August–18 September 1960, catalog, text by P.F. Althaus.

Zurich, Kunsthaus, *Sammlung G. David Thompson, Pittsburgh*, 15 October–27 November 1960, catalog.

Paris, Musée National d'Art Moderne, *Les*

ARTE ITALIANA DEL XX SECOLO

DA COLLEZIONI AMERICANE

"SILVANA" EDITORIALE D'ARTE - MILANO

Milan, *Arte italiana del XX secolo da collezioni americane*, 1960.

New York, *Giorgio Morandi. Oils, Watercolors, Drawings, Etchings*, 1960–1961.

sources du XXe siècle. Les arts en Europe de 1884 à 1914, 4 November 1960–23 January 1961, catalog, texts by G.C. Argan, J. Cassou and N. Pevsner.

New York, World House Galleries, *Giorgio Morandi. Oils, Watercolors, Drawings, Etchinngs*, 6 December 1960–14 January 1961, catalog.

Rome, Galleria La Nuova Pesa, *Arte italiana e straniera in piccolo formato*, 22 December 1960–8 January 1961, catalog.

New York, The Museum of Modern Art, *The James Thrall Soby Collection*, 1–25 February 1961, catalog, texts by A.H. Barr Jr., B.H. Rockefeller and J.Th. Soby.

Milan, *Trenta opere di Giorgio Morandi*, 1959–1960.

Milan, Ente Internazionale d'Arte e Cultura, *Maestri della pittura italiana contemporanea*, 29 March–29 April 1961, catalog, text by E. Mastrolonardo.

Chicago, Illinois Institute of Technology, *The Maremont Collection of Twentieth-Century Art*, 5–30 April 1961.

Turin, Galleria La Bussola, *La figura nell'arte italiana contemporanea*, 3–29 June 1961, catalog, text by G. Ballo.

Turin, Palazzo a Vela, *Mostra della moda stile costume. Da Boldini a Pollock. Pittura e scultura del XX secolo*, exhibition organized on occasion of *Italia '61*, curated by L. Carluccio, T. d'Albisola, F. Russoli, G. Russoli, M. Tapié de Celeyran and M. Valsecchi, June 1961, catalog (then Milan, Padiglione d'Arte Contemporanea, 12 October–5 November 1961).

Siena, Pinacoteca Nazionale, *Mostra di grafica italiana contemporanea dalla collezione di Paolo Cesarini*, July-September 1961, catalog, texts by A. Cairola and E. Carli.

Amsterdam, Stedelijk Museum, *Polariteit. Het appolinische en het dionysische in de kunst*, curated by T. Grochwiak, H.L.C. Jaffè, W. Sandberg, A. Schröder and A. Schulze-Vellinghausen, 22 July–18 September 1961, catalog.

Turin, Galleria Narciso, *Il paesaggio nella pittura italiana contemporanea*, 24 September–15 October 1961, catalog, text by L. Carluccio.

Milan, Galleria Bergamini, *Opere scelte di recente e vecchia data*, 16 December 1961–12 January 1962, catalog, text by G. Giani.

Rome, Galleria Chiurazzi, *Carrà, de Chirico, de Pisis, Guttuso, Maccari, Mafai, Morandi, Permeke, Rosai, Sironi, Tomea. 18 opere*, December 1961, catalog.

London, Royal Academy of Arts, *Primitives to Picasso*, 6 January–7 March 1962, catalog, texts by P. James, B. Nicolson and C. Wheeler.

Modena, Caffè Nazionale, *Opere scelte della Collezione Fogliani*, 14–28 January 1962, catalog.

Turin, Galleria Narciso, *Motivi d'arte contemporanea*, 17 March–10 April 1962, catalog.

Venice, Giardini di Castello, *XXXI Esposizione biennale internazionale d'arte*, 16 June–7 October 1962, catalog, texts by various authors, special exhibition at Ca' Pesaro, *I Grandi Premi della Biennale 1948–1960*, curated by R. Pallucchini.

Turin, Galleria Gissi, *Maestri del '900 italiano*, 28 June–14 July 1962, catalog.

Salzburg, Galerie Welz, *Italienische Meister des XX. Jahrhunderts*, summer 1962, catalog.

Vienna, Museum des 20. Jahrhunderts, *Kunst von 1900 bis heute*, 21 September–4 November 1962, catalog, text by W. Hofmann.

Siegen, Haus Seel am Markt, *Rubenspreis der Stadt Siegen. Giorgio Morandi*, 27 October–17 November 1962, catalog, text by U. Apollonio.

London, *Primitives to Picasso*, 1962.

Turin, Galleria La Bussola, *Il disegno italiano contemporaneo*, from 8 December 1962, catalog.

Milan, Galleria Lorenzelli, *Magini-Morandi*, December 1962, catalog, text by M. Valsecchi.

Turin, Galleria Galatea, *Giorgio Morandi*, December 1962.

Milan, Galleria Sacerdoti, *Viaggio nel tempo di*

Siegen, *Rubenspreis der Stadt Siegen. Giorgio Morandi*, 1962.

un mercante-amatore, catalog, text by M. Monteverdi, [dates unknown] 1962.

Towson (Maryland), Goucher College, *Selections from the Collection of Mrs. Henry Epstein*, 13 January–13 February 1963, catalog, texts by O.F. Kraushaar and L.F. Johnson Jr.

Turin, Galleria Narciso, *Italian Still-Life Paintings XXth Century*, 20 January–24 February 1963, catalog.

Naples, Galleria Il Centro, *Giorgio Morandi, incisioni*, 26 January–8 February 1963.

Naples, Galleria Il Centro, *I grandi maestri della pittura moderna*, 9–26 February 1963.

Ivrea, Centro Culturale Olivetti, *Disegni italiani moderni*, February 1963, catalog, text by G. Carandente.

Rome, Galleria Don Chisciotte, exhibition organized in collaboration with the Galleria Galatea, Turin, *Quaranta incisioni di Giorgio Morandi*, February 1963.

Cape Town, South African National Gallery, *Modern Italian Painting*, from 4 March 1963, catalog, text by M. Bokhorst.

Milan, Galleria Sianesi, *Maestri moderni*, from 29 March 1963, catalog.

Rome, Galleria Zanini, *Maestri contemporanei*, from 8 April 1963, catalog.

Florence, Galleria Santacroce, *Cinquanta incisioni di G. Morandi*, from 20 April 1963, catalog.

Turin, Galleria Narciso, *Motivi d'arte contemporanea*, 20 May–14 June 1963, catalog.

Paris, Galerie de Seine, *[Group show]*, 10 June–25 July 1963.

Strasbourg, Musée des Beaux-Arts, *La grande aventure de l'art du XXe siècle*, June-September 1963.

Viareggio, Galleria Nettuno, *Giorgio Morandi, acqueforti*, from 7 July 1963.

Rimini, Galleria La Riva, *Maestri grafici del XX secolo*, 3–31 August 1963, catalog, texts by A. Emiliani and M. Zuffa.

Hamburg, Kunstverein, *Italien 1905–1925. Futurismus und Pittura Metafisica*, 28 September–3 November 1963, catalog (then Frankfurt, Kunstverein, Kuratorium Kulturelles, Steinernes Haus Römerberg, 16 November 1963–5 January 1964, catalog).

Milan, Galleria Sacerdoti, *Umanesimo del "Novecento" pittorico italiano*, 22 October–10 November 1963, catalog, text by M. Monteverdi.

Bologna, Galleria Indipendenza, *Maestri contemporanei*, 26 October–10 November 1963, catalog.

Beirut, Istituto Italiano di Cultura, *Dipinti italiani d'oggi*, October-November 1963.

New York, Marlborough-Gerson Gallery, *Artists and Maecenas. A Tribute to Curt Valentin*, 2 November–21 December 1963.

New York, The Solomon R. Guggenheim Mu-

GIORGIO MORANDI

Geneva, *Giorgio Morandi*, 1963.

seum, *20th-Century Master Drawings*, 6 November 1963–5 January 1964 (then Minneapolis, University Gallery, University of Minnesota, 3 February–15 March 1964; Cambridge, The Fogg Art Museum, Harvard University, 6 April–24 May 1964), single catalog, texts by E. Rauh and S. Simon.

Rome, Galleria L'Obelisco, *Morandi*, from 7 November 1963, catalog.

Geneva, Galerie Krugier, *Giorgio Morandi*, 14 November–14 December 1963, catalog, text by G. Floersheim.

Biella, Circolo degli artisti, *Premio Biella per l'incisione*, November-December 1963, catalog, text by L. Carluccio.

Washington, D.C., National Gallery of Art, *Paintings from the Museum of Modern Art, New York*, 17 December 1963–1 March 1964, catalog, text by A.H. Barr Jr.

Milan, Galleria Bergamini, *Opere di Campigli, Carrà, Cassinari, Morandi*, 21 December 1963–24 January 1964, catalog.

Turin, Galleria Narciso, *Motivi d'arte contemporanea*, 15 February–18 March 1964, catalog, text by L. Carluccio.

Livorno, Bottega d'Arte, *Maestri italiani della pittura contemporanea*, 7–20 March 1964, catalog.

Ringenberg, Galerie Schloss Ringenberg, *Giorgio Morandi. Gemälde, Aquarelle, Druck-Grafik*, 14 March–5 April 1964, catalog, texts by G. de Chirico and W. Haftmann (then Stuttgart, Galerie Lutz & Meyer, 16 May–13 June 1964, catalog, texts by G. de Chirico and W. Haftmann).

Zurich, Galerie Obere Zäune, *Giorgio Morandi*, exhibition organized in collaboration with the Galerie Krugier, Geneva, March 1964, catalog.

Bielefeld, Städtisches Kunsthaus, *Giorgio Morandi. Gemälde, Aquarelle, Druckgraphik*, exhibition organized in collaboration with the Galerie Schloss Ringenberg, Ringenberg, 19 April–10 May 1964, catalog, texts by G. de Chirico and W. Haftmann.

London, Tate Gallery, *54–64. Painting & Sculpture of a Decade*, exhibition organized by the Calouste Gulbenkian Foundation, 22 April–28 June 1964, catalog ed. by R. Fior and E. Wright.

Caracas, Fundación Eugenio Mendoza, *Preferencias de los coleccionistas*, 17–31 May 1964, catalog, text by G. Meneses.

Lausanne, Palais de Beaulieu, *Chefs-d'œuvres des collections suisses de Manet à Picasso*, May-October 1964, catalog, text by M. Huggler.

Venice, Giardini di Castello, *XXXII Esposizione biennale internazionale d'arte*, 20 June–18 October 1964, catalog, texts by various authors.

Karlsruhe, Badischer Kunstverein, *Giorgio Morandi. Gemälde, Aquarelle, Zeichnungen, Radierungen*, 22 June–26 July 1964, catalog, text by W. Haftmann.

Kassel, Alte Galerie, Museum Fridericianum, Orangerie, *Documenta III. Internationale Ausstellung*, 27 June–5 October 1964, catalog, texts by A. Bode and W. Haftmann, special section *Handzeichnungen*, catalog, text by W. Haftmann.

Ancona, Palazzo del Liceo Scientifico, *Premio Marche 1964. 8ª Mostra nazionale di arti figurative*, 6–29 September 1964, catalog, text by G. Marchiori, speciale exhibition *Omaggio a Giorgio Morandi*, text by G. Marchiori.

Darmstadt, Mathildenhöhe, *Die Internationale*

LA NATURA MORTA ITALIANA

1964 - Napoli - Palazzo Reale

ALFIERI & LACROIX - MILANO

Naples, *La natura morta italiana*, 1964–1965.

der Zeichnung, 12 September–15 November 1964.

Munich, Galerie Atelier Monti, *Giorgio Morandi*, September-October 1964.

Milan, Galleria delle Ore, *Omaggio a Morandi*, 17–30 October 1964, catalog, text by G. Fumagalli.

Pittsburgh, Carnegie Institute, *The 1964 Pittsburgh International Exhibition of Contemporary Painting and Sculpture*, 30 October 1964–10 January 1965, catalog, text by G. von Groschwitz.

Florence, Galleria Santacroce, *Antologia di maestri contemporanei*, October 1964, catalog.

Naples, Palazzo Reale, *La natura morta italiana*, October-November 1964, catalog, text by S. Bottari (then Zurich, Kunsthaus, December 1964–February 1965; Rotterdam, Museum Boymans-van Beuningen, March-April 1965, single catalog, texts by V. Bloch, S. Bottari, E. Hüttinger and F. Russoli).

Hanover, Kestner-Gesellschaft, *Morandi*, 17 November–6 December 1964, catalog, texts by G. de Chirico, E. Roditi and W. Schmied.

Bibliography 1950–1964

Following is the most complete possible bibliography for the period covered by the present exhibition. It includes in alphabetical order by author or, if this is missing, by title: monographs, general studies, articles, and reviews in newspapers and magazines. When initials are the only indication of an author, but identification has been possible, the full name is given between parentheses. When a publication has no title or date, the missing element has been attributed by the compiler and indicated between square brackets.
The numeral 1 following an author's name or a title identifies the items mentioned by Flavio Fergonzi in his Catalog of Works.

A.B., "Mostra di pittura italiana contemporanea nelle collezioni pratesi," *Arte Figurativa Antica e Moderna*, Milan, September-October 1958.

a.b., "Acqueforti di Morandi alla Galleria delle Stagioni di Padova," *Il Resto del Carlino*, Bologna, 25 January 1959.

A.B., "Meditative Stille," *Der Kurier. Der Gag*, Berlin, 1 December 1964.

A.C., "Giorgio Morandi," *Le Monde*, Paris, 26 June 1964.

a.d.g. (Del Guercio A.), "La scomparsa di un grande pittore. Gli 'interminati spazi' di Giorgio Morandi," *Rinascita*, Rome, 27 June 1964.

A.J., ["Giorgio Morandi"], *St. Galler Tagblatt*, St. Gallen, 26 July 1952.

A.L., "Morandi," *St. Galler Tagblatt*, St. Gallen, 26 July 1952.

A.M., "È morto Giorgio Morandi fra i grandi maestri del pennello," *Corriere del Giorno*, Taranto, 19 June 1964.

a. mnz., "È morto Giorgio Morandi il pittore delle bottiglie," *Messaggero Veneto*, Udine, 19 June 1964.

A.N., "Cronache d'arte. Omaggio a Morandi," *L'Unità*, Milan, 23 October 1964.

a.t. (Trombadori A.), "Morandi. La luce di via Fondazza," *Vie Nuove*, Rome, 25 June 1964.

A.V., "Giorgio Morandi," *La Mercanzia*, Bologna, July 1964.

"A Morandi il 'Premio Rubens,'" *L'Unità*, Rome, 27 October 1962.

"A Venezia vince la pop-art," *Gazzetta del Mezzogiorno*, Bari, 20 June 1964.

Aliprandi G., "Giorgio Morandi visto da Cesare Brandi," *Gazzetta del Veneto*, Padua, 16 January 1961.

Andren G., "Nutida italiensk Konst," *Ny Tid*, Göteborg, 22 March 1953.

Apollonio U., *Pittura metafisica*, Edizioni del Cavallino, Venice, 1950.

Apollonio U., *Pittura italiana moderna*, Neri Pozza, Venice, 1950.

Apollonio U., "Pienezza del suo linguaggio," *La Fiera Letteraria*, Rome, 25 September 1955, special issue dedicated to Giorgio Morandi.

Apollonio U., Valsecchi M., *Panorama dell'arte italiana*, Lattes, Turin, 1950.

Apollonio U., Valsecchi M., *Panorama dell'arte italiana*, Lattes, Turin, 1951.

Apollonio U., "Capolavori d'arte moderna nelle raccolte private," *Arte Figurativa Antica e Moderna*, Milan, November-December 1959.

Apollonio U., "Morandi," *Das Kunstwerk*, Baden-Baden, September 1960.

Apuleo V., "La scomparsa di Giorgio Morandi," *La Voce Repubblicana*, Rome, 19 June 1964.

Apuleo V., "Umanità di Morandi," *La Voce Repubblicana*, Rome, 26 June 1964.

Apuleo V., "Evoluzione di un linguaggio," *La Voce Repubblicana*, Rome, 21 July 1964.

Apuleo V., "Segnato dal Caravaggio il destino della natura morta," *La Voce Repubblicana*, Rome, 23 October 1964.

Arbasino A., "Aria di Londra. Spender a tavola," *Il Mondo*, Rome, 23 July 1957.

Arcangeli F., "La peinture italienne en 1920," *Cahiers d'Art*, no. 1, Paris, 1950, special issue for the 25th year, *Un demi-siècle d'art italien*, introduction by C. Zervos, texts by various authors.

Arcangeli[1] F., *12 opere di Giorgio Morandi*, Edizioni del Milione, Milan, 1950.

Arcangeli F., "Picasso 'Voce recitante,'" *Paragone*, no. 47, Florence, November 1953.

Arcangeli F., "Gli ultimi naturalisti," *Paragone*, no. 59, Florence, November 1954.

Cinotti M., "Giorgio Morandi," *Le Carte Parlanti*, Florence, July-September 1950.

Cinotti M., "Giorgio Morandi," *Via*, Milan, September 1950.

Cinti I., "L'arte di Giorgio Morandi," *La Famèja Bulgnèisa*, Bologna, 3 July 1964.

Coates R.M., "The Art Galleries. The Quadriennale," *The New Yorker*, New York, January 1956.

Cogniat R., Fourny M., Waldemar G., *Encyclopédie de l'art international contemporain*, Prisme des Arts, Paris, 1958.

Colacicchi G., "La crisi della pittura italiana rispecchiata nella Quadriennale," *La Nazione*, Florence, 30 November 1955.

"Collezione Estorick," *Sele Arte*, no. 29, Florence, March-April 1957.

"Commemorato Morandi," *Il Resto del Carlino*, Bologna, 24 June 1964.

Contini E., "A Morandi il 'Rubens,'" *Avanti!*, Bologna, 20 May 1962.

Corazza C., "Disegni di Morandi e testo di Ramous," *Portici*, Bologna, 1 September 1950.

Corazza C., "Studenti di Belle Arti all'Accademia e alla Galleria del Voltone," *L'Avvenire d'Italia*, Bologna, 21 June 1953.

Corazza N.C., "Giorgio Morandi ha fede nell'uomo," *Colloqui*, no. 28, Milan, October 1956.

Corazza N.C., "È morto Morandi," *L'Avvenire d'Italia*, Bologna, 19 June 1964.

Costantini V., *Architettura, scultura, pittura contemporanea europea in un secolo di materialismo*, Ceschina, Milan, 1951.

Courir D., "Giorgio Morandi compie oggi settant'anni. Un classico," *Il Resto del Carlino*, Bologna, 20 July 1960.

Courthion P., *L'art indépendant. Panorama international de 1900 à nos jours*, Albin Michel, Paris, 1958.

Cramer H.M., "Giorgio Morandi im Haag," *Welt Kunst*, no. 10, Munich, 15 May 1954.

"Critics Abroad," *The Times*, London, 27 September 1963, literary supplement.

Cucchi I., "Estremo omaggio di Bologna alla salma di Giorgio Morandi," *Carlino Sera*, Bologna, 20 June 1964.

"Current and Forthcoming Exhibitions," *The Burlington Magazine*, London, February 1961.

D.L., "L'arte solitaria di Morandi," *L'Ora*, Palermo, 19 June 1964.

"Da Caravaggio a Morandi," *L'Unità*, Milan, 3 October 1964.

Da Vià G., "L'idea nella pittura di Giorgio Morandi," *L'Osservatore Romano*, Vatican City, 15 July 1964.

Dagnini G., "Fra breve lo perderemo," *Il Resto del Carlino*, Bologna, 24 July 1964.

Damigella A.M., "La 'natura morta' italiana dai caravaggiani ai metafisici," *Espresso Sera*, Catania, 26 October 1964.

D'Ancona P., "I maestri italiani del '900 a Parigi," *Le Vie d'Italia*, Milan, June 1950.

D'Ancona P., *I classici della pittura italiana del Novecento*, Edizioni del Milione, Milan, 1953.

Dannecker H., "Deutsche und italienische Kunst in München," *Schwäbische Landeszeitung*, Augsburg, 11 June 1957.

Daval J.-L., "A la Galerie Krugier vernissage Morandi," *Courrier de Genève*, Geneva, 15 November 1963.

Daval J.-L., "Patient, solitaire, concentré: Giorgio Morandi," *Journal de Genève*, Geneva, 23–24 November 1963.

Daval J.-L., "Hommage à Giorgio Morandi," *Journal de Genève*, Geneva, 19 June 1964.

de Begnac Y., "Come se Morandi fosse sempre qui," *Gazzetta di Vigevano*, Vigevano, 23 July 1964.

de Begnac Y., "Come se Morandi fosse sempre qui," *Il Giornale di Pavia*, Pavia, 23 July 1964.

de Begnac Y., "Ha ritrovato il tempo perduto," *Gazzetta di Mantova*, Mantua, 24 July 1964.

de Begnac Y., "Come se Morandi fosse sempre qui," *Gazzetta di Reggio*, Reggio Emilia, 24 July 1964.

de Begnac Y., "Come se Morandi fosse sempre qui," *Gazzetta dell'Emilia*, Modena, 24 July 1964.

de Begnac Y., "Come se Morandi fosse vivo," *L'Arena*, Verona, 29 July 1964.

de Begnac Y., "Come se Morandi fosse vivo," *Il Giornale di Vicenza*, Vicenza, 29 July 1964.

de Begnac Y., "Morandi pigia ancora i secoli all'interno delle sue bottiglie," *Il Piccolo*, Trieste, 30 July 1964.

de Begnac Y., "Come se Morandi fosse sempre qui," *La Tribuna del Mezzogiorno*, Messina, 31 July 1964.

de Begnac Y., "Lo spirito di Giorgio Morandi è rimasto nella sua Bologna," *La Gazzetta di Parma*, Parma, 31 July 1964.

De Giorgio E., "La natura morta nella pittura italiana contemporanea," *Corriere del Giorno*, Taranto, 25 June 1964.

De Grada R., "Cronache d'arte. Un pittore puro," *L'Unità*, Rome, 5 January 1950.

De Gruyter J., "Arte di oggi e di tutti i tempi: Giorgio Morandi," *Her Valderland*, The Hague, 15 April 1954.

de Jayme M., "Morandi: un mestre no meio do caos," *O Estado de São Paulo*, São Paulo, 20 September 1957.

de Libero L., "Dalla luce aurorale alla dorata fermezza," *La Fiera Letteraria*, Rome, 25 September 1955, special issue devoted to Giorgio Morandi.

de Marchis G., "Cronaca di Roma," *Art International*, New York, 25 April 1963.

de Marchis G., "La mostra a Firenze," *Art International*, New York, 25 May 1963.

De Witt A., *L'incisione italiana*, Hoepli, Milan, 1950.

Degenhart B., *Italienische Zeichner der Gegenwart*, Gebr. Mann Verlag, Berlin, 1956.

Del Boca A., "Ha perdonato sette volte il pittore delle bottiglie," *Gazzetta Sera*, Turin, 6 October 1953.

Del Boca A., "Un pittore dalla figura di un frate giottesco: Morandi, quello delle bottiglie ha perdonato sette volte ai suoi allievi," *Il Mattino dell'Italia Centrale*, Florence, 23 October 1953.

Dell'Acqua G.A., "La peinture 'métaphisique,'" *Cahiers d'Art*, no. I, Paris, 1950, special issue for the 25th year, *Un demi-siècle d'art italien*, introduction by C. Zervos, texts by various authors.

Della Pergola P., "La pittura di Morandi," *Paese Sera*, Rome, 17 April 1964.

Della Pergola P., "Le magiche lastre di Giorgio Morandi," *Paese Sera*, Rome, 31 December 1964.

Dentice F., "Gli ostinati," *L'Espresso*, Rome, 25 February 1962.

Desideri F., "I grandi maestri sentono la terra," *L'Agricoltura*, Rome, March 1956.

Dh., "Abkehr vom menschlichen Antlitz: Giorgio Morandi wird in Hamburg, ausgestellt," *Hamburger Anzeiger*, Hamburg, 20 May 1954.

"Digestible Moderns," *Time*, New York, 10 November 1952.

Disegni e dipinti della RAI-Radiotelevisione Italiana, ERI, Edizioni della RAI-Radiotelevisione Italiana, Turin, 1962.

"Disegni italiani moderni," *Sele Arte*, no. 28, Florence, January-February 1957.

II. Documenta '59. Kunst nach 1945. Internationale Ausstellung, exh. cat., Museum Fridericianum, Kassel, 11 July–11 October 1959.

"Domani s'inaugura la Biennale d'arte," *Il Gazzettino*, Venice, 19 June 1964.

Dorfles G., "La settima Quadriennale," *Aut Aut*, Milan, January 1956.

Dorival B., *Les peintres du XXe siècle. Du cubisme à l'abstraction 1914–1957*, Tisné, Paris, 1957.

Dossena G.M., "Il pittore del silenzio," *L'Europeo*, Milan, 28 June 1964.

Dossena G.M., "Il pittore del silenzio," *Il Progresso Italo-Americano*, New York, 14 July 1964.

Dragone A., "Si inaugura oggi a Roma la VII Quadriennale d'arte," *Il Popolo Nuovo*, Turin, 22 November 1955.

Dragone A., "L'omaggio del governo italiano ai nostri più significativi artisti," *Il Popolo Nuovo*, Turin, 22 February 1956.

Dragone A., "La sua prima mostra durò un giorno, adesso un Morandi è pagato milioni," *Stampa Sera*, Turin, 6–7 August 1962.

Dragone A., "Quattro secoli di natura morta dal Caravaggio a Giorgio Morandi," *Il Nostro Tempo*, Turin, 22 October 1964.

E.F. (Fezzi E.), "A Taranto la mostra della natura morta," *La Provincia*, Cremona, 19 August 1964.

E.F. (Fezzi E.), "Giorgio Morandi pittore," *La Provincia*, Cremona, 13 September 1964.

E.G., "Giorgio Morandi," *Herald Tribune*, New York, 1 January 1961.

Elmo F., "Giorgio Morandi," *Gazzettino del Jonio*, Siderno, 3 July 1964.

"È morto a Bologna Giorgio Morandi," *L'Eco di Bergamo*, Bergamo, 19 June 1964.

"È morto a Bologna Giorgio Morandi," *Corriere degli Italiani*, Buenos Aires, 22 June 1964.

"È morto Giorgio Morandi," *Gazzetta del Mezzogiorno*, Bari, 19 June 1964.

"È morto Giorgio Morandi," *Il Mattino*, Naples, 19 June 1964.

"È morto Giorgio Morandi il 'pittore delle bottiglie,'" *Libertà*, Piacenza, 19 June 1964.

"È morto Giorgio Morandi il 'pittore delle bottiglie,'" *La Provincia*, Como, 19 June 1964.

"È morto il pittore Giorgio Morandi," *Gazzetta dell'Emilia*, Modena, 19 June 1964.

"È morto il pittore Giorgio Morandi," *Gazzetta di Reggio*, Reggio Emilia, 19 June 1964.

"È morto il pittore Giorgio Morandi," *Paese Sera*, Rome, 19 June 1964.

"È morto Morandi," *Il Telegrafo*, Livorno, 19 June 1964.

"È morto un grande artista," *La Settimana Incom Illustrata*, Milan, 5 July 1964.

"È morto un grande pittore," *Alba*, Milan, 5 July 1964.

Entità A., "Attendendo a Catania Morandi con la sua mostra d'arte nazionale," *Giornale dell'Isola*, Catania, 6 September 1950.

Espariat D., "Constantes et variations de l'art italien. Une étude d'André Chastel," *Contacts Franco-Italiens*, Milan, March-April 1957.

Ettinger P., "L'arte italiana contemporanea a Mosca," *Sele Arte*, no. 9, Florence, November-December 1953.

F.B., "L'ultimo maestro," *La Tribuna*, Rome, 5 July 1964.

F.P. (Porter F.), "Giorgio Morandi [World House]," in *Art News*, New York, November 1957.

Fahlstrom O., "Biennal i Stockholm," *Eskilstuna-Kurinen*, Stockholm, 21 March 1953.

"Fatica della gloria," *Corriere Lombardo*, Milan, 9 January 1953.

Federici R., "Arte contemporanea italiana in Germania," *Il Nuovo Corriere*, Florence, 5 November 1950.

Federici R., "Cinquant'anni di pittura moderna in Italia," *Sele Arte*, no. 49, Florence, January-February 1961.

Federici R., "L'uomo e il pittore nella vecchia casa di Bologna," *Paese Sera*, Rome, 19 June 1964.

Ferrante L., *Arte e realtà*, Fantoni, Venice, 1952.

Ferrara L., "Arte italiana contemporanea alla VII Quadriennale," *Nuova Antologia*, Rome, January 1955.

Ferri L.C., "L'opera grafica di Giorgio Morandi," *La Voce Repubblicana*, Rome, 5 April 1957.

Ferri L., "Ricordo di Morandi," *La Carovana*, Rome, June 1964.

Ferriani L., "Ricordo di Giorgio Morandi," *La Prealpina*, Varese, 21 June 1964.

Fezzi E., "Note di pittura. Il Grand Prix a Giorgio Morandi," *La Provincia*, Cremona, 3 October 1957.

Fezzi E., "Giorgio Morandi pittore," *La Provincia*, Cremona, 13 September 1964.

Fierens P., "L'art italien au Palais des Beaux-Arts de Bruxelles," *Arts*, Brussels, 3 February 1950.

Fin M., "Variazione sul tema Morandi," *Bollettino della Galleria Annunciata*, no. 50, Milan, 1959–1960.

Floersheim G., "Art. Good Man with a Bottle," *Time*, New York, 30 September 1957.

Floersheim G., *Ist die Malerei zu Ende?*, Atlantis, Zurich, 1959.

Floersheim G., "Morandi," *Prévues*, no. 115, Paris, September 1960.

Floersheim G., "Giorgio Morandi," *National Zeitung*, Basel, 24 June 1964.

Formaggio D., *L'arte come comunicazione: I. Fenomenologia della tecnica artistica*, Nuvoletti, Milan, 1953.

Franceschini G., "2000 umetněčkih dela od 900 umetnika na VII. Kvadrijenali umetnosti u Rimu," *Italjug*, Rome, December 1955.

Francia E., "Morandi e Guidi," *Il Popolo*, Rome, 19 January 1950.

Francia E., "Mostre d'arte: Morandi alla Medusa," *Il Popolo*, Rome, 8 November 1955.

Francia E., "Dalla crisi dell'Ottocento alla rinascita della pittura italiana," *Il Popolo*, Rome, 9 December 1955.

Francia E., "La VII Quadriennale d'arte a Roma. Dalla crisi dell'Ottocento alla rinascita della pittura italiana," *Il Quotidiano Sera*, Cagliari, 11 December 1955.

Francia E., "Vecchi maestri alla VII Quadriennale: con de Chirico, Morandi e Carrà l'arte italiana diventa europea," *La Voce del Popolo*, Brescia, 18 February 1956.

Francia E., *Pittura e scultura moderna nelle Collezioni Vaticane*, Lorenzo del Turco, Rome, 1961.

g.a., "Le incisioni di Morandi," *Il Secolo XIX*, Genoa, 31 December 1964.

G.F., "Le mostre a Roma," *Il Paese*, Rome, 14 December 1955.

g.m. (Marussi G.), "Una mostra di Giorgio Morandi," *Le Arti*, Milan, November-December 1959.

G.M., "È morto Giorgio Morandi francescano osservatore della verità," *Il Piccolo*, Trieste, 19 June 1964.

G. Mar. (Marchiori G.), "Cronache milanesi del nuovo anno: Morandi pittore senza fratture," *La Fiera Letteraria*, Rome, 8 January 1950.

G.P., "Saggi, Cesare Brandi, 'Ritratto di Morandi,'" *Espresso Mese*, Rome, December 1960.

G.P., "Die sogenannte Natur," *Frankfurter Allgemeine Zeitung*, Frankfurt, 2 June 1964.

G.P., "Un ricordo di Morandi," *Domus*, Milan, September 1964.

G.R. (Raimondi G.), "Pomerio. L'arte che si capisce," *L'Immagine*, no. 14–15, Rome, [1950].

g.ru. (Ruggeri G.), "Consegnato il Premio Rubens. Un brindisi in casa Morandi," *Il Resto del Carlino*, Bologna, 19 December 1962.

g.z., "Negli ultimi giorni contemplò Picasso," *Gazzetta del Popolo*, Turin, 20 June 1964.

g.z., "L'addio di Bologna al pittore Morandi," *Gazzetta del Popolo*, Turin, 21 June 1964.

Galdi E., "L'antologia della pittura e della scultura italiana (1910–1930)," *Il Nazionale*, Rome, 4 December 1955.

Galdi E., "La VII Quadriennale," *Il Nazionale*, Rome, 11 December 1955.

Galdi E., "Il gigante solitario. È scomparso Giorgio Morandi," *Il Nazionale*, Rome, 5 July 1964.

Galvao P., "Representaçao italiana na Bienal paulista e um congressinho de criticos de arte," *Fanfulla*, São Paulo, 28 September 1951.

"Gäste aus dem Süden im Haus der Kunst," *Donau-Kurier*, Ingolstadt, 8 June 1957.

Geiger B., "Come per ottanta lire ho comperato un Morandi," *Il Gazzettino*, Venice, 1 July 1964.

Geiser G., *Moderne Malerei. Von Cézanne bis zur Gegenwart*, Knorr & Hirth, Munich-Hanover, 1963.

Geist H.-F., "Giorgio Morandi, Erinnerungen an eine Ausstellung," *Werk*, no. 7, Zurich, July 1957.

Genaille R., *La peinture contemporaine*, F. Nathan, Paris, 1955.

Gendel M., "The Italians from the Dying Renaissance to the Futurist Explosion," *Art News*, New York, October 1959.

"Genfer Kunstbrief," *Luzerner Neueste Nachrichten*, Lucerne, 16 December 1963.

"Genfer Kunstbrief," *Der Bund*, Bern, 3–4 January 1964.

Platte H., *Die Kunst des 20. Jahrhunderts. Malerei*, R. Piper & Co., Munich, 1957.

Plaza J.L., "Ultima visita a Morandi," *El Nacional*, Caracas, 23 August 1964.

Poncet M., "Antologia di pittori," *Arte Figurativa Antica e Moderna*, Milan, March-April 1956.

Ponente N., "La Quadriennale," *Letteratura*, Rome, September 1955.

Ponente N., "La Quadriennale," *Commentari*, Rome, October-December 1955.

Ponente N., "Era il più grande pittore italiano del nostro secolo," *Avanti!*, Milan, 19 June 1964.

Ponente N., "Il più grande pittore italiano," *Avanti!*, Rome, 19 June 1964.

Portalupi M., "Morandi e Soffici pittori paesisti," *Nazione Sera*, Florence, 9 October 1964.

Pozzi P., "Si è spento il poeta degli antichi silenzi," *Eco di Biella*, Biella, 22 June 1964.

Prange J.M., "Morandi: variaties op de soberheid," *Parool*, Amsterdam, 8 May 1954.

Priori L., "Artisti italiani. Destino europeo di Giorgio Morandi," *La Fiera Letteraria*, Rome, 1 April 1951.

Puccini M., "Tra le sue bottiglie Morandi dipinge i sogni," *La Settimana nel Sud*, Salerno, 28 March–4 April 1953.

Puccini M., "Giorgio Morandi il pittore semplice," *Gazzetta di Mantova*, Mantua, 12 June 1957.

Quaretti L., "Davanti alla Biennale con Morandi e Licini," *Stampa Sera*, Turin, 19–20 June 1958.

"IV Bienal de São Paulo: Morandi, da Italia, conquistou o Grande Premio internacional," *O Estado de São Paulo*, São Paulo, 17 September 1957.

Querel A., "Mercato d'arte," *La Settimana a Roma*, no. 5, Rome, 7 February 1963.

Querel A., "Art Centre," *This Week in Rome*, no. 6, Rome, 14 February 1963.

R. (Ragghianti C.L.), "Arte italiana moderna," *Sele Arte*, no. 6, Florence, May-June 1953.

R., "Ritratto di Morandi," *L'Avvenire d'Italia*, Bologna, 30 September 1960.

r.d.g. (De Grada R.), "Cronache d'arte. Un pittore puro," *L'Unità*, Milan, 6 January 1950.

R.F., "Morandi," *Paese Sera*, Rome, 9 December 1960.

R.H., "Winterthur: Giorgio Morandi, Giacomo Manzù," *Werk*, no. 8, Zurich, August 1956.

r.l.[1] (Longhi R.), "I fiamminghi e l'Italia," *Paragone*, no. 25, Florence, January 1952.

r.l. (Longhi R.), "La mostra della natura morta all'Orangerie,'" *Paragone*, no. 33, Florence, September 1952.

R.O., "Morandi ha visto tutto senza muoversi dallo studio," *Grazia*, Milan, 24 June 1956.

Ragghianti C.L., *L'arte e la critica*, Vallecchi, Florence, 1951.

Ragghianti C.L., "Acquaforte," *Sele Arte*, no. 3, Florence, 1952.

Ragghianti C.L., [Untitled], in *Arte moderna in una raccolta italiana*, exh. cat., Palazzo Strozzi, Florence, April-May 1953.

Ragghianti C.L., "Giorgio Morandi," *Critica d'Arte*, no. 1, Florence, January 1954.

Ragghianti C.L., *Il pungolo dell'arte*, Neri Pozza, Venice, 1956.

Ragghianti C.L., "Disegni italiani moderni," *Sele Arte*, no. 28, Florence, January-February 1957.

Ragghianti C.L., *Diario critico. Estetica critica linguistica*, Neri Pozza, Venice, 1957.

Ragghianti C.L., *Il Selvaggio*, Neri Pozza, Venice, 1959.

Ragghianti C.L., "Arte italiana al 1960," *Sele Arte*, no. 48, Florence, October-December 1960.

Ragghianti C.L., "Un'antologia pittorica di Morandi. Un artista solo," *La Stampa*, Turin, 24 March 1964.

Ragghianti[1] C.L., "Una antologia di Morandi," *Critica d'Arte*, no. 62, Florence, May 1964.

Raimondi G., "Giorgio Morandi," in *Panorama dell'arte italiana*, ed. by M. Valsecchi and U. Apollonio, Lattes, Turin, 1950.

Raimondi G., "La congiuntura metafisica Morandi-Carrà," *Paragone*, no. 19, Florence, July 1951.

Raimondi G., "Morandi," *Il Mondo*, Rome, 22 September 1951.

Raimondi G., "Pensosa armonia," *La Fiera Letteraria*, Rome, 25 September 1955, special issue devoted to Giorgio Morandi.

Raimondi G., "Sensibilidad y metafísica en la pintura de Giorgio Morandi," *Latina*, Caracas, October 1955.

Raimondi G., "La valigia delle Indie. La carriera di Morandi," *Il Mondo*, Rome, 8 January 1957.

Raimondi G., "La pittura metafisica: de Chirico, Carrà, Morandi," *Comunità*, Milan, December 1957.

Raimondi G., "Morandi: un ideale di perfezione. La sua lezione," *Il Resto del Carlino*, Bologna, 19 June 1964.

Raimondi G., "Morandi 1916," *Il Resto del Carlino*, Bologna, 15 August 1964.

Raimondi G., "Sempre viva la natura morta," *Il Resto del Carlino*, Bologna, 20 October 1964.

Rainer W., "Stumme Würde des Gegenstands. Zur Ausstellung Giorgio Morandi in Karlsruhe," *Stuttgarter Zeitung*, Stuttgart, 23 July 1964.

Raini A., *Morandi*, Ph.D. diss., Università degli Studi, Bologna, 1958–1959, advisor A.M. Brizio.

Raini A., "Mostre a Milano," *Le Arti*, no. 1, Milan, January 1963.

Raynal M., *Peinture moderne*, Skira, Geneva, 1953 (2nd ed., 1958).

Redeker H., "De zeer eigen wereld van Professor Giorgio Morandi," *Haagsche Post*, The Hague, 22 May 1954.

Reetz H., "Giorgio Morandi zum Gedächtnis," *Die Rheinpfalz*, Ludwigshafen, 27 June 1964.

Reindl L.E., "Nur ein paar zierliche Gefässe. Ein Gedenkblatt für italienischen Maler G. Morandi," *Südkurier*, Constance, 16 July 1964.

Répaci L., "Dio può essere chiuso in un tubetto di colore," *Tempo*, Milan, 20 May 1958.

Rey S., "Retour à l'art italien," *Le Phare Dimanche*, Brussels, 12 February 1950.

Ricci P., "Le correnti figurative alla Quadriennale," *L'Unità*, Rome, 16 December 1956.

Ricci P., "Un grande pittore, un uomo libero," *L'Unità*, Rome, 19 June 1964.

Rieux A., "Au Palais des Beaux-Arts de Bruxelles. Art italien contemporain," *L'Indépendance*, Charleroi, 14 February 1950.

Rieux A., "Moderne italiaanse kunst," *Soldatenpost*, Brussels, 16 February 1950.

Rinaldi A., "Giorgio Morandi, il pittore nascosto," *Successo*, Milan, August 1963.

Rinaldo G., "Italiensk form och färg," *Göteborgs Tidningen*, Stockholm, 13 March 1953.

Rizzi P., "È morto Giorgio Morandi pittore delle forme pure," *Il Gazzettino*, Venice, 19 June 1964.

Rocco A., "Visita alla casa di Morandi," *Corriere Mercantile*, Genoa, 16 June 1964.

Rocco E., "Prima di Natale verrà fissato il nuovo volto del Parlamento," *Settimo Giorno*, Milan, 6 November 1962.

Roda E., "Natura falsa. Giorgio Morandi," *Tempo*, Milan, 16 December 1961.

Roditi E., *Dialogues on Art*, Secker & Warburg, London, 1960 (German ed., Insel-Verlag, Frankfurt, 1960).

Rodriguez F., "Ricordo di Giorgio Morandi," *La Famèja Bulgnèisa*, Bologna, 3 July 1964.

Romani B., "Morandi: o del creare senza fretta in una cella ingombra di bottiglie," *Il Secolo XIX*, Genoa, 21 April 1959.

Rosenberg P., *Chardin*, Skira, Geneva, 1963.

Rossi A., "Morandi il poeta delle 'nature morte,'" *Selezionando*, Turin, June 1964.

Rossi P., "Morto il pittore Giorgio Morandi," *Voce Adriatica*, Ancona, 19 June 1964.

Rouve P., "European Moments in Italian Art," *Art News and Review*, London, 20 May 1950.

Rouve P., "Portrait of the Artist: Morandi," *Art News and Review*, no. 24, London, 22 December 1956.

Ruggeri G., "Morandi: un ideale di perfezione. Una vita fra Bologna e Grizzana," *Il Resto del Carlino*, Bologna, 19 June 1964.

Ruggeri G., "La lezione di Morandi," *Carlino Sera*, Bologna, 19 June 1964.

Ruggeri G., "La lezione di Morandi," *Nazione Sera*, Florence, 19 June 1964.

Ruggeri G., "Splende Morandi al Premio Marche," *Il Resto del Carlino*, Bologna, 25 September 1964.

Ruggeri G., "Quattro secoli di natura morta," *Il Resto del Carlino*, Bologna, 3 October 1964.

Russoli F., "Maestri famosi e poco noti alla Quadriennale," *Settimo Giorno*, Milan, 13 December 1955.

Russoli F., "Una collezione esemplare," *Settimo Giorno*, Milan, March 1958.

Russoli F., "Pretesti e appunti: . . . La mostra Magini-Morandi, o della polivalenza della natura morta," *Pirelli*, Milan, January-February 1963.

S.B. (Branzi S.), "A Morandi il Gran Premio della IV Biennale brasiliana," *Il Gazzettino*, Venice, 18 September 1957.

S.B., "In ricordo di Giorgio Morandi," *Arte Antica e Moderna*, Florence, July-September 1964.

S.W., "Heitere Bemühung um den Gegenstand," *Rhein-Neckar Zeitung*, Mannheim, 30 October 1964.

Sachs P.J., *Modern Prints & Drawings*, Knopf, New York, 1954.

Sala A., "Morandi, addio," *Corriere d'Informazione*, Milan, 19 June 1964.

Salvaneschi E., "Giorgio Morandi," *Scena Illustrata*, no. 2, Florence, February 1950.

Salvini R., *Guida all'arte moderna*, Garzanti, Milan, 1954 (2nd ed., 1956).

Sandler D., "Giorgio Morandi. His Work Reflects His Life: 'So Simple, Clear,'" *The Daily American*, Rome, 8 December 1957.

Santini P.C., "La VII Quadriennale di Roma. Una rassegna d'arte troppo folta," *Il Nuovo Corriere*, Florence, 25 November 1955.

Sapori L., "È morto Giorgio Morandi il 'pittore delle bottiglie,'" *La Gazzetta del Sud*, Messina, 19 June 1964.

Sauvage T., *Pittura italiana del dopoguerra (1945–1957)*, Schwarz, Milan, 1957.

Savonuzzi C., "Ricordo di Morandi," *Il Mondo*, Rome, 30 June 1964.

Scafa T., "Una tradizione che scompare. Morandi," *Il Cittadino*, Taranto, 4 July 1964.

Schettini A., "Giorgio Morandi," *Corriere di Napoli*, Naples, 20 June 1964.

Schildt G., "Italiens moderna Konst," *Konstrevy*, no. 2–3, Stockholm, 1953.

Sciortino G., "Incontri con l'uomo e con l'artista," *La Fiera Letteraria*, Rome, 25 September 1955, special issue devoted to Giorgio Morandi.

Sciortino G., "Morandi grafico," *La Fiera Letteraria*, Rome, 17 March 1957.

Sciran P., "Giorgio Morandi o delle 'nature morte,'" *Città di Vita*, no. 4, Florence, July-August 1964.

"Scompare con Giorgio Morandi un maestro dell'arte italiana," *L'Arena*, Verona, 19 June 1964.

Sebastiani A., "VII Quadriennale d'arte," *Cronache*, Rome, December 1955.

Serra L., "La VII Quadriennale di Roma," *Rivista Latina*, Rome, December 1955.

Severi A., "'Per me sono tutti matti' diceva sapendo che i suoi quadri si pagavano milioni," *Corriere Mercantile*, Genoa, 19 June 1964.

Severini M., *La collezione Sebastiano Timpanaro delle stampe e dei disegni*, Neri Pozza, Venice, 1959.

"Si è spento a Bologna il pittore Giorgio Morandi," *La Nuova Sardegna*, Sassari, 19 June 1964.

"Si è spento Giorgio Morandi," *Giornale del Mattino*, Florence, 19 June 1964.

"Si è spento Giorgio Morandi il pittore delle 'nature morte,'" *La Sicilia*, Catania, 19 June 1964.

"Si è spento ieri a Bologna il pittore Giorgio Morandi," *Gazzetta di Mantova*, Mantua, 19 June 1964.

"Si è spento tra le braccia delle sorelle," *La Provincia*, Cremona, 19 June 1964.

Sicre J.G., "Visita a la IV Bienal de São Paulo," *Américas*, no. 10, Washington, D.C., February 1958.

Silvi N., "È morto Morandi 'poeta delle cose,'" *Momento Sera*, Rome, 19 June 1964.

Simonsson I., "Nutida italiensk Konst," *Sydsvenska Dagbladet*, Stockholm, 7 April 1953.

Sinisgalli L., *Pittori che scrivono*, Meridiana, Milan, 1954.

Soby J.Th., *Giorgio de Chirico*, The Museum of Modern Art, New York, 1955.

Soby J.Th., *Modern Art and the New Past*, introduction by P.J. Sachs, University of Oklahoma Press, Norman, 1957.

Soby J.Th., "Giorgio Morandi," *Saturday Review*, New York, 4 January 1958.

Soby J.Th., "Genesis of a Collection," *Art in America*, no. 1, New York, 1961.

Soffici A., *Trenta artisti moderni italiani e stranieri*, Vallecchi, Florence, 1950.

Solari S., "Ricordo di Morandi," *L'Educatore Italiano*, Milan, 15 October 1964.

Soldi R., "Arte moderno italiano. La Colección Remorino," *Ars*, no. 58, Buenos Aires, 1952.

"Solenni funerali a Bologna alla salma di Giorgio Morandi," *Corriere di Sicilia*, Catania, 21 June 1964.

Sosset L.-L., "L'art italien contemporain à Bruxelles," *La Nouvelle Gazette de Bruxelles*, Brussels, 9 February 1950.

Speich K., "Neuerwerbungen in Kunstmuseum," *Neues Winterthurer Tagblatt*, Winterthur, 4 May 1963.

Spinelli de Santelena G., "L'VIII Premio Marche," *Bari Sport*, Bari, 23 September 1964.

Stabell W., "Italiensk kunst," *Morgenbladet*, Oslo, 22 August 1950.

Staber M., "Radierung und Zeichnung bei Giorgio Morandi," *Art International*, New York, 16 January 1964.

Staber M., "Die Irrealität des Realen," *Zürcher Woche*, Zurich, 6 March 1964.

Staber M., "Das Stilleben bei Giorgio Morandi," *Nachrichten Kunst*, Lucerne, November 1964.

Stehelin R., "Exposition Giorgio Morandi à Genève," *Dernières Nouvelles d'Alsace*, Strasbourg, 16 December 1963.

Steinbruker C., "Moderne Italienische Malerei und Plastik," *Der Kunsthandel*, Heidelberg, July 1960.

Sterling C., *La nature morte de l'antiquité à nos jours*, Tisné, Paris, 1959.

"Storia della pittura. 11: Giorgio Morandi," *Il Gatto Selvatico*, no. 2, Rome, February 1957.

Surchi S., "Capogrossi, Manzù e Morandi aprono la stagione romana," *La Nazione*, Florence, 25 September 1964.

Sutton D., "Trends in Italian Art," *Country Life*, London, 28 July 1950.

T.C., "Ricordo di Giorgio Morandi," *Cooperazione Sud*, Lecce, 28 June 1964.

Tafani A., "Giorgio Morandi fuori dalla leggenda," *Il Centro*, Rome, 28 June 1964.

Tafani A., "Giorgio Morandi fuori dalla leggenda," *L'Argine*, Ravenna, 4 July 1964.

Tagliacozzo P., "Incontro con Morandi," *Paese Sera*, Rome, 19 June 1964.

Tassi R., "L'opera grafica di Morandi," *Palatina*, no. 4, Parma, October-December 1957.

Tassi R., "Giorgio Morandi," *L'Approdo Letterario*, no. 26, Florence, April-June 1964.

Tea E., "Morandi Giorgio," *Il Ragguaglio Librario*, Milan, September 1951.

Tebano N., "Inaugurata a Venezia la XXXII Biennale d'arte," *Corriere del Giorno*, Taranto, 22 June 1964.

Testori G., "Le meditazioni di Morandi e le 'cucine' del Magini," *Settimo Giorno*, Milan, 8 January 1963.

Tillim S., "Month in Review," *Arts*, New York, December 1960.

Tramontana Botti E., "Austera solitudine di Giorgio Morandi," *L'Eco di Brescia*, Brescia, 26 June 1964.

Trezzi M., "Con le acqueforti di Morandi si è aperta a Viareggio la galleria d'arte 'Nettuno,'" *Nazione Sera*, Florence, 17 July 1963.

Tridenti C., "Primo sguardo alla VII Quadriennale," *Giornale d'Italia*, Rome, 20 November 1955.

Trier E., *Zeichner des 20. Jahrhunderts*, Gebr. Mann, Berlin, Buchergilde Gutenberg, Frankfort, 1956.

Trombadori A., "Morandi," *L'Unità*, Milan, 5 June 1950.

Trombadori A., "La VII Quadriennale," *Il Contemporaneo*, Rome, 3 December 1955.

Trombadori A., "Commosso saluto di Bologna a Morandi," *L'Unità*, Rome, 21 June 1964.

Trucchi L., "La settima Quadriennale," *Leggere*, Rome, 15 March 1956.

U.P., "Strano mondo pittorico nei quadri di Giorgio Morandi," *Stampa Sera*, Turin, 9 May 1957.

"Un omaggio a Giorgio Morandi la mostra della natura morta," *Il Mattino*, Naples, 26 September 1964.

"Una mostra di Morandi si apre domenica ad Ancona," *Paese Sera*, Rome, 4 September 1964.

"Una mostra grafica di Giorgio Morandi alla Galleria Nettuno," *Il Giornale del Mattino*, Viareggio, 7 July 1963.

"Una mostra in omaggio di Morandi ad Ancona," *Giornale del Mattino*, Florence, 4 September 1964.

"Una tela di Morandi pagata sei milioni," *La Tribuna del Mezzogiorno*, Messina, 2 December 1964.

Ungaretti G., *Pittori italiani contemporanei*, Cappelli, Bologna, 1950.

Valeri D., "Sironi, Morandi," *La Biennale*, Venice, January 1951.

Valeri D., "Un'incisione di Morandi," *Lo Smeraldo*, no. 1, Milan, 30 January 1964.

Valeri D., "Un'incisione di Morandi," *Il Gazzettino*, Venice, 30 June 1964.

"Vallecchi 1951," *Le Carte Parlanti*, no. 9, Florence, 31 January 1951.

Valsecchi M., "In mostra a Milano le celebri bottiglie del pittore bolognese," *Oggi*, Milan, 19 January 1950.

Valsecchi M., "Parigi a bocca aperta. L'esposizione della pittura italiana del quindicennio 1910–1925 ha lasciato sorpresi ed entusiasti i francesi," *Oggi*, Milan, 8 June 1950.

Valsecchi M., *24 dipinti in una raccolta d'arte moderna*, Edizioni del Milione, Milan, 1952.

Valsecchi M., "Mezzo secolo a Firenze," *Tempo*, Milan, 23 May 1953.

Valsecchi M., "Tre chilometri di arte italiana," *Tempo*, Milan, 8 December 1955.

Valsecchi M., "Una buona stagione della pittura," *L'Illustrazione Italiana*, Milan, December 1955.

Valsecchi M., "Neorealisti e astratti alla Quadriennale di Roma," *L'Illustrazione Italiana*, Milan, January 1956.

Valsecchi M., "Una rete d'oro l'incisione di Morandi," *Tempo*, Milan, 11 April 1957.

Valsecchi M., "I capolavori del bulino non trovano amatori," *Il Giorno*, Milan, 30 August 1957.

Valsecchi M., "Gran Premio a San Paolo. Il massimo premio è stato vinto da Morandi," *Tempo*, Milan, 17 October 1957.

Valsecchi M., "Profeti dell'arte moderna. Gli eroi diventano manichini," *Il Giorno*, Milan, 24 November 1957.

Valsecchi M., *Maestri moderni*, Garzanti, Milan, 1957.

Valsecchi M., "Escluso da Amsterdam," *Il Giorno*, Milan, 16 September 1958.

Valsecchi M., "Morandi l'inaccessibile infrange il voto del silenzio," *Il Giorno*, Milan, 22 September 1959.

Valsecchi M., *Profilo della pittura moderna*, Garzanti, Milan, 1959.

Valsecchi M., "La pittura metafisica," *Art Club*, Milan, March-May 1961.

Valsecchi M., "Picasso e Morandi," *Il Giorno*, Milan, 18 December 1962.

Valsecchi M., "L'incisione italiana fra due secoli," in *Cinquanta incisioni di artisti italiani*, Prandi, Reggio Emilia, 1963.

Valsecchi M., "Ha dato agli oggetti sentimenti umani," *Il Giorno*, Milan, 19 June 1964.

Valsecchi M., "Giorgio Morandi," *Rivista Italsider*, Genoa, June-September 1964.

Valsecchi M., "Duecento opere ma soprattutto Morandi," *Il Giorno*, Milan, 12 September 1964.

Valsecchi M., *Morandi*, Garzanti, Milan, 1964 (2nd ed., 1966).

"Variazioni nella borsa dell'arte," *L'Elefante*, Rome, 18–24 October 1950.

Vehmans E.J., "Italien nykytaiteen näyttely," *Uusi Suomi*, Helsinki, 10 May 1953.

Veira J.G., "IV Bienal de São Paulo: Italia," *Folha da Manha*, São Paulo, 13 October 1957.

"Veliki umetnik Giorgio Morandi," *Primorski Dnevnik*, Trieste, 20 June 1964.

"Venduta per sei milioni una 'natura morta' di Morandi," *Espresso Sera*, Catania, 1 December 1964.

Venturi L., "Quarante ans de peinture et de sculpture," *Les Beaux-Arts*, no. 479, Brussels, 1950.

Venturi L., "Gusto internazionale," *Commentari*, Rome, April-June 1952.

Venturi L., *La peinture italienne. Du Caravage à Modigliani*, Skira, Geneva, 1952.

Venturi L., "La rivoluzione della fantasia: VII Quadriennale," *L'Espresso*, Rome, 27 November 1955.

Venturi L., "Tre generazioni allo specchio," *L'Espresso*, Rome, 11 December 1955.

Venturi L., *Arte moderna*, Bocca, Rome, 1956.

Venturi L., *Saggi di critica*, Bocca, Rome, 1956.

Venturi L., "Acqueforti di Morandi," *L'Espresso*, Rome, 21 April 1957.

Venturi[1] L., "Giorgio Morandi," in *Giorgio Morandi. Retrospective. Paintings, Drawings, Etchings 1912–1957*, exh. cat., World House Galleries, New York, 5 November–7 December 1957.

Venturi L., "Introduction," in *Painting in Post-War Italy 1945–1957*, exh. cat., La Casa Italiana of Columbia University, New York, 1958.

Venturoli M., "Viaggio intorno alla VII Quadriennale," *La Rassegna*, Pisa, November-December 1955.

Venturoli M., "Viaggio attraverso la VII Quadriennale. Siamo parenti o nemici dei maestri di avanguardia?," *Paese Sera*, Rome, 8 December 1955.

Venturoli M., "La settima Quadriennale," *Mondo Operaio*, Rome, 10 December 1955.

Venturoli M., "I maestri della pittura e della scultura premiati alla VII Quadriennale d'arte," *Paese Sera*, Rome, 21 February 1956.

Venturoli M., "Intervista con Morandi," *Europa Letteraria*, Rome, 29 May 1964.

Venturoli M., "Morandi sta male," *Le Ore*, Rome, 18 June 1964.

Venturoli M., "Morandi e il Premio Marche," *Le Ore*, Rome, 8 October 1964.

Venturoli M., "I meravigliosi trofei della natura," *Le Ore*, Rome, 5 November 1964.

Vergani O., "Giorgio Morandi," *L'Illustrazione Italiana*, Milan, March 1953.

Vergani O., *Pittori di ieri e di oggi*, Pizzi, Milan, [1954].

Vergani O., "Puro Morandi," *Corriere d'Informazione*, Milan, 15–16 May 1957.

Vergani O., "Morandi ammalato," *Tempo*, Milan, 23 May 1964.

Vernetti L., "Il positivismo di Ardigò nell'interpretazione di Rodolfo Modolfo," *Critica Sociale*, Milan, 5 June 1964.

Verzellesi G.L., "Pitture di Morandi," *Gazzetta di Mantova*, Mantua, 17 December 1957.

Verzellesi G.L., "Un'antologia di Morandi," *Nuova Rivista di Varia Umanità*, no. 1, Verona, January 1958.

Verzellesi G.L., "Iconografia di Morandi," *Il Giornale di Vicenza*, Vicenza, 15 December 1960.

Verzellesi G.L., "Iconografia di Morandi," *L'Arena*, Verona, 15 December 1960.

Verzellesi G.L., "Un ritratto di Morandi," *La Gazzetta di Mantova*, Mantua, 26 December 1960.

Verzellesi G.L., "La tacita rivolta di Giorgio Morandi," *Il Giornale di Vicenza*, Vicenza, 20 June 1964.

Verzellesi G.L., "La tacita rivolta di Giorgio Morandi," *L'Arena*, Verona, 20 June 1964.

Verzellesi G.L., "L'esempio di Morandi," *Gazzetta di Mantova*, Mantua, 12 August 1964.

Verzellesi G.L., "I critici e Morandi," *Il Giornale di Vicenza*, Vicenza, 10 September 1964.

Verzellesi G.L., "I critici e Morandi," *L'Arena*, Verona, 10 September 1964.

Veth C., "Werk van Giorgio Morandi in het Gemeentemuseum," *Haagsche Courant*, The Hague, 3 June 1954.

Vic., "Alla Galleria d'Arte. Pittori alla ribalta," *Il Setaccio*, Salerno, 7 July 1951.

Vice, "Le mostre d'arte romane: Morandi alla Medusa," *L'Unità*, Rome, 8 November 1955.

Vice, "Mostre a Roma: Giorgio Morandi alla Galleria La Medusa," *Il Giornale d'Italia*, Rome, 13 November 1955.

Vice, "Arte. La VII Quadriennale di Roma," *Le Vie d'Italia*, Milan, January 1956.

Vice, "Morandi alla Selecta," *Il Tempo*, Rome, 30 May 1959.

Visentini G., "È morto Giorgio Morandi," *Il Messaggero*, Rome, 19 June 1964.

Visentini G., "È morto Giorgio Morandi," *Il Secolo XIX*, Genoa, 19 June 1964.

Vitali L., *Preferenze*, Domus, Milan, 1950.

Vitali L., *Giorgio Morandi. Opera grafica*, Einaudi, Turin, 1957, with 113 plates (2nd expanded and revised ed., 1964; 3rd expanded and revised ed., 1978; 4th expanded ed., 1989).

Vitali L., "Giorgio Morandi," *Notizie Olivetti*, no. 70, Ivrea, January 1961.

Vitali L., "Giorgio Morandi," *Du*, no. 241, Zurich, March 1961.

Vitali L., *Giorgio Morandi*, Olivetti, Ivrea, 1961.

Vitali L., "Giorgio Morandi," *Goya*, no. 49, Madrid, July-August 1962.

Vitali L., *Giorgio Morandi pittore*, Edizioni del Milione, Milan, 1964 (2nd expanded ed., 1965; 3rd expanded ed., 1970).

Vivaldi C., "Girando per le 93 sale della VII Quadriennale d'arte," *L'Ora*, Palermo, 24 November 1955.

Viviani R., "Giorgio Morandi," *Corriere degli Artisti*, Milan, 15 January 1950.

Volpe C., "La mostra nazionale per il Premio del Fiorino," *Il Nuovo Corriere*, Florence, 25 April 1951.

Volpe C., *L'arte del Novecento*, series "Storia dell'Arte Italiana," Principato, Milan-Messina, 1957.

Volpe C., "Giorgio Morandi," *La Biennale di Venezia*, no. 55, Venice, 1964.

Wallis N., "Calm," *The Observer*, London, 4 July 1954.

Washington L., "IV Bienal de São Paulo. Premiado o mais alto vôo lirico da pintura figurativista moderna," *Correio Paulistano*, São Paulo, 21 September 1957.

"Werk van Giorgio Morandi in Gemeentemuseum," *Haagsche Courant*, The Hague, 3 April 1954.

Wingen E., "Morandi verwierf met flessen wereldnaam," *Telegraf*, Amsterdam, 20 June 1964.

Wretholm E., "Ung italiensk Konst," *Svenska Morgonbladet*, Stockholm, 11 March 1953.

Y.D.B., "L'eredità di Morandi," *L'Unione Sarda*, Cagliari, 18 August 1964.

Zamberlan G., *Il mercante in camera*, Vallecchi, Florence, 1959.

Zanotti G., "Il pittore Giorgio Morandi è deceduto ieri a Bologna," *Roma-Napoli*, Rome, 19 June 1964.

Zanuccoli L., "Posta dall'Olanda. Due esposizioni di rilievo: pitture di Giorgio Morandi all'Aja," *La Nazione*, Florence, 14 May 1954.

Zardi F., "Vendeva per trecentomila lire quadri da venti milioni," *Il Telegrafo*, Livorno, 20 June 1964.

Zervos C., "Vue d'ensemble sur l'art italien moderne," *Cahiers d'Art*, no. I, Paris, 1950, speciale issue for the 25th year, *Un demi-siècle d'art italien*, introduction by C. Zervos, texts by various authors.

Zorzi E., "La mostra organizzata a Stoccolma dalla Biennale. L'arte italiana contemporanea," *Il Gazzettino*, Venice, 18 March 1953.

"Zum Tode von Giorgio Morandi," *Das Kunstwerk*, Baden-Baden, July-September 1964.

Zurlini V., "Peinture. Giorgio Morandi," *L'Express*, Paris, 4 January 1962.

Select Bibliography

The bibliography includes all the monographs, general studies, and newspaper and magazine articles published before or after the period covered by the present exhibition that are felt to be essential for a reconstruction of the artist's career. Where the date of publication was missing, the compiler has attributed one, indicated by square brackets. The numeral 1 following an author's name identifies the items Flavio Fergonzi mentions in his Catalog of Works.

Abramovicz J., "The Artist's Artist: Giorgio Morandi," *Arts Canada*, Toronto, April-May 1978.

Abramovicz J., "The Liberation of the Object," *Art in America*, no. 3, New York, March 1983.

A.P. (Podestà A.), "La lezione di Morandi," *Emporium*, Bergamo, May 1948.

Apollonio U., "The Paintings of Giorgio Morandi," *Horizon*, no. 115, London, July 1949.

Arcangeli F., "Novità di Morandi," *Il Mondo*, Florence, 5 October 1946.

Arcangeli F., "Tre pittori italiani dal 1910 al 1920," in *XXIV Esposizione biennale internazionale d'arte. Catalogo*, Giardini di Castello, Venice, 29 May–30 September 1948.

Arcangeli F., *Dal romanticismo all'informale*, Einaudi, Turin, 1977, 2 vols.

Arcangeli F., *Giorgio Morandi*, Editura Meridiane, Bucharest, 1987.

Arcangeli F., *Arte e vita. Pagine di galleria*, introduction by D. Trento, Accademia Clementina, Bologna, 1994.

Argan G.C., "Pittura italiana e cultura europea," *Prosa*, no. 3, Florence, 1946.

Argan G.C., *L'arte moderna 1770–1970*, Sansoni, Florence, 1970.

Arnheim R., *Il potere del centro. Psicologia della composizione nelle arti visive*, Einaudi, Turin, 1984 (1st ed. University of California Press, Berkeley-Los Angeles, 1982).

Arrigoni L., *Giorgio Morandi*, Capitol, Bologna, 1974.

Bacchelli M., "Giorgio Morandi," *Magazine of Art*, Washington, October 1947.

Bacchelli R., "Giorgio Morandi," *Il Tempo*, Rome, 29 March 1918.

Baker K., "Redemption through Painting. Late Works of Morandi," in *Giorgio Morandi*, exh. cat., Museum of Modern Art, San Francisco, 24 September–1 November 1981.

Ballo G., "Morandi," *Domus*, no. 443, Milan, 1966.

Barilli R., *L'arte contemporanea. Da Cézanne alle ultime tendenze*, Feltrinelli, Milan, 1984.

Barilli R., "Morandi e il secondo Novecento," in *Morandi e il suo tempo*, ed. by F. Solmi, exh. cat., Galleria Comunale d'Arte Moderna, Bologna, 9 November 1985–10 February 1986.

Barilli R., "Giorgio Morandi," *Storia Illustrata di Bologna*, no. 12/V, AIEP, Milan, 1990.

Bartolini, L., "Un pittore tra i pittori della Quadriennale," *Quadrivio*, no. 16, Rome, 12 February 1939.

Bartolini L., "Diario romano. Dedicato alla critica ermetica," *Quadrivio*, no. 21, Rome, 19 March 1939.

Basile F., *Morandi incisore*, La Loggia Edizioni d'Arte, Bologna, 1985.

Beccaria A., *Giorgio Morandi*, series "Arte moderna italiana," Hoepli, Milan, 1939.

Beccaria A., "A proposito di Morandi," *Corrente di Vita Giovanile*, Milan, 15 January 1940.

Bell J., "Messages in Bottles: the Noble Grandeur of Giorgio Morandi," *Art News*, New York, March 1982.

Berengo Gardin G., *Lo studio di Giorgio Morandi*, Charta, Milan, 1993.

Bigongiari P., *Dal barocco all'informale*, Cappelli, Bologna, 1980.

Bigongiari P., "Le immagini dell'assenza," *La Nazione*, Florence, 31 August 1993.

Birolli Z., "Pittura ed intimità poetica," *NAC*, no. 3, Milan, 1968.

Bloch V., "L'homme et sa peinture," *Le Monde*, Paris, 10 February 1971.

Bontempelli M., "Giorgio Morandi," *Corriere della Sera*, Milan, 20 August 1941.

Borsini O.C., "Bottiglie nell'arte. 'Gli umili vetri' di Morandi," *Notiziario CE.T.IM.*, Milan, October 1971.

Bortolon L., "Il pittore del silenzio," *Grazia*, no. 1418, Milan, 21 April 1968.

Boschetto A., *La collezione Roberto Longhi*, Sansoni, Florence, 1971.

Boston R., "Perfectly Formed," *The Guardian*, London, 24 May 1993.

Brandi C., "Cammino di Morandi," *Le Arti*, no. 3, Rome, February-March 1939.

Brandi C., *Morandi*, Le Monnier, Florence, 1942 (2nd revised ed., 1952).

Brandi C., "Morandi," *Comunità*, no. 6, Milan, October 1946.

Brandi C., "Europeismo e autonomia di cultura nella moderna pittura italiana (II-VIII)," *L'Immagine*, no. 2, Rome, June 1947.

Brandi C., "La mostra dell'arte italiana moderna a New York," *L'Immagine*, no. 13, Rome, [1949].

Brandi C., *Morandi lungo il cammino*, Rizzoli, Milan, 1970.

Brandi C., *Scritti sull'arte contemporanea*, Einaudi, Turin, 1976.

Brandi C., "Morandi merita un museo nel cuore di Bologna," *Corriere della Sera*, Milan, 23 December 1982.

Brandi C., *Morandi*, introduction by V. Rubiu, *Carteggio Brandi-Morandi 1938–1963*, ed. by M. Pasquali, Editori Riuniti, Rome, 1990.

Branzi S., "Morandi senza mito," *Il Giornale*, Milan, 25 October 1974.

Brolatti G., "Morandi, è fatta," *Carlino*, Bologna, 18 April 1985.

Burger A., *Die Stilleben des Giorgio Morandi. Eine koloritgeschichtliche Untersuchung*, Georg Holms Verlag, Hildesheim-Zurich-New York, 1983.

Buzzati D., "Solitudine di Morandi," *Corriere della Sera*, Milan, 6 May 1969.

Calvesi M., *La metafisica schiarita. Da de Chirico a Carrà, da Morandi a Savinio*, Feltrinelli, Milan, 1982.

Calvesi M., Sgarbi V., "Morandi, più che un Museo," *Quadri e Sculture*, no. 4, Rome, 1993.

Carluccio L., *La faccia nascosta della luna*, selected writings ed. by R. Tassi, Allemandi, Turin, 1983.

Caroli F., "Una luce di calce e ombre colorate," *Il Sole 24 Ore*, Milan, 10 October 1993.

Carrà C., "Giorgio Morandi," *L'Ambrosiano*, Milan, 25 June 1925.

Carrà C., "Giorgio Morandi," *L'Ambrosiano*, Milan, 9 February 1935.

Carrà M., "Carrà e Morandi," *L'Arte Moderna*, no. 75, Fabbri, Milan, 1967.

Carrieri R., "Giorgio Morandi," *Tempo*, Milan, 16 May 1940.

Cecchi E., *Taccuini*, Mondadori, Milan, 1976.

Cecchi E., *Lettere da un matrimonio*, ed. by M. Ghilardi, Sansoni, Florence, 1990.

Chastel A., "Giorgio Morandi," *Le Monde*, Paris, 2 January 1969.

Ciarrocchi A., "Quinta visita alla Quadriennale," *La Fiera Letteraria*, Rome, 23 August 1948.

50 acquarelli di Giorgio Morandi, texts by R. Guttuso, J. Leymarie, J. Rewald and V. Zurlini, ILTE, Turin, 1973.

Colombo F., "Lo shock di Morandi a New York," *La Stampa*, Turin, 10 December 1981.

"Current and Forthcoming Exhibitions," *The Burlington Magazine*, London, July 1965.

de Giorgi E., *I coetanei*, Leonardo, Milan, 1992 (1st ed., Einaudi, Turin, 1955).

De Grada R., "Posizione di Morandi," *L'Illustrazione Italiana*, Milan-Rome, 12–19 August 1945.

Dell'Acqua G.A., *La donazione Emilio e Maria Jesi*, Amici di Brera, Milan, 1981.

Demetrion J.T., "Collection of 20th-Century Italian Art in the United States," *Bollettino d'Arte*, Rome, supplement 1982.

De Micheli M., "Realismo e poesia," *Il '45*, no. 1, Milan, [1946].

Dunlop I., "Still-Life of Perfection," *Apollo*, London, December 1970.

Eco U., "Morandi, l'arte della variazione infinita," *Corriere della Sera*, Milan, 5 October 1993.

Fagiolo dell'Arco M., "The World in a Bottle. Morandi's Variations," *Artforum International*, no. 4, New York, December 1987.

Folon J.-M., *Fleurs de Giorgio Morandi*, Alice, Geneva, 1985.

Forge A., [Untitled], in *Giorgio Morandi*, exh. cat., Rotonda della Besana, Milan, May-June 1971.

Fossati P., *Valori Plastici, 1918–1922*, Einaudi, Turin, 1981.

Fossati P., *La "pittura metafisica,"* Einaudi, Turin, 1987.

Fossati P., *Storie di figure e di immagini*, Einaudi, Turin, 1995.

Fox Weber N., "The Morat Institute in Freiburg Celebrates the Artist's Work," *Architectural Digest*, Los Angeles, September 1992.

Fox Weber N., "A Struggle of the Titans," *Art & Auction*, New York, November 1995.

Franchi R., "Giorgio Morandi," *La Raccolta*, Bologna, 15 November–15 December 1918.

Ghirri L., *Atelier Morandi*, text by G. Messori, Palomar, Bari, 1992.

Giuffrè G., *Giorgio Morandi*, series "I Maestri del Novecento," Sansoni, Florence, 1970.

Gnudi C., *Morandi*, Edizioni U, Florence, 1946.

Gombrich E.H., *The Story of Art*, Phaidon Press, London, 1995.

Graham-Dixon A., "The Still, Small Voice of Turmoil," *The Independent*, London, 1 June 1993.

Graham-Dixon A., *Paper Museum*, Harper Collins, London, 1996.

Gregori M., *La Fondazione Roberto Longhi a Firenze*, Electa, Milan, 1980.

Gualdoni F., "L'ultimo Morandi," in *Giorgio Morandi 1890–1900. Mostra del centenario*, ed. by M. Pasquali, exh. cat., Galleria Comunale d'Arte Moderna, Bologna, 12 May–2 September 1990.

Guerrini M., "Perché la pittura," *Forma 1*, Rome, April 1947.

Hall D., "Morandi's Still Life with Bottles," *The Burlington Magazine*, London, January 1966.

Hertzsch W., *Giorgio Morandi*, E.A. Seeman, Leipzig, 1979.

Jouvet J., Schmied W., *Giorgio Morandi. Ölbilder, Aquarelle, Zeichnungen, Radierungen*, Diogenes, Zurich, 1982.

La collezione Jucker acquistata dal Comune di Milano, Finarte, Milan, 1992.

La pittura in Italia. Il Novecento / 1. 1900-1945, ed. by C. Pirovano, Electa, Milan, 1992, 2 vols.

Lega A., "Giorgio Morandi," *Il Selvaggio*, Florence, 30 July 1927.

Lepore M., "Figure caratteristiche del Novecento. Triste non credo, ma claustrale il modo di vivere di Morandi," *Il Sabato del Lombardo*, Milan, 28 December 1946.

Leymarie J., *Gli acquarelli di Morandi*, Edizioni De' Foscherari, Bologna, 1968.

Linker K., "Giorgio Morandi," *Artforum*, New York, February 1981.

Locarnini N., "L'astrattista che si ispirava a Morandi," *Arte*, no. 239, Milan, April 1993.

Longanesi L., "Morandi," *L'Italiano*, no. 16–17, Bologna, 31 December 1928.

Longhi R., "Momenti della pittura bolognese," *L'Archiginnasio*, no. 1–3, Bologna, 1935.

Longhi R., "Giorgio Morandi," *Il Mondo*, Florence, 21 April 1945.

Longhi R., *Da Cimabue a Morandi*, Mondadori, Milan, 1973.

Longhi R., *Scritti sull'Otto e Novecento 1925–1966*, Sansoni, Florence, 1984.

Maccari M., "Giorgio Morandi," *Il Resto del Carlino*, Bologna, 8 June 1928.

Magnani L., *Il mio Morandi. Un saggio e cinquantotto lettere*, Einaudi, Turin, 1982.

Mandelli P., "Giorgio Morandi 1907–1913," *Analisi*, Bologna, 15 October 1978.

Mandelli P., "Il 'Morandi' di Francesco Arcangeli," *Analisi*, no. 6, Bologna, 15 June 1981.

Mandelli P., "Storia di una monografia," *Ac-*

cademia Clementina. Atti e Memorie, no. 35–36, Bologna, 1995–1996.

Marchiori G., "La II Quadriennale d'arte a Roma. Evoluzioni e conquiste della pittura contemporanea," Corriere Padano, Ferrara, 5 February 1935.

Marchiori¹ G., "Alla terza Quadriennale. Giorgio Morandi," Corriere Padano, Ferrara, 23 February 1939.

Marchiori G., "Giorgio Morandi," Domus, Milan, February 1939.

Marchiori G., Giorgio Morandi, Editrice Ligure di Arti e Lettere, Genoa, 1945.

Marchiori G., Arte moderna all'Angelo, Neri Pozza, Venice, 1948.

Marchiori G., Giorgio Morandi. Le incisioni, Ronzon, Rome, 1969.

Marti L., Morandi, series "I Classici della Pittura," Armando Curcio, Milan, 1980.

Meltzoff S., "Italy: Report on Recent Painting," Magazine of Art, Washington, February 1946.

Morat F.A., Giorgio Morandi. Ölbilder, Aquarelle, Zeichnungen, Radierungen, F.A. Morat, Freiburg, 1979.

Oppo C.E., "Pittura di Morandi," L'Italia Letteraria, Rome, 10 April 1932.

Pasini R., Morandi, CLUEB, Bologna, 1989.

Pasquali M., "Morandi," Art e Dossier, supplement no. 50, Florence, October 1990.

Pasquali M., Morandi. Acquerelli. Catalogo generale Electa Milan, 1991.

Pasquali M., Museo Morandi Bologna, il catalogo, texts by various authors, Charta, Milan, 1993.

Pasquali M., Museo Morandi. Catalogo generale, texts by various authors, Grafis, Bologna, 1996.

Pasquali M., Solmi F., Vitali L., Morandi, Rizzoli International Publications, New York, 1988.

Pasquali M., Tavoni E., Morandi. Disegni. Catalogo generale, systematic cataloging, dating and iconographic comparisons by M. Pasquali in collaboration with L. Selleri, Electa, Milan, 1994.

Pellicano I., "Arriva Morandi in casa Scialoja," La Tribuna Illustrata, Rome, 6 February 1949.

Peygnot J., "Silence, Morandi," Connaissance des Arts, no. 228, Paris, February 1971.

Pontiggia E., "Le ragioni dello sguardo. Temi e orientamenti delle principali interpretazioni morandiane da Bacchelli ad Arcangeli (1918–1964)," in Morandi e Milano, ed. by various authors, exh. cat., Palazzo Reale, Milan, 22 November 1990–6 January 1991.

Pozza N., Morandi. . . i disegni. . ., Franca May, Rome, 1976.

Pozzati C., "I Morandi prima di Morandi, i Morandi dopo Morandi," in Quaderni moran-

diani n. 1. I Incontro internazionale di studi su Giorgio Morandi: Morandi e il suo tempo, Mazzotta, Milan, 1985.

Quaderni morandiani n. 1. I Incontro internazionale di studi su Giorgio Morandi: Morandi e il suo tempo, Mazzotta, Milan, 1985.

Ragghianti C.L., "Picasso e l'astrattismo," Critica d'Arte, no. 2, Florence, 1 July 1949.

Ragghianti C.L., "Bologna cruciale 1914," Critica d'Arte, no. 106–107, Florence, 1969.

Ragghianti C.L., Bologna cruciale 1914 e saggi su Morandi, Gorni, Saetti, Calderini, Bologna, 1982.

Raimondi G., "Cartella di disegni: Giorgio Morandi," Le Arti, Rome, February-March 1941.

Raimondi G., "Giorgio Morandi," Les Arts Plastiques, no. 3–4, Brussels, March-April 1949.

Raimondi G., "Le cose dell'uomo nell'opera di Morandi," La Fiera Letteraria, Rome, 27 November 1949.

Raimondi G., I divertimenti letterari (1915–1925), Mondadori, Milan, 1966.

Raimondi G., Anni con Giorgio Morandi, Mondadori, Milan, 1970.

Raini A., "Retrospettiva di Giorgio Morandi," Le Arti, no. 7–8, Milan, July-August 1966.

Ramous M., Giorgio Morandi, Cappelli, Bologna, 1949.

Renzi R., La città di Morandi, Cappelli, Bologna, 1989.

Rewald J., "Visit with Morandi," in Morandi, exh. cat., Albert Loeb & Krugier Gallery, New York, 18 May–17 June 1967.

Roditi E., Dialogues. Conversations with European Artists at Mid-Century, Bedford Arts Publishers, San Francisco, 1990.

Ruggeri G., Tavoni E., Morandi, amico mio, Charta, Milan, 1995.

Salvagnini S., "Giuseppe Marchiori, anonimo del Novecento," in Giuseppe Marchiori e il suo tempo. Mezzo secolo di cultura artistica e letteraria eruopea visto da un critico d'arte, ed. by S. Salvagnini, Palazzo Roncale, Rovigo, 5–28 November 1993.

Salvini R., Guida all'arte moderna, series "L'Arco," Vallecchi, Florence, 1949.

Scheiwiller G., Giorgio Morandi, Chiantore, Turin, [1943].

Scialoja T., "La 'metafisica' e il 'tono' nella pittura italiana contemporanea," Il Mondo, no. 33, Florence, 3 August 1946.

Siblík J., Giorgio Morandi, Současné Světové Umění, Prague, 1965.

Skira P., La nature morte, Skira, Geneva, 1989.

Soavi G., La polvere di Morandi, Elli & Pagani, Milan, 1982.

Soby J.Th., "Painting and Sculture since 1920," in J.Th. Soby, A.H. Barr Jr, Twentieth-Century

Italian Art, exh. cat., The Museum of Modern Art, New York, 1949.

Soffici A., "Morandi," L'Italiano, no. 10, Bologna, March 1932.

Solmi F., Morandi: storia e leggenda, Grafis, Bologna, 1978.

Solmi S., "Giorgio Morandi," in Pittori di ieri e di oggi, Ferrania, Milan, 1949.

Strauss E., Koloritgeschichtliche Untersuchungen zur Malerei seit Giotto und andere Studien, Deutsch Kunstverlag, Berlin-Munich, 1983.

Szucs J.P., Morandi, Corvina Kiadó, Budapest, 1974.

Tassi R., "Gli acquerelli di Morandi," L'Approdo Letterario, Florence, January-March 1969.

Tassi R., "Alla natura chiese permesso," La Repubblica, Rome, 10 August 1993.

Tavoni E., Morandi. Disegni, La Casa dell'Arte, Sasso Marconi, 1981–1984, 2 vols. (vol. 1, texts by M. Valsecchi and G. Ruggeri; vol. 2, texts by G.C. Argan and F. Basile).

Testori G., "Giorgio Morandi o la capacità di resurrezione," Corriere della Sera, Milan, 20 August 1978.

Tillim S., "Morandi: A Critical Note and a Memoir," Artforum, New York, September 1967.

Tobino M., "Accenno a Morandi," Corrente di Vita Giovanile, Milan, 31 May 1940.

Trombadori A., "Serietà e limiti di Morandi," Rinascita, Rome, May-June 1945.

Venturi L., Pittura contemporanea, Hoepli, Milan, 1947.

Venturi L., "New York. . . . The New Italy Arrives in America," Art News, New York, June-August 1949.

Visconti L., Il mio teatro, ed. by C. d'Amico de Carvalho and R. Renzi, vol. 1, 1936–1953, Cappelli, Bologna, 1979.

Vitali L., "L'incisione italiana del Novecento. I Selvaggi: Giorgio Morandi," Domus, Milan, December 1930.

Vitali L., L'incisione italiana moderna, Hoepli, Milan, 1934.

Vitali L., "Giorgio Morandi," Werk, Winterthur, August 1946.

Vitali L., "Giorgio Morandi," in Atti della Accademia Nazionale di San Luca, Rome, 1965.

Vitali L., Morandi. Catalogo generale, Electa, Milan, 1977, 2 vols. (2nd expanded ed., 1983).

Wilkin K., "The Eloquent Whispers of Giorgio Morandi," The New Criterion, no. 5, New York, January 1994.

Zucchini C.L., "Quante facce ha la realtà?," L'Eco di Bergamo, Bergamo, 6 March 1993.

Zurlini V., Il tempo di Morandi, Prandi, Reggio Emilia, 1975.

Photographic Credits

Photographs of the works
Luca Carrà, Milan
Coopers Professional Photographic Services, London
Tarcisio Dal Gal, Verona
Foto Scala, Florence
Giuseppe Schiavinotto, Rome
Hartmut W. Schmidt - Fotografie, Freiburg

Offsets by Franco Bestetti and Bruno Castellani, CdG - Milano srl

Illustrations
Archivio del '900 (Maurizio Fagiolo dell'Arco), Rome
Archivio Storico delle Arti Contemporanee della Biennale (ASAC), Venice
Archivio Storico del Cinema /AFE, Rome
Galleria dello Scudo archive, Verona
Galleria Il Milione archive, Milan
Giovanardi archive, Milan
Mattioli archive, Milan
Museo Morandi archive, Bologna
Sammlung Oskar Reinhart archive, Winterthur
Vitali archive, Milan
Günther Becker, Kassel
Luciano Calzolari, Bologna
Pietro Carrieri, Milan
Christie's, New York
Giorgio Colombo, Milan
Foto Dainesi, Milan
Mario De Biasi, Milan
Corrado Degrazia, Rome
Documenta Archiv, Kassel
Claudio Emmer, Milan
Luigi Ghirri, Reggio Emilia
Antonio Guerra, Bologna
Franz Hubmann, Vienna
Leo Lionni, Radda in Chianti
Gianni Mari, Milan
Antonio Masotti, Bologna
Ugo Mulas, Milan
Foto Saporetti, Milan
Sotheby's, London
Carlo Vannini, Reggio Emilia
A. Villani & Figli, Bologna

The Solomon R. Guggenheim Foundation

Honorary Trustees in Perpetuity
Solomon R. Guggenheim
Justin K. Thannhauser
Peggy Guggenheim

Chairman
Peter Lawson-Johnston

President
Ronald O. Perelman

Vice Presidents
Wendy L-J. McNeil
Stephen C. Swid

Director
Thomas Krens

Treasurer
Stephen C. Swid

Trustees
Giovanni Agnelli
Jon Azua
Peter M. Brant
The Earl Castle Stewart
Mary Sharp Cronson
Elizabeth T. Dingman
Gail May Engelberg
Daniel Filipacchi
Barbara Jonas
David Koch
Thomas Krens
Peter Lawson-Johnston
Samuel J. LeFrak
Rolf-Dieter Leister
Peter B. Lewis
Peter Littmann
Wendy L-J. McNeil
Edward H. Meyer
Ronald O. Perelman
Frederick Reid
Richard A. Rifkind
Denise Saul
Rudolph B. Schulhof
Terry Semel
James B. Sherwood
Raja Sidawi
Seymour Slive
Stephen C. Swid
John S. Wadsworth, Jr.
Cornel West
Michael F. Wettach
John Wilmerding
William T. Ylvisaker

Honorary Trustee
Claude Pompidou

Trustee Ex Officio
Luigi Moscheri

Director Emeritus
Thomas M. Messer

Peggy Guggenheim Collection Advisory Board

President
Peter Lawson-Johnston

Honorary Chairman
Claude Pompidou

Honorary Co-Chairmen
H.R.H. The Grand Duchess
of Luxembourg
Rose-Anne D. Bartholomew

Honorary Member
Olga Adamishina

Members
Luigi Agrati
Steven Ames
Giuseppina Araldi Guinetti
Maria Angeles Aristrain
Rosa Ayer
Marchese Annibale Berlingieri
Alexander Bernstein
Mary Bloch
Patti Cadby Birch
Wilfred Cass
The Earl Castle Stewart
Claudio Cavazza
Fausto Cereti
Sir Trevor Chinn
Franca Coin
Elizabeth T. Dingman
Christine Ehrmann
Isabella del Frate Eich
Rosemary Chisholm Feick
Mary Gaggia
Danielle Gardner
Marino Golinelli
Jacques Hachuel M.
Gilbert W. Harrison
Robert A. Hefner III!
W. Lawrence Heisey
William M. Hollis, Jr.
Evelyn Lambert
Jacques Lennon
Samuel H. Lindenbaum
June Lowell
Cristiano Mantero
Achille Maramotti
Valeria Monti
Luigi Moscheri
Raymond D. Nasher
Christina Newburgh
Giovanni Pandini
Maria Pia Quarzo-Cerina
Annelise Ratti
Benjamin B. Rauch
Richard A. Rifkind
Nanette Ross
Aldo Sacchi
Gheri Sackler
Sir Timothy Sainsbury
Denise Saul

Evelina Schapira
Hannelore Schulhof
James B. Sherwood
Marion R. Taylor
Roberto Tronchetti Provera
Melissa Ulfane
Leopoldo Villareal F.
Jean Wagener
Nancy Pierce Watts
Ruth Westen Pavese

Emeritus Members
Enrico Chiari
William Feick, Jr.
Umberto Nordio
Anna Scotti
Kristen Venable

Peggy Guggenheim Collection Family Committee
David Hélion
Fabrice Hélion †
Nicolas Hélion
Laurence and Sandro Rumney
Clovis Vail
Julia Vail and Bruce Mouland
Karole P.B. Vail
Mark Vail

Finito di stampare nel giugno 1998
presso le Arti Grafiche Salea di Milano
per conto delle Edizioni Gabriele Mazzotta